Chinese agriculture has experienced some radical changes over the past twenty years. Following the successful introduction of the household production system in the early 1980s, difficulties were encountered in establishing a unified domestic agricultural market in the later 1980s and 1990s. Through a comprehensive analysis of the changes in the Chinese agricultural institutions between the late 1970s and the mid-1990s, this study attempts to provide some answers to the main questions presently facing the agricultural sector. It focuses on the key elements of the pre-reform agricultural institutions, reviews the ways these institutions were refashioned and assesses the resulting changes in agricultural development. The implications of different policy choices are carefully considered with the assistance of a computable general equilibrium model. The author argues that China should push forward with its market-oriented reform measures and introduce the rigours of international competition into the agricultural sector.

Agricultural reform in China

TRADE AND DEVELOPMENT

A series of books on international economic relations and economic issues in development

Academic editor
Ron Duncan, *National Centre for Development Studies,*
   The Australian National University

Advisory editors
Ross Garnaut, *The Australian National University*
Reuven Glick, *Federal Reserve Bank of San Francisco*
Enzo R. Grilli, *The World Bank*
Mario B. Lamberte, *Philippine Institute for Development Studies*

Executive editor
Maree Tait, *National Centre for Development Studies,*
   The Australian National University

Other titles in the series
Helen Hughes (ed.), *Achieving industrialization in East Asia*
Yun-Wing Sung, *The China–Hong Kong connection: the key to China's open door policy*
Kym Anderson (ed.), *New Silk Roads: East Asia and world textile markets*
Rod Tyers and Kym Anderson, *Disarray in world food markets: a quantitative assessment*
Enzo R. Grilli, *The European Community and developing countries*
Peter Warr (ed.), *The Thai economy in transition*
Ross Garnaut, Enzo Grilli and James Riedel (eds.), *Sustaining export-oriented developments: ideas from East Asia*
Donald O. Mitchell, Merlinda D. Ingco and Ronald C. Duncan (eds.), *The world food outlook*
David C. Cole and Betty F. Slade, *Building a modern financial system: the Indonesian experience*
Ross Garnaut, Guo Shutian and Ma Guonan (eds.), *The third revolution in the Chinese countryside*
David Robertson (ed.), *East Asian trade after the Uruguay Round*

Agricultural reform in China

Getting institutions right

YIPING HUANG

The Australian National University, Canberra

PUBLISHED BY THE PRESS SYNDICATE OF THE UNIVERSITY OF CAMBRIDGE
The Pitt Building, Trumpington Street, Cambridge CB2 1RP, United Kingdom

CAMBRIDGE UNIVERSITY PRESS
The Edinburgh Building, Cambridge CB2 2RU, United Kingdom
40 West 20th Street, New York, NY 10011–4211, USA
10 Stamford Road, Oakleigh, Melbourne 3166, Australia

© Cambridge University Press 1998

This book is in copyright. Subject to statutory exception and to the provisions of relevant collective licensing agreements, no reproduction of any part may take place without the written permission of Cambridge University Press.

First published 1998

Printed in the United Kingdom at the University Press, Cambridge

Typeset in Palatino 10/12$\frac{1}{2}$ pt [CE]

A catalogue record for this book is available from the British Library

Library of Congress cataloguing in publication data
Huang, Yiping, 1964–
Agricultural reform in China: getting institutions right / Yiping Huang.
    p.   cm. – (Trade and Development)
Includes bibliographical references (p.   ) and index.
ISBN 0 521 62055 4 (hc)
1. Agriculture and state – China.
2. China – Economic policy – 1976–
3. Agriculture – Economic aspects – China.
I. Title. II. Series: Trade and Development (Cambridge, England)
HD2098.H82   1998
338.1'851 – dc21   97–12182   CIP

ISBN 0 521 62055 4 hardback

For my mother and my daughter

Contents

List of figures	page x
List of tables	xi
Acknowledgements	xiii
1 Getting markets to work in the countryside	1
2 Institutional distortions in pre-reform agriculture	17
3 Getting farmers back to work	38
4 Getting prices right	54
5 Adjustments in rural markets bring structural change	76
6 An agricultural economy without freedom to trade	96
7 China's agricultural policy choices	118
8 Chinese farmers can adapt	139
9 Getting reform right in agriculture	156
Appendix: The China model	171
References	192
Index	223

Figures

1.1	Growth rates of agricultural and grain output, 1979 to 1994	*page* 2
2.1	Inward-looking versus outward-looking policies	33
3.1	Agricultural yields, 1952, 1978 and 1984	48
4.1	State and market prices for grain, 1952 to 1990	57
4.2	The dual-market system for grain	62
4.3	Government monopsony in state grain transactions	64
4.4	The state and free markets for grain	67
5.1	Per capita rural output, 1980 to 1994	79
5.2	Relative growth of agriculture in the economy, 1978 to 1994	79
5.3	Composition of rural output, 1980 to 1992	81
5.4	Relative market prices of agricultural products, 1979 to 1993	82
5.5	Relative price and production decisions	87
5.6	Policy restrictions and a truncated production possibility frontier	88
7.1	International and Chinese cereal prices, 1993 to 1994	120
9.1	China's net imports of cotton and world cotton prices, 1972 to 1993	169
A.1	Agricultural production	173
A.2	Technology of current production	174
A.3	Industry output decisions: the case of the livestock industry	176
A.4	Household consumption	177

Tables

1.1	Economic growth and agricultural prices, 1978 to 1995	*page* 3
2.1	Composition of exports and imports, 1953 to 1979	24
2.2	Collectivisation, 1950 to 1958	29
2.3	Industry output growth in the pre-reform period, 1952 and 1979	31
3.1	Adoption of different responsibility systems, 1979 to 1983	41
3.2	Changes in private plot policy, 1955 to 1980	45
3.3	Agricultural output growth before and after the reform, 1952 to 1984	49
3.4	Quantitative assessments of the household responsibility system reform, 1965 to 1985	50
4.1	Indices of state purchase prices for agricultural products, 1952 to 1990	55
4.2	Coefficient estimates of the system equations	72
4.3	Predicted bargaining coefficients and their derivatives, 1979 to 1990	72
5.1	Per capita agricultural production, 1952 to 1994	80
5.2	Resource allocation and relative prices in the farming sector, 1978 to 1990	83
5.3	Variables affecting agricultural performance, 1978 to 1994	84
5.4	Development of the TVP sector, 1984 to 1994	89
5.5	Changes in farmers' truncated production frontier, 1978 to 1995	90
5.6	State bank loans to TVP and agricultural sectors, 1978 to 1989	92
6.1	Inflation of grain prices, 1993 and 1994	103
6.2	Grain demand and supply, 1989 to 1994	105
6.3	Growth of money and the inflation rate, 1979 to 1994	107
6.4	Grain stocks, 1970 to 1994	112
7.1	Nominal rate of protection for grain and oil crops, 1978 to 1994	119

xii *List of tables*

7.2	Producer subsidy equivalent estimates for agriculture, 1986 to 1994	122
7.3	Effects of agricultural trade liberalisation on international prices	124
7.4	Population and agricultural resources in selected countries, 1992	125
8.1	Pursuing self-sufficiency in grain	148
8.2	Maintaining existing policy regimes	150
8.3	Implementing the Uruguay Round agreement	151
8.4	Welfare impacts of agricultural trade liberalisation	152
8.5	Liberalisation beyond the Uruguay Round	153
A.1	Sector details of the China model	172
A.2	Equations of the China model	182
A.3	Variables of the China model	187
A.4	Coefficients and parameters of the China model	189

The following symbols are used
- .. not available
- — zero
- . insignificant
- n.a. not applicable

Acknowledgements

This book is an outcome of my work on China's agricultural reform in the past several years, developed at the Australia–Japan Research Centre, The Australian National University between 1991 and 1993 and at the Department of Economics, Research School of Pacific and Asian Studies, The Australian National University between 1994 and 1995.

I owe a great debt to three distinguished economists, Peter Drysdale, Peter Warr and Ross Garnaut. Peter Drysdale provided both the opportunity to study in Australia as well as stimulation, encouragement and guidance for my research. The effort he made in terms of time, passion and resources is beyond measure. Ross Garnaut has recently provided me with an opportunity to work with him on China's agricultural reform among other topics. His writings on East Asian growth and China's agricultural policy were a key inspiration for my research. Many of my views reflected in this book, especially those on agricultural trade policy, were absorbed from his earlier analyses or formulated during collaborative work done with him. I have also benefited greatly from Peter Warr's critical but constructive insights at various stages of this study.

Maree Tait also played an irreplaceable role in the production of this book. She voluntarily helped to polish the English and restructure the arguments, and also provided constant encouragement for me to complete the manuscript. Without Maree's friendship and selfless help, I would never have been able to complete a book of this quality within such a short period. I wish to thank Justin Yifu Lin for providing many opportunities and generous support for my pursuit of an academic career at various stages.

My research interest in China's agricultural reform started in 1987 when I became a member of the research staff at the Development Institute of the then Research Centre for Rural Development of the State Council in China. I benefited greatly from my colleagues of the institute, especially Chen Xiwen, Justin Yifu Lin, Lu Mai, Zhou Qiren, Du Ying, Deng Yingtao, Xiang Ning, Cui Xiaoli and Yu Baoping, from their broad knowledge about the Chinese rural economy and their patient introduction to the subject. Gao Xiaomeng, a senior colleague of the Development Institute, in particular played an important role in my years in China as a policy analyst. He guided me on several research projects, took me with him on field trips and patiently instructed me on China's grain policy.

I have also received encouragement and comments from Yujiro Hayami, Kym Anderson, Wing Thye Woo, Ron Duncan, Dwight Perkins, K. P. Kalirajan, Ken Clements, Christopher Findlay, Guo Shutian, Cai Fang and many others.

While working on this study I received financial assistance from the Australian Wool Corporation, the Australian Centre for International Agricultural Research, the International Monetary Fund and the Organisation for Economic Cooperation and Development.

My parents and my brother have always supported me with deep love, without which I would not have been able to achieve anything. My wife Tina Chen provided me with the needed support to pursue this work.

1

Getting markets to work in the countryside

The 'dilemma' posed by China's agricultural reform

Why was China's agricultural reform so successful before 1985 but frequently problematic after that? In which policy direction should China proceed in the 1990s – introducing agricultural protection or internationalising agricultural production? And what is the best strategy for achieving domestic food security as well as sustaining rapid economic growth? These are questions that puzzle many Chinese policy analysts and Western economists who are closely watching China's economic reform and development.

Agricultural reform in China started at the end of 1978. Reform in the early stages, mainly the giving back of responsibility to farming households and increases in state purchase prices for agricultural products, led to large improvements in agricultural production. From 1979 to 1984, agricultural production expanded by 7.4 per cent per annum and grain output grew at an annual rate of 5 per cent. From 1982 to 1984 growth was spectacular with grain output increasing, on average, by 27 million tonnes a year (about 8 per cent of the annual output) (figure 1.1). Agricultural reform was widely regarded as being very successful, with the extraordinary growth recorded in the wake of the initial reforms being called a 'miracle' (Longworth 1989; Huang 1993a).

After 1985, when the government pushed forward with market reforms, problems were felt in agricultural performance. Growth rates in agriculture dropped back to less than 4 per cent. The average annual growth rate of agriculture was 3.8 per cent during the period 1984–94. Although not low by international standards, this rate of growth represented a considerable slowdown. Grain output increased by only 0.9 per cent per annum. Grain output dropped significantly first in 1985 and then, to a lesser extent, in 1988, 1991 and 1994 (figure 1.1). More seriously, increasing agricultural prices in 1993–95 and reduced grain output caused significant macroeconomic problems. According to the

2 Agricultural reform in China

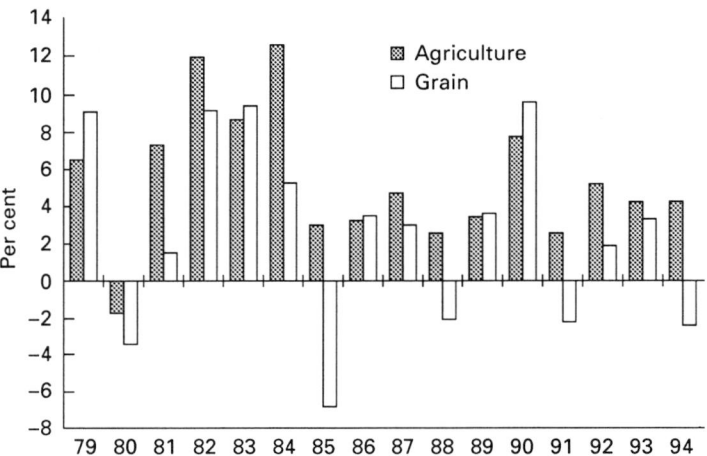

Fig. 1.1. Growth rates of agricultural and grain output, 1979 to 1994.
(*Source:* SSB, *China Statistical Yearbook 1995.*)

Chinese State Statistical Bureau, food prices rose by 32 per cent in 1994 contributing about 12.1 percentage points (or 55.8 per cent) to overall inflation.[1] High inflationary pressures were transmitted to consumers' cost of living, to enterprise production costs and, partially, to the government's budget. As a result state intervention in agricultural production became more pronounced in 1994 and 1995.

The sharp contrast in agricultural performance between the periods before and after 1985 fuelled criticisms of reform policies (table 1.1). Many economists pointed to declining investment in agricultural infrastructure on the part of both farmers and the government. Others questioned the direction of agricultural reform. Rural market reform introduced in the mid-1980s was regarded as a premature and overly-optimistic policy response (Niu and Calkins 1986). Calls for re-collectivisation of agricultural production were also made, particularly around 1988. Liberalisation of grain prices in the early 1990s was criticised as being reckless. Some Chinese economists stressed the special significance of grain production within the Chinese economy and recommended special policy measures to achieve food security and political stability. It was seriously suggested that agriculture should be exempted from trade liberalisation. These discussions caused inconsistent changes in agricultural policies throughout the reform period. While market reform was often pushed forward when agricultural supplies were abundant, resumption of state intervention and controls was frequently observed when domestic agricultural products were in short supply.

Table 1.1. *Economic growth and agricultural prices, 1978 to 1995*

	GNP growth (per cent)	Agricultural growth (per cent)	Grain output (million tonnes)	GNP per capita (yuan) (1985 prices)	Price indices	
					Agricultural purchases[a]	Food markets[b]
1978	12.3	3.9	304.8	398	59.9	81.4
1979	7.0	6.4	332.1	420	73.2	83.4
1980	6.4	−1.8	320.6	442	78.4	88.4
1981	4.9	7.1	325.0	457	83.0	90.0
1982	8.2	11.8	354.5	487	84.8	91.5
1983	10.0	8.5	387.3	529	88.5	91.9
1984	13.6	12.9	407.3	593	92.1	92.9
1985	13.5	2.7	379.1	663	100.0	100.0
1986	7.7	3.0	391.5	703	106.4	106.1
1987	10.2	4.5	403.0	762	119.2	112.6
1988	11.3	2.3	394.1	835	146.6	132.1
1989	3.7	3.2	407.6	853	168.6	156.7
1990	5.1	7.5	446.2	881	164.2	160.9
1991	7.7	2.3	435.3	936	160.9	163.7
1992	12.8	5.0	442.7	1047	166.4	170.2
1993	13.4	4.0	456.4	1174	182.5	182.1
1994	11.8	4.0	446.2	1295	264.6	240.3
1995	10.2	5.9	460.0	1409	306.9	288.4

Notes: [a] Agricultural purchase prices are weighted averages of both state and market purchase prices.
[b] Food prices are prices in rural markets.
Sources: SSB, *China Statistical Yearbook 1995*; Asia Pacific Economics Group, 1996.

The events after 1985 presented a dilemma for China's agricultural reforms. On one hand, it was widely agreed among government officials and economists, and in the public arena, that the ultimate objective of reform was to develop an agricultural market economy in which consumers and producers would make their own decisions, resources would be allocated between sectors according to relative prices and market prices determined by demand and supply conditions. On the other hand, the reform measures being introduced by the Chinese government to achieve these ends, seemed to be causing serious problems – from grain shortages to high inflation. This dilemma is clearly illustrated by the difficult choices posed by continuing grain policy reform in the 1990s. To encourage domestic grain production, prices needed to be raised further and controls removed. But increases in grain and food prices, were already 'unbearable' for consumers and the government. Chinese policymakers in the mid-1990s are not sure that market reform is the right direction for Chinese agriculture.

Reform – a process of getting institutions right

There is evidence that market reforms in China's agriculture since 1985 have not been successful in delivering all that was expected of them, but this evidence does not give grounds for the conclusion that free market mechanisms are not appropriate to Chinese agriculture. Although distortions are a widespread phenomenon in agriculture, even in the developed world, agricultural development is steady and stable in most of the developing world where free markets are in use. There is evidence – from the former Soviet Union and pre-reform China – of the inappropriateness of the central planning system. The 'problems' incurred in Chinese agriculture have arisen in the process of reform and are associated with the transition to a market system rather than with the direction of the reform. It is to be expected that in an economy that is transforming its institutions, special problems will be generated by time lags in institutional adaptability, the incompleteness of the reform and a lack of experience in policy implementation.

In the economic literature, an institution is a broad concept on which economists do not agree completely.[2] According to North, 'institutions are the rules of the game in a society, more formally, are the human devised constraints that shape human interaction' (1990: 3). Theoretically, institutions represent a varied array of elements ranging from cultural values to contracts, labour unions and political parties. Markets for agricultural products, labour and capital are institutions because they define the rules for exchange and mechanisms for price determination. Government purchase and marketing policies are institutions for similar reasons. Subsidies, taxes and state plans are institutions because they constrain producers' and consumers' behaviour. Ownership and production organisations, including production teams and household farming, are also institutions because they determine an individual's involvement in the production process and resultant income distribution. Cultural values and codes of conduct are also important institutions, but they will not be considered in this study. The institutions of concern to this study are those governing relationships among individual farmers, between farmers, consumers and the government, between agriculture and other sectors, and between China's agriculture and the world economy. The focus is on flows of factors, outputs and other resources (including income), and the way they are organised – through either administrative or market measures.

Two broad institutions lie at the centre of a study of Chinese institutions: one is the central planning system and the other is the market mechanism. From an institutional perspective, 'market' does not narrowly mean the market-place where products are exchanged. Market is an institution that contains rich assumptions about consumer/producer behaviour (or characteristics of production and utility functions), information, transaction costs and rules for exchange. In the real world there are different forms of markets. The market in Japan is sometimes regarded as operating differently to those in Europe and North America. Different forms of market are defined by their different institutional structures.

In theory, two optimality theorems of welfare economics are attainable in the market economy: first, if there is perfect competition, resource allocation is Pareto-efficient; second, any specified Pareto-efficient resource allocation that is technically feasible can be achieved by establishing free markets and an appropriate pattern of factor ownership. The operation of a market economy is, at the same time, influenced by other institutions, including government intervention. Well-defined property rights are another critical institution for the proper working of market mechanisms.

Even after nineteen years of reform China has not established typical market institutions. China had about thirty years' experience of central planning. The pre-reform Chinese economy was one of institutional distortions that affected all areas of economic activity – from property rights to factor flows and from price determination to production/consumption decisionmaking. None of the important assumptions for attaining welfare efficiency existed. Institutions in pre-reform China were determined by state ideology that relied on bureaucratic decisions and not value in the market-place to determine how resources were used. Central planners believed that any equilibrium reached by market mechanisms could be achieved by a planning system. Prices would arrive at market equilibrium levels because the planners would observe (see Kowalik 1994) the differences between demand and supply and changing price levels. Public ownership would help to achieve economic benefits, including scale economies, while preserving the advantages of private ownership. The central planning system would overcome market failures. The autarchic system was brought to China from the Soviet Union where it had been inspired and created by Marx, Lenin and Stalin. Thus development strategy based on giving priority to heavy industry was fundamental to the rationale of allocating resources. Central planning would deliver a more efficient allocation of resources, particularly of scarce resources which needed to be directed to the development of 'leading sectors' of the economy. Central planners aimed to build a 'more efficient' planning system to replace market institutions.

Some success was achieved by the central planners in the early years with investment in new activities, but the industries selected for promotion in China were not appropriate to its resource endowments.

Experience worldwide has demonstrated that market equilibrium and welfare optimisation have never been achieved under a central planning system because of the difficulties and expense in monitoring economic activity and the time lags involved in government responses. Heavy state interventions proved vastly inferior to a free market system in the allocation of resources.

In an analysis of agricultural price policies, Timmer (1986) observed that many developing economies tried to get agricultural prices 'correct' though policies. He observed that instead of 'getting prices right' governments that tried to influence prices usually got them wrong in the end. Similarly, 'getting institutions right' was not the end of the story in countries where central planning and heavy state intervention were introduced, but 'getting institutions wrong' usually was. 'Wrong institutions' existed not only in the former centrally planned economies but also in many developing and industrial economies. Wrong institutions reduced an economy's efficiency and prevented the growth of income and productivity.

After several decades governments which had adopted central planning systems started to move back to market institutions. Changes in agricultural policies in China in the past nineteen years are one such example. Economic reform is a process which aims to eliminate institutional distortions and establish market mechanisms to get institutions right. Increases in state purchase prices for agricultural products in China were an attempt to get rid of price distortions. The introduction of free markets was an important step in phasing out administrative intervention in the market. And the introduction of household responsibility was targeted at correcting the distorted microeconomic system for agricultural production – formerly the commune system.

The removal of institutional distortions is not an easy job. It is difficult enough to identify what the distortions are. Economic reform is, therefore, a process of institutional learning and innovation. Institutions within any economy are interdependent and individual. An institution which works effectively in one economy may not do so in another. Institutions can sometimes evolve 'inefficiently'. An institutional change is only desirable if it achieves 'institutional efficiency', usually defined as a reduction in transaction costs and an improvement in productivity.

There are circumstances where efficient institutional innovations are reversed because of the special interests of some dominant groups, or of the government.

The process of 'getting institutions right' can be either gradual or radical. Different approaches to economic reform of formerly centrally planned economies have been applied. In the former Soviet Union reform was abrupt ('shock therapy'), while in China it was gradual.

Hayami and Ruttan (1985) proposed a theory of induced institutional innovation extending their work on induced technological change. It can be applied to Chinese institutional reform. The choice of institutional arrangements and realisation of institutional change are endogenous and determined by various economic forces. In an economy like China which adopts a gradual approach, economic forces play a greater role in defining the direction and paths of institutional change.

Agricultural reform in China

China has taken a gradual approach to agricultural reform as it has to reforms in other areas of the economy.[3] At the Communist Party's Third Plenum, held in December 1978, the Chinese leadership put revolutionary politics and class struggle aside and set out to make the nation wealthy and powerful. At that time agricultural production was not meeting the demands of China's huge population, or even farmers themselves in many areas. The government moved to increase state investment in agriculture and to raise the purchase price for agricultural products.

At the beginning the government did not intend to change the commune regime and the central planning system. All practices that disrupted the existing system of agricultural organisation were strictly prohibited. Farmers in some poor areas, however, experimented with household-based production responsibility systems. At first the new systems were permitted by the government in poor areas only. But they spread and were adopted as a national policy at the beginning of the 1980s. By the end of 1983, about 98 per cent of production teams throughout China had adopted the household responsibility system. Meanwhile, the government continued to raise state purchase prices.

In 1985, rural market reforms were introduced to abolish the unified purchasing and marketing system. All agricultural products were assumed to be bought and sold in free markets. State purchases of grain, cotton and edible oil were maintained but through a newly instituted contract system under which both quantities and prices of state purchases were determined mutually by the government and farmers.

A number of other policies were also implemented to encourage diversification of non-agricultural, non-grain production in the Chinese countryside. Feedgrain sales were subsidised with the aim of stimulating the growth of the animal husbandry industry, while tax-exempt and subsidised bank loans were devised to encourage rural industrial development. But reform in agriculture was not to proceed smoothly as the government struggled to overcome instability in the wider economy induced by the inflationary effects of higher agricultural prices while at the same time trying to best guess supply responses to price changes.

The government response to agricultural difficulties in the mid-1980s was to retreat from some areas of reform. Stop-go reform was the result for the decade after 1985. Following significant falls in production, contract purchases of grain and cotton were quickly made mandatory again in 1985 and 1986 although liberalisation policies for other agricultural products were maintained. In 1988 and 1989, to avoid confusion caused by the form of 'purchase contract' and associated difficulties in meeting procurement targets, the term 'state purchase quota' was officially re-introduced, implying the revival of a unified purchasing and marketing system for these products.

On the other hand, in May 1988, the government made its first attempt to reform marketing policies for non-staple food in urban areas. Lump-sum subsidies were paid to urban consumers in an effort to abolish existing price subsidies on consumption of agricultural products. At the same time, a series of experiments was carried out to reform grain policies and the land tenure system.

From 1989, the government again raised state purchase prices for grain in response to several years' stagnation in grain production. Alongside the implementation of the wider austerity programme to cool down the 'overheated' economy, state intervention through quotas for the purchase of grain was re-iterated in policy. Previous preferential policies toward the livestock sector and rural industry were terminated.

In 1991, grain market reform accelerated. Based on experiences of the 1988 reform of the non-staple food policy and regional policy reform experiments, the government, for the first time in about thirty years, significantly raised state market prices for grain. Again, in 1992, urban market prices were brought to the levels of rural purchase prices. By so doing, the government expected to remove the increasing burden of grain subsidies on the state budget. The state still intended to buy certain amounts of grain, but prices were to be determined by the market. In

1994, the government abolished the State Price Bureau, signalling the end of forty years' massive state intervention in prices.

Owing to dramatic increases in grain and food prices in 1993–95, many administrative measures were revived. The government stressed the importance of maintaining basic self-sufficiency in grain and a new grain policy was announced in March 1995 requiring every provincial governor to be responsible for grain supply for his/her own province. Grain coupons again became a fact of life in many cities in 1994 and the State Price Bureau was re-established in May 1995.

Some outstanding questions

In the middle of the 1990s, plotting the future directions of agricultural reform in China is causing confusion among policy analysts and policy-makers. There are broadly three competing arguments. The first stresses the special role that agricultural products, especially grain, play in the cultural, social and economic life of the whole country. The argument is that because political stability and food security are of crucial importance for a country's sustainable growth, grain is not a normal but a political commodity. Recent changes in China's grain market following policy liberalisation – including supply shortages and sharp price rises – are used to support this argument. Markets will lead to greater fluctuations in supply and price which will threaten the economy's stability and are, thus, undesirable.

The second argues that grain is a commodity (although with some special features) that can be regulated by market mechanisms. This view has it that the problems that occurred in grain markets during the early 1990s were not caused by the introduction of reform policies but by the incompleteness of the reforms introduced. The only way to eliminate the problems being experienced is to complete market reform. Agricultural trade liberalisation, if appropriately introduced, will help to stabilise the domestic grain market and prevent the rapid rise of domestic food prices.

The third line of argument runs that, while fully operating markets should always be held as the ultimate objective of reform, including reform of grain policies, a certain degree of state intervention in prices and grain procurement is necessary. To the supporters of this argument complete liberalisation of agricultural markets is not compatible with China's current economic conditions because of the high Engel coefficient in consumption and the government's limited fiscal abilities.

These important policy issues are taken up in this study in a systematic way by applying an institutional approach. Three broad questions are asked in the process of the analysis, and these are introduced in the following paragraphs.

- What was wrong with the pre-reform agricultural institutions?

To understand what the problems of the current system are, it is helpful to start from an analysis of the pre-reform regime. Pre-reform agricultural institutions provided a complete set of policies carefully designed for the purpose of promoting heavy industrial development. Different components had different functions, but they all worked to serve the chosen development strategy. It is particularly useful to analyse which functions of a market institution were distorted by those policies and how individual institutional elements constrained individuals' behaviour in the pre-reform period.

- What institutional distortions have been corrected during the reform period and how successful were these reforms?

While a return to household responsibility, increases in purchase prices and liberalisation of state controls are commonly regarded as the most important reforms in agriculture, it is important to relate these changes to the functioning of the market mechanism. Economic reforms can facilitate the proper working of markets only if they help to eliminate effectively those factors that blocked the operation of free markets in pre-reform China. Some policy changes may be effective and others may not. Some policy changes may bring about new problems while eliminating 'old factors'. Such analysis helps to assess the usefulness and effectiveness of past reform and provide understanding of current problems.

- What are the major problems with the current agricultural institutions?

Agricultural reform in China has experienced difficulties in recent years because of unexpected changes in agricultural production and prices, following the introduction of policy changes. The analysis of the problems of the existing agricultural regime can begin with the examination of these new problems and exploration of their causes. Generally, there can only be two conclusions about recent changes in agricultural markets – they were either normal responses of the market mechanisms or they were abnormal, at least in magnitude. If they were normal outcomes, efforts should be made to seek additional policy instruments that can smooth market fluctuations and confine them within an acceptable range. On the other hand, if the changes were abnormal, correction should be sought in the choice of policy instruments, the process of implementation and the compatibility between different measures of the existing institutions. Unexpected fluctuations may also occur if some important components are missing from the existing set.

Analytical framework

The institutional approach to economic reform proposed here has two important components – one positive, the other normative. The positive analysis looks at the process of reform and the implementation of individual reform policies. It is concerned with how the institutions were changed and how they look post-reform. Quantitative assessment of the reform process may further improve understanding of the impact of the policy changes and performance of the new institutions. The normative analysis compares the reformed economic system with the stylised institutions of a market economy. It looks at how reformed institutions perform and what institutions are still necessary for the market to operate properly and smoothly. A combination of both the positive and normative approaches contributes to analysis of the impact of reform policies, examination of the working of the existing institutions, and to recommendations for further improvements of the institutional framework.

Many studies of Chinese agricultural reform have looked directly at policy adjustments and associated changes within the agricultural sector. These studies have often come to oversimplified conclusions. A reform policy is often welcome if agricultural supply increases, but strongly criticised if agricultural output decreases. To trace the true source of agricultural growth or market fluctuation, it is necessary to analyse the new policies together with existing instruments. It is important to take a broader perspective on the impact of policy change. Market fluctuations may be brought about by the new policy, they may also be caused by some elements of the 'old regime'. It is dangerous simply to reverse policy reforms whenever these appear to cause fluctuations in the market, without establishing true causation.

China's experience of agricultural reform provides many interesting case studies of institutional change – involving learning and innovation by both farmers and the government. Farmers created the model for agricultural organisation – the household responsibility system – basing it on their memories of the pre-collectivisation period and their experiences of the household-based production system experiments in the commune era. They did it within the political constraint of public ownership of land. The government also undertook a learning process, from initial total prohibition, through partial recognition to finally adopting household responsibility as a national policy.

Grain policy reform is another interesting case. The government first tried to reform the unified purchasing and marketing system for grain in 1985 but retreated quickly when other constraints came into play. From 1987, the government created local experiments that were designed as experiments in reform, but were localised in small areas of the countryside. From these experiences the government gained the confidence to expand the reforms more widely. In the early 1990s, the government liberalised grain policies. The process of institutional innovation for grain, however, is still far from complete because state purchase and marketing policies were resumed in 1995. Careful observation and, more importantly, analysis of these processes of institutional learning (looking both forward and backward) help to identify the critical issues for reform in the future. As well they provide excellent cases for research in institutional economics.

Most economic analysis of China's agricultural reform focuses on policy change within the agricultural sector. This was adequate for the period before 1985 because at that time non-agricultural opportunities were very limited and the rest of the economy was still frozen. After 1985 the situation changed dramatically. Following the introduction of rural market reform, resources began to move out of agriculture. Farmers found jobs in the rural township, village and private enterprises (TVP) and in the urban areas.

Agricultural performance can be influenced by economy-wide policies as well as agricultural policies. A policy encouraging exports of labour-intensive manufactured goods, for instance, may adversely affect agricultural production by drawing labour and other resources away from agriculture. A general austerity programme, on the other hand, may have some positive effects on agricultural production. As urban and rural industries are hurt by tight monetary policy and other measures, non-agricultural opportunities for investment and employment decrease dramatically, forcing some farmers to go back to their farm households and to increase agricultural production.

In the years before 1985, agricultural output increased whenever agricultural prices rose. As the agricultural sector has gradually integrated with the rest of the economy, increases in agricultural prices have not necessarily led to increases in agricultural production (it may even have declined) because prices in other sectors have risen even faster. This potential illustrates the importance of a general equilibrium perspective in analysing agricultural policy reforms.

Because of the increasing interdependence of different parts of the economy, a particular policy may have positive effects in one area but negative effects in others. Evaluating the ups and downs makes policy-making difficult for the government. In this study, a computable general equilibrium (CGE) model of the Chinese economy is applied to assess more accurately the outcomes of institutional changes. Through quantitative analysis, a picture of the 'true' (net) impact of institutional changes is built up because the CGE model captures not only the direct but also the indirect, second-round policy effects of reform.

The process of reform

Like the former Soviet Union, China adopted a heavy-industry oriented development strategy in the 1950s to try and fulfil its ambitions to catch up with, and overtake, industrial economies as quickly as possible. To facilitate such a development strategy, a complete set of agricultural institutions was established. The essence of that agricultural regime was a low price for agricultural products. By providing urban consumers and industries with cheap food, the industrial sectors were able to exploit resources from agriculture and produce profits which could be invested in more industrial development. The government intervened in every aspect of the agricultural economy to reduce the resistance to this discriminatory policy and to sustain resource transfers. The core of that institution was formed by three elements: an inward-looking strategy, a unified purchasing and marketing system for agricultural products, and the collectivisation of agricultural production (chapter 2).

The resulting set of agricultural institutions caused severe problems for agricultural development. At the end of 1978, China started its agricultural reforms and has fundamentally changed its pre-reform agricultural institutions since.

One of the most important reform measures in agriculture focused on household responsibility. There has been a great deal written about its effectiveness over the previous commune system and its contribution to the growth of agricultural output and productivity. Economists agree that the reform was a dramatic policy change that brought enormous change within a very short period. From an institutional perspective it is interesting to note that the household responsibility reform involved a long process of institutional learning by both the government and farmers before it was adopted as national policy (chapter 3).

In much empirical work, the contribution of the household responsibility reform to agricultural and economic growth stopped in 1984 because the proportion of production teams adopting this new system reached its maximum (Lin 1992a). But the new system continued to contribute to the improvement of farmers' income and welfare. The establishment of household responsibility provided autonomy to farmers in decisionmaking. At the same time, it made farmers increasingly powerful in negotiations (implicitly or explicitly) with the state and consumers over a number of policy variables. Continuous increases in state purchase prices for grain in the reform period were partly a result of the improvement in farmers' bargaining power. Taking grain policy as a case study where consumers could be isolated out of the picture because of the unchanged marketing policies, farmers were able to lobby strongly for further increases in state prices. The current study, by applying a co-operative game-theoretic model, changes the conventional methodology of treating policies as exogenous variables. By involving the different parties that influence policy decisions in the game, we can understand changes in policies (chapter 4).

The household responsibility and price reforms from 1978 were very successful, inducing fast agricultural growth. This situation, however, changed dramatically after 1985 when a programme to reform rural markets was implemented. Agricultural production stagnated and grain output fell. Shortages of many agricultural products occurred. A number of explanations for these changes have been put forward – from adverse terms of trade to poor weather conditions, but none of these captures the real reason agricultural output declined. In explaining changes in agricultural performance after 1985, economists continue to restrict their analysis to factors within the sector while, in reality, the agricultural sector was increasingly integrated with the rest of the economy. An important reason for the decline in agricultural production lay in the new opportunities that market reforms created for farmers. Because these new opportunities presented higher returns, resources moved quickly out of agriculture in the pursuit of higher income (chapter 5).

Rapidly rising grain and food prices became a serious problem after 1985, especially between 1993 and 1995. This happened after the complete liberalisation of grain policy – the 'third revolution'. Questions were raised about the direction and timing of this reform. Some economists attribute the dramatic price changes in the grain market to a reduction of grain output in 1994, while others attribute them to the mismanagement of monetary policy. These arguments are correct to some extent, but the most important explanation lies in the incompleteness of the market reform. Regional agricultural markets are segmented from each other and the domestic market is isolated from the international market. It is shown that the lack of freedom to trade creates significant uncertainties and reduces the market's ability to accommodate changes. This has been the dominant influence on the dramatic fluctuations in the agricultural markets. Large fluctuations in prices due to small changes in production occurred often in 1994. Similar price instability was evident in other small closed food markets. The special mechanisms of monetary and fiscal policies and the soft-budget problem of the state sector magnified changes in agricultural markets and transformed some into macroeconomic problems, such as high inflation (chapter 6).

The sharp rise in agricultural prices in 1994 pushed Chinese agriculture to a historical turning point. The agricultural sector was for long discriminated against during both the pre- and post-reform periods. But changes in the early 1990s not only drove most domestic agricultural prices very close to or even higher than international prices, but also reduced producer subsidy equivalents (PSEs) from about -50 per cent of product value in the mid-1980s to near zero in 1994. Before the turn of the century the Chinese government must make an important policy choice – to introduce agricultural protection or to internationalise its agricultural sector. This study evaluates a number of conceptions about agricultural trade liberalisation. The policy decision in China, of course, will not be independent of the prevailing political economy. Currently, the opposition to agricultural protection is weak because consumers are always compensated by the government whenever food prices rise by a large margin. The opposition will be stronger if consumers have to absorb all the price changes incurred during the process of economic reform, but will be weaker as income grows and the share of food in living expenditure falls. The main supporters of agricultural protection are, however, not farmers themselves but the professional agricultural economists and agricultural bureaucrats. They are able to influence farmers to act against their own interests by highlighting short-term costs and ignoring long-run benefits. Dissemination of correct information on the costs and benefits of trade protection and liberalisation is, therefore, important to influencing the future direction of policy reform and domestic political economy. International trade negotiations are another important instrument helpful in influencing the domestic political economy of trade liberalisation (chapter 7).

Many arguments in favour of agricultural protection emphasise that free trade hurts agriculture and farmers (both in terms of income and adjustment costs). But it is important to examine these arguments in a sophisticated quantitative framework. A number of policy choices, ranging from self-sufficiency, through implementation of the Uruguay Round agreement, to complete liberalisation, are simulated using the China model. The results suggest that agriculture will not be damaged by free trade. On the contrary, trade liberalisation not only brings higher income and welfare to the whole economy, but also promotes rural development and raises farmers' real income (chapter 8).

The objective of economic reform in China is to establish a market economy. Agriculture is an important part of the whole programme and should not be exempt from trade liberalisation. Agricultural reform is important for China not only in the usual sense of income growth and welfare improvement. It is also an important signal with which China can demonstrate to the world that it believes in free trade – if China gives this signal it is more likely to be accommodated within the world economy. On the other hand, it is in the international community's interest to encourage China in further reforms. If China's agricultural policy is moved onto a protection path, not only China but also the world will find itself in a difficult situation (chapter 9).

Notes

1 Grain prices increased by 51 per cent, contributing about 2.6 percentage points (or 12.4 per cent) to overall inflation.
2 Lin and Nugent (forthcoming) provide a thorough review of different definitions of institutions and the role of institutions in economic development.
3 There is a large literature on aspects of agricultural reform in China; see Ash (1988), Perkins (1988), Lin (1992a) and Huang (1993a).

2

Institutional distortions in pre-reform agriculture

Earlier reliance on investment in heavy industry

China copied its economic system from the Soviet Union in the early 1950s (Xue 1981; World Bank 1983; Fan and Nolan 1994). The 'Soviet model' adopted was a comprehensive economic system implemented by bureaucratic decisions. An underlying premise of this system was that the quick road to development lay in forcing growth of heavy industries.

When Mao Zedong led the Communists to power in 1949, the new government inherited a war-torn agrarian economy. The ravages of the war had reduced production by 25 per cent in agriculture, 30 per cent in light industry and 70 per cent in heavy industry. The founding of Communist China initiated three years of rehabilitation bringing about significant recovery and dramatic growth to the economy. Grain output rose from 103 million tonnes in 1949 to 166 million tonnes in 1952. Similar rapid growth was experienced in cotton, up from 450,000 tonnes to 1.3 million tonnes, and steel, 160,000 tonnes to 1.4 million tonnes. Coal production jumped from 32 million to 66 million tonnes. The 1952 levels of output were far above the highest pre-liberalisation levels (Xue 1981: 22).

But the Chinese economy as a whole was still a poor agrarian one, particularly by international standards (Lin, Cai and Li 1994a). China had a population of nearly 600 million occupying a land area comparable in size to the United States or Canada. The majority of the population, 88 per cent, were farmers living in rural areas. Per capita grain output in 1952 was 285 kilograms, barely sufficient to support life. Agricultural production, however, accounted for about 45 per cent of total society output (TSO, *shehuo zhong chanzhi*). Light and heavy industries were a very small part of the economy in 1952, accounting for 22 and 12 per cent of TSO respectively. Industrial output on a per capita basis was particularly small – cloth 6.7 metres, sugar 0.8 kilograms, raw coal 0.1 tonnes, raw oil 0.8 kilograms, electricity 12.7 kW hour and steel 2.3 kilograms

(SSB, *China Statistical Yearbook*, 1984–95). Such a poor industrial base presented a large challenge for the economic ambitions of the Chinese leaders.

Marx and Engels had first assumed that the socialist revolution would be successful in the most developed capitalist economies, such as Britain, France, Germany and the United States, perhaps all at once (Marx 1959). It did not happen. Instead the socialist revolution occurred in less developed (pre-)capitalist economies like Russia and China.[1] 'Building socialism in such a country was much more difficult and complicated than it would be after the victory of the revolution in a developed capitalist country where industrialisation had been completed and the small-scale peasant economy was insignificant' (Xue 1981: 292). The difficulties were to fashion economic policies aimed at developing the nascent communist economies.

Raising living standards became a major objective for the new Chinese communist government for both political and economic reasons. The Chinese leadership observed the feature common to the advanced economies of North America and Western Europe – the high proportion of industry, especially heavy industry. Development of heavy industry was, therefore, seen as the avenue to economic modernisation (Xue 1981; Lin, Cai and Li 1994a). Many and vibrant heavy industries were taken as a necessary symbol of a modern and advanced economy. Technological progress and productivity growth in other sectors of the economy including the agricultural sector would be facilitated by developing heavy industry (through the supply of modern production equipment). At this point in history the Soviet Union appeared to provide a good model. Its economic growth in the 1930s impressed the world, especially in contrast with most of the Western economies which were experiencing severe depression at the time.[2] Economic growth continued at a high rate in the immediate post-war period, recording 2.4 percentage points higher than the world average in the 1950s.[3] In fact, a heavy-industry oriented development strategy was adopted by many non-socialist, less developed economies, such as South Asian and Latin American economies.

The development of heavy industry was assigned top priority by the Chinese government. The First Five-Year Plan (1953–57) launched a massive industrialisation programme. It was intended to concentrate on implementing a programme for industrial construction, consisting of 694 'above norm' projects (and 2,300 'below norm' projects), and having as its nucleus 156 key-point projects planned with Soviet aid. These key-point projects were critical to the government's policy:

we must concentrate our strength primarily on guaranteeing the completion according to plans of these 156 construction projects. Because the major enterprises are heavy industrial enterprises, these 156 construction projects include modern integrated iron and steel enterprises, non-ferrous metal smelting and coal-mining enterprises, thermal and hydroelectric power stations, heavy machinery manufacturing factories, vehicle, tractor and aeroplane-manufacturing factories, chemical factories, etc. (Wang 1955: 10–12).

Production of iron and steel was assigned top priority among all economic activities, being regarded as the benchmark for success. Ambitious plans were set for Chinese production to overtake steel production in Britain and Canada within ten to twenty years.[4] As a result, resources were mobilised and concentrated on heavy industrial production. The share of state capital construction investment in heavy industry, for instance, rose from 36.2 per cent during the period of the First Five-Year Plan to 54 per cent in the Second Five-Year Plan (1958–62) and remained around 50 per cent until economic reform (Lin, Cai and Li 1994a). The proportion of workers in 'secondary' industry (mainly light and heavy industrial processing) also increased – from 7.4 per cent in 1952 to a peak of 26.4 per cent in 1958.[5]

Development strategies and agricultural institutions

Implementation of a development strategy that was oriented to heavy industry was incompatible with China's economic resources. As a poor, densely populated developing economy, its comparative advantage lay in labour-intensive sectors, not capital- and knowledge-intensive sectors. To facilitate the development of heavy industries, a comprehensive central planning system was instituted. A set of macroeconomic measures including a depressed interest rate and an overvalued foreign exchange rate was introduced. Administrative measures dominated almost all areas of resource allocation. The banking and financial system was restructured, with the People's Bank of China at its core. Foreign exchange allocation was also centralised. Foreign trade was monopolised by a handful of large trading companies which were arms of the central government. The relatively scarce foreign exchange was only spent on imports of modern equipment and advanced technology. Public ownership was enforced to facilitate the smooth implementation of the development strategy. Factories in urban areas were gradually nationalised through a process called 'socialist transformation'. The newly established heavy industry factories were exclusively owned by the state, partly to ensure that the artificially high profits (created basically by taxing agriculture) were handed over to the state or re-invested in heavy industry.

But where could the resources possibly come from for heavy industrial development in a poor agrarian economy? The only answer was from agriculture, although agriculture itself was very vulnerable. The difficulty was that, while massive construction of heavy industry required tremendous resource outflows from agriculture on one hand, stable and increasing supplies of agricultural products were also crucial for the success of industrialisation on the other. Although agricultural development did not stand high on the policy agenda and the government did not have resources for agricultural investment, it was in the interest of the government, aiming at rapid industrialisation, to keep agricultural output increasing at a similar pace to industrial development. Continued supplies of agricultural products to the urban areas were a decisive influence on the success of the industrialisation policy. The government was not able to import large quantities of agricultural products, even when there was domestic crop failure, not only because trade relations with the major agricultural exporting countries were not good but also because scarce foreign exchange had to be used for imports of modern, large-scale equipment and advanced technologies, mainly from the Soviet Union. Domestic agricultural supply was, therefore, the only source of farm products.

Policies introduced during the period of rehabilitation (1949-52), including land reform and stabilisation of domestic prices, brought about significant recovery in agricultural production. But, at the same time, agriculture did not present itself as a sector which could potentially support industrialisation. First, the growth potential of agriculture was very limited because of a lack of agricultural investment and technical progress. Second, increases in output did not reduce the gap between supply and demand in major agricultural markets. Alongside increases in agricultural output and income, farmers consumed more grain.[6] As a result, the commodity rate of agricultural production and even net amounts of supply to the market fell (the *commodity rate* measures the ratio of output marketed to total output). On the other hand, because of the expansion of the urban population, partly related to the planned industrialisation, market demand rose significantly in urban areas. Third, changes in agricultural demand and supply caused significant rises in agricultural prices and their increasing instability. Increased market fluctuations created obstacles to implementation of the government's plans. Furthermore, there was concern that if agricultural prices, especially grain prices, rose in the market, they would be transmitted to workers' wage rates and to the production costs of the urban sectors and they would eventually slow the pace of industrialisation. This was the last thing the government wanted to happen.

A set of 'new' agricultural institutions was devised to facilitate the overly ambitious industrialisation programme. There are two ways to tap agricultural resources (or surpluses) for industrialisation – one is through heavy agricultural taxes and the other is through low prices for agricultural products. China chose the latter option.[7] Lower than market equilibrium agricultural prices secured lower subsistence costs for industrial workers and, in turn, ensured low wages and cheap raw materials.[8] Lower production costs, in turn, enabled industry to generate high profits which were then re-invested in industrial development, either by enterprises themselves or through the government.

To implement lower agricultural prices, the government needed a central planning system and various government bodies to make and enforce agriculture plans. As well, the government had to cut linkages between the domestic economy and the international market because enforcement of the comprehensive economic plans would have been extremely difficult otherwise. This notion of domestic insulation was reinforced at that time by the fact that China had virtually no trading relationships with the world's major market economies.

When the domestic agricultural markets were in place (even at the margin), the government found that the transaction costs of fulfilling plans for purchasing agricultural products were prohibitively high as agricultural products could be easily slipped from the planning system to free markets. Hence, free markets for agricultural products had to be restricted or totally abolished. State agencies monopolised the purchase and marketing of all agricultural products, under the unified purchase and marketing system (UPMS).

To guarantee the success of heavy industry, agricultural production also had to meet strict quantity and structural targets as set out in detail by the state plan. But as households were the basic units of agricultural production, their objective was to maximise total income, not to fulfil state plans. Fulfilment of the state plan was only important to farmers when plan enforcement was effective and when the penalty for not fulfilling the plan was high. Theoretically, even in the absence of a free market, farmers could choose to consume more leisure if agricultural prices were too low. Consequently farm households often failed to produce and deliver planned quotas.

The next institutional element to be introduced to the agricultural sector to fulfil the government's central objective was the abolition of the household production unit and the introduction of the commune system. A commune was usually organised with three levels: commune, brigade and production team. The production team, consisting of about thirty households, served as the basic unit of production and accounting. Land and other production means were pooled and all production activities were determined by the team leader and carried out by collective labour. Distinguished from household heads, team leaders behaved differently. Collectivisation of agricultural production significantly reduced the transaction costs of plan enforcement.

The pre-reform agricultural institutions, therefore, contained three major components:

- an inward-looking approach
- a unified purchase and marketing system
- a commune regime.

These three interdependent policies created the main areas in which market institutions were distorted in the pre-reform period.

Looking inward

The heavy-industry oriented development strategy was built on the idea of a closed economy. If China had been exposed to international competition, its comparative advantage would have led it to develop its more labour-intensive industries. It would have had no reason to develop its large-scale heavy industry. But, to the Chinese leadership, development of heavy industry was paramount. Heavy industry was seen as the source of modernisation and of productivity growth in other sectors. To pursue the heavy-industry oriented development strategy, China cut off its economic linkages with the outside world by raising barriers and imposing direct control to trade. Thus in the pre-reform period China relied on import substitution. This message was clearly carried in policy statements by trade officials, cited by Lardy (1992: 16):

> Export is for import and import is for the country's socialist industrialisation (Ye Jizhuang, then Minister of Foreign Trade).

> (T)he purpose of importing more industrial equipment from the Soviet Union is to lay the foundation of China's industrial independence, so that in the future China can produce all of the producer goods it needs and will not have to rely on imports from the outside (Zhang Huadong, then Director of the Ministry's Import Bureau).

Derived from this inward-looking approach, the international trade of pre-reform China had four distinguishing characteristics. First, trade was kept to the lowest possible level (Garnaut and Huang 1995). International trade was not applied effectively to improve the economy's efficiency and to raise incomes. Imports and exports occurred only when they were necessary to balance domestic markets, such as food imports in 1962–64, and to meet industrialisation objectives, such as the import of machinery. Second, China's trade occurred primarily with other communist groups, especially the Soviet Union – the so-called 'leaning to one side'. This was at the time when major Western countries adopted policies that blocked the People's Republic's economic and political relations with the outside world. At the beginning of the 1960s, China broke from the Soviet Union in defence of its own ideology and the unity of its own economy. Thereafter, Japan became the primary source of large equipment and plant imports. Third, China's trade pattern was determined by policy priorities rather than the economy's comparative advantage. Over 90 per cent of imports were producer goods. This contrasted remarkably with the trade pattern in the pre-liberation period. The largest imports in the first half of the century were typically cotton goods, cotton yarn and raw cotton, followed by grain, flour, sugar and tobacco. The major producer goods of petroleum, transport equipment, chemicals and metals were only 10–14 per cent of total imports in the first three decades (Lardy 1992). Machinery imports increased from only 2–3 per cent of imports in the 1930s to 20–40 per cent in the pre-reform period. On the other hand, from being an import in the pre-liberation era food became a major export. On average, food accounted for about 30 per cent of total imports between 1953 and 1979 (table 2.1). This dramatic shift was, of course, not a result of changing comparative advantage because at the time when China exported huge amounts of food to the Soviet Union, it still had big food problems at home.

Agricultural trade (or food export) was necessary because agriculture was the only source for foreign exchange earnings. Food imports increased in 1962 following severe crop failure and widespread famine, but were quickly scaled back as economic recovery gathered pace and agriculture, again, became a major contributor of foreign exchange.

International trade in agriculture was strictly monopolised by the government. The government purchased agricultural products, for the purpose of exporting, at state purchase prices according to plans. The linkage between international and domestic markets was cut (there was in fact no agricultural market in most years of the pre-reform period). Changes in prices received for exported goods were never transmitted to farmers.

Table 2.1. *Composition of exports and imports, 1953 to 1979*

	Total exports (US$ billion)	Total raw materials (US$ billion)	Shares of total exports (per cent)		
			Textile fibres[a]	Food	Total manufacturing
1953–55	3.6	39.2	9.0	42.7	18.1
1956–58	5.2	42.2	6.5	29.3	28.5
1959–61	5.6	31.7	6.9	19.3	49.0
1962–64	5.1	24.5	4.1	22.2	53.3
1965–67	6.7	24.2	4.9	28.9	46.9
1968–70	6.5	21.5	5.1	29.8	48.7
1975	7.3	26.6	3.3	29.7	43.6
1979	13.7	30.1	3.7	20.1	49.9

	Total imports (US$ billion)	Total raw materials (US$ billion)	Shares of total imports (per cent)		
			Textile fibres	Food	Total manufacturing[a]
1953–55	4.3	15.8	84.1	..	8.0
1956–58	5.0	22.1	77.0	..	8.6
1959–61	5.5	23.7	70.6	41.0	6.3
1962–64	4.0	25.0	60.0	5.0	12.5
1965–67	6.3	17.0	63.3	21.5	14.1
1968–70	6.1	16.7	64.4	15.4	16.2
1975	7.4	13.5	74.7	29.2	11.9
1979	15.7	15.5	71.8	26.7	10.1

Note: [a] In the exports sub-table, textile fibres is a sub-group of all raw materials, and in the imports sub-table, machinery and chemicals are sub-groups of all manufacturing.
Source: Sung 1994.

Unifying purchase and marketing systems

State purchase and marketing of agricultural products, mainly grain, began in 1950. At that time, however, the state bought from markets at market prices and competed with other commercial agents.

The unexpected and, to some extent, undesirable events of the early 1950s necessitated stronger and stricter state intervention in agricultural markets. For grain, for instance, the gap between state purchase and marketing prices widened rapidly. In 1952, the volume of state purchases increased only 11.6 per cent over 1951 levels. State sales volumes, however, increased by 44.7 per cent. The government found it increasingly difficult to purchase grains from farmers. The share of state purchases (including grain buying by other commercial agencies) in Hunan and Hubei provinces in total grain purchases declined significantly from 60–70 per cent in earlier years to 10–30 per cent in 1953 (Gao and Xiang 1992). Such problems not only caused economic and political instability but also threatened the new industrialisation programme.

In October 1953, the government decided to introduce for grain a unified purchase and marketing system which included four major policy elements:

- the state purchased grain from farmers according to grain purchase plans (unified purchase)
- the state sold grain to urban residents and rural grain-deficit farmers (unified marketing)
- the government regulated grain markets through a policy prohibiting participation of any private commercial agencies in grain purchase and marketing
- responsibility for grain policy management was divided between the central and local governments.

Edible oil was included in the UPMS shortly after the introduction of the new policy for grain. The core of this new policy was government monopoly in grain markets and determination of quantities and prices for producers and consumers.[9]

The number of commodities covered by this UPMS expanded quickly in the following years: cotton was included in July 1954, pork in January 1955, and tobacco, tea and another dozen agricultural commodities in October 1956. In 1957, the UPMS was further extended to cover fruits and herbal medicine. In 1961, the government formally separated all agricultural products into three categories which were governed by different purchase and marketing policies. The first category contained grain, cotton and edible oil, which were governed by a unified purchase policy (*Tong Ge*). The second category included other important consumption goods, raw materials for industrial production and infrastructural construction and agricultural products for export. The second category was regulated by the so-called designated purchase policy (*Pai Ge*). All other agricultural products were included in the third category and purchased by the state at negotiated prices (*Yi Ge*). Free markets were strictly prohibited for the first category and allowed to operate for the second category only after fulfilment of state purchase quotas. In practice, there was no significant difference between policies for the first two categories. Prices for the third category were, according to the policy, to be determined between farmers and the state. But, in practice, farmers never had a say in price determination.

Agricultural purchase prices were adjusted several times in order to encourage agricultural production, especially in the early years of the pre-reform period. State purchase prices were raised for pork by 10.5 per cent in 1953 and 12.7 per cent in 1957. In 1961, following widespread crop failures, purchase prices were increased by 25 per cent for grain, 13 per cent for edible oil, 26 per cent for pork and 37 per cent for poultry and eggs. Significant and wide-ranging price increases for agricultural products occurred in 1962. Purchase prices for grain were increased by 17.1 per cent on average. After that, however, most prices were left unadjusted for one and a half decades until economic reform in 1979.

While the government purchased agricultural products at low prices it also devised some compensation measures. Farmers or production teams who fulfilled state purchase quotas were entitled to certain allocations of agricultural inputs including agricultural machinery, fertilisers, pesticides, electricity and diesel oil and small farm tools at subsidised prices. This compensation, though only symbolic in value terms, reduced resistance to state purchase of agricultural products.

The UPMS was a very important element of China's urban industrialisation programme. First, it was devised to secure necessary urban agricultural supplies. Second, agricultural resources were channelled to urban industry through depressed agricultural prices engineered by the UPMS. Third, the UPMS guaranteed foreign exchange earnings through forced agricultural exporting. The foreign exchange was used to import industrial equipment and advanced technologies.

To enforce the UPMS in the countryside the government instituted a set of facilitating or related policies. Agricultural production was determined by central plans. Under the commune system, production plans were first formed by the central government based on estimated requirements and then divided and assigned to local governments, from provinces to counties. Each level of government added new or additional components to the plans according to regional requirements. At the level of production teams, team leaders had virtually no autonomy in production. Agricultural plans often detailed variety, yield and production techniques including the timing of planting, irrigation and fertiliser application. No matter how inefficient and ridiculous these plans were, they nonetheless helped the government control the structure and quantity of agricultural production.

Collectivisation of agricultural production

Shortly after the communist government came to power, it introduced national land reform to keep political promises made during the civil war. The programme started in June 1950 and was completed by

September 1952. Estimates are that about 300 million farmers acquired some 700 million mu (or 47 million hectares) of arable land (S. Guo et al. 1989). After acquiring land poor peasants fared much better, and farmhands became producers. In spite of farmers' enthusiasm, problems arose. Farmers could not prosper on the small pieces of land they had acquired and some lost their land because of poor management skills. Re-emergence of a polarisation between rich and poor was frequently reported. More importantly, the government deemed that small-scale individual farming was unlikely to be able to support the industrialisation programme, especially given the discriminatory policies against agriculture.[10]

The government faced a dilemma. On one hand, it required a steadily growing agricultural sector, while on the other, it had to implement low-price polices for agricultural products and had no extra resources to invest in agriculture. Collectivisation was seen as a critical step toward maintenance of steady growth in agriculture and, thus, facilitation of heavy industrial development. Growth of agricultural output was only possible through the mobilisation of massive labour resources in the construction of agricultural infrastructure and through intensive inputs per unit of land area (Lin 1991c). As Chen Yun (1984: 238) observed on the advantages of the collectives: 'According to the past experiences, yields can be raised by 15–30 per cent on average. A 30 per cent increase in yield implies about 50 billion kilograms of grain. Furthermore, yield-raising measures can only be easily effective after agricultural collectivisation.'

Collectivisation in China went through four stages – mutual-aid teams, elementary and advanced production co-operatives, and communes. In the liberated areas the Communists began to collectivise agricultural production before 1949. In December 1952, the government introduced a national policy encouraging collectivisation in the countryside. The most popular form of collectivisation at that time was the mutual-aid team, in which four or five neighbouring households pooled their labour, draught-animals and farm tools for peak seasons on a temporary or permanent basis (table 2.2). In 1953, about 40 per cent of farmers joined various forms of mutual-aid teams, most of which were temporary. These mutual-aid teams, formed voluntarily, overcame some of the disadvantages of small-scale farming and promoted significant labour productivity gains. It was reported that per capita income in terms of grain was 10–30 per cent higher for members of mutual-aid teams (S. Guo et al. 1989).

In addition to encouraging mutual-aid teams, the government helped to develop and establish Rural Supply and Marketing Co-operatives (RSMCs) and Rural Credit Co-operatives (RCCs). The RSMCs were mainly responsible for the supply of agricultural inputs to, and the purchase of agricultural products from, farmers and served as a connection or extension of the state in urban areas. In the early 1950s, the RSMCs were truly co-operative organisations and membership increased quickly from 26 million in 1950 to 161 million in 1954. The aim of the RCCs was to mobilise surplus funds from farmers for lending to the other farmers. The number of RCCs also exploded, from 33 in 1950 to 21,281 in 1954, and RCCs later became an important capital source for rural construction and development.

During 1954 and 1955, elementary co-operatives developed rapidly, increasing from 15,000 in 1953 to 114,000 in 1954 to 633,000 in 1955. In an elementary co-operative, while retaining private ownership, peasants pooled their land for common use and management. Draught-animals and large farm implements also remained under private ownership but were used jointly by co-operative members. Income from the co-operative was distributed according to both work and investment in the form of land, draught-animals and farm implements.

It is often noted that the official approach to collectivisation at this point was cautious and gradualist (Xue 1981; Lin 1991c), although some also argue that the rapid growth of co-operatives in 1954 and, particularly, in 1955 indicated a strong involuntary element (S. Guo et al. 1989: 114). In 1955, however, there was an important debate about how fast collectivisation should proceed and the proponents of collectivisation within the party won. This dramatically accelerated the process of collectivisation. In 1956 and 1957 advanced co-operatives began to predominate as a form of collectivisation. In an advanced co-operative, land, draught-animals and farm implements became publicly owned property, with compensation paid to former owners (table 2.2). Agricultural inputs were distributed solely according to work loads.

By the end of 1956 about 96 per cent of the country's farm households were members of various co-operatives, among which advanced co-operatives numbered 540,000 and their members accounted for 88 per cent of total farm households. This rapid progress after 1955 shortened the period of collectivisation from the planned fifteen years to less than five years. Not only did almost all farm households join co-operatives, but the size of each co-operative also became larger. The size of an advanced co-operative, for instance, was initially about 30 households but increased to encompass all households in a village – from 150 to 200 (table 2.2).

Table 2.2. *Collectivisation, 1950 to 1958*

	1950	1953	1954	1955	1956	1957	1958
Mutual-aid teams							
number (million)	2.7	7.5	9.9	7.1	0.9	..	..
households per team	4.2	6.1	6.9	8.4	12.2	..	..
Elementary co-operatives							
number (thousand)	..	15.0	114.0	633.0	216.0	36.0	..
households per co-op.	10.4	18.1	20.0	26.7	48.2	44.5	..
Advanced co-operatives							
number (thousand)	..	0.2	0.2	0.5	540.0	753.0	..
households per co-op.	32.0	137.3	58.6	75.8	198.9	158.6	..
Communes							
number (thousand)	..	..	..	..	..	..	24.0
households per commune	..	..	..	..	..	..	5,000.0

Source: Lin 1994.

In 1958 all agricultural co-operatives became People's Communes. While farmers had had some freedom in deciding whether or not to join a production co-operative, from 1958 it became compulsory for every farm household to be a member of the local people's commune. People's communes were both political and economic organisations. They performed most of the local government functions, including police, justice, welfare, administration of various policy programmes and operation of schools and hospitals. More importantly for this study, the communes had monopoly power over economic affairs – assignment of production plans to brigades and production teams, allocation of procurement quotas and control over the leadership of brigades and teams (Johnson 1988). In most cases, the production team was a basic unit for production, accounting and income distribution.[11] All means of production were owned by the team or the commune. Production activities were arranged and assigned to each member by the team leader on a daily basis. Income (both cash and physical output), after deducting agricultural taxes, state purchase quotas and collective welfare funds, was distributed among team members at the end of the year according to a hybrid of egalitarian and working-points systems. Some products, mainly necessities such as grain and crop residues, were allocated on a per capita basis regardless of working effort throughout the year. The rest (income) was distributed according to an individual's accumulation of working points and the value of each working point. Individuals' working points were determined by effort, skill and political attitude toward their collective work (Perkins 1988).[12] At the end of 1978 there were 52,780 communes, each consisting of about thirteen brigades which, in turn, each had about seven to ten production teams (Johnson 1988).

Most official documents indicate that the objective of agricultural collectivisation was to modernise backward, small-scale individual agricultural units. Underlying this, however, was the view that collectivisation was an important tool for the maintenance and development of agricultural production without the usual price incentives and that it facilitated the operation of the UPMS (Lin 1991c; Gao and Xiang 1992). This motivation was hinted at in an article by Chen Yun (1984: 276):

> Faced with such a large number of individual farm households, we had difficulties in fulfilling the unified purchase and marketing of grain. The difficulties not only came from a lack of experience with the unified purchase and marketing system, but more importantly, because it is no easy task to estimate output, to identify shortage and surplus and their quantities.

Development and management of plans for agriculture became much easier when farm households were organised into production teams and communes. Resistance from household heads to state purchase of agricultural products at low prices was strong because of the direct link between prices and households' income and welfare. Under the commune system, administrative management governed economic relations between production teams and the government. Team leaders, unlike most household heads, also took political power into account in maximising their utility. A small marginal cost (to themselves or their own families) could potentially generate large marginal (political) returns, although the other members of the teams had to share costs with them. Thus production teams and team leaders became an amalgamation of both state and farmer interests. The government could relatively easily fulfil its agricultural plans for the purpose of industrialisation without directly confronting farmers.

The commune system, together with household registration, effectively restricted labour flows between sectors and regions. For farmers belonging to a commune, planned agricultural production within their production teams was the only possible employment. In the absence of price incentives, the necessary inputs to agricultural production were further guaranteed.

Evaluation of the pre-reform institutions

The pre-reform agricultural institution was an integrated economic system devised to facilitate the nation's industrialisation. A fundamental element of that system was the bias of policies toward urban areas. Resources were mobilised for, and concentrated on, urban industrial

Table 2.3. *Industry output growth in the pre-reform period, 1952 and 1979*

	Output 1952 (billion yuan)	Output 1979 (billion yuan)	Annual growth rate 1952–79 (per cent)
Heavy industry	12.4	263.6	13.6
Light industry	22.5	204.5	9.3
Agriculture	46.1	169.8	2.9

Note: Output values for 1952 and 1979 are in current prices while the growth rates are calculated according to constant price output values.
Source: SSB, *China Statistical Yearbook,* various issues.

development. The inward-looking approach, the UPMS and the commune system were all designed to secure continuing and adequate agricultural output while only minimum investment was made in agriculture.

Effectiveness in facilitating industrial development

Putting aside questions of efficiency, pre-reform industrialisation policy was generally effective in promoting heavy industrial development (table 2.3). Between 1952 and 1979, government revenue totalled 1,404 billion yuan which accounted for about 35 per cent of national output. Budget spending on state industrial investment summed to 622 billion yuan, about 15.5 per cent of national income or 52 per cent of national investment. In 1979, total industrial output was 4,237 billion yuan, 6.8 times higher than that in 1952, in accordance with an annual growth rate of 8.2 per cent. State industry accounted for 78 per cent of national industry and grew by 8.3 per cent per annum between 1952 and 1979.

After some thirty years, China had established a relatively complete and independent national industrial sector, even if inefficient resource use was widespread. Investment even contributed to specialisation in some capital-intensive sectors and promoted export growth during the reform period.

Inefficient agricultural policies

The pattern of development in the pre-reform period was not sustainable because it was not consistent with principles of economic efficiency and welfare optimisation. On average, agriculture managed a reasonable rate of growth, but it still presented a stringent constraint on overall growth because of serious institutional problems.

The drawbacks associated with an inward-looking approach to economic development are often not easily perceived. This is one reason why the inward-looking approach (or the import-substitution strategy) was widely adopted among developing economies in the 1950s and early 1960s. But experiences of post-war economic development have provided clear evidence of the inefficiencies of *dirigiste* strategies. None of the economies which adopted inward-looking policies has delivered sustained rapid economic growth. After forty years virtually no *dirigiste* economy had significantly changed its world income ranking. In sharp contrast, economies that adopted an outward-looking approach, mainly the East Asian economies and others like Botswana, Malta and Mauritius, achieved extraordinary economic growth in the post-war period (World Bank 1994; Hughes 1995).

The serious disadvantage of the inward-looking approach lies in its efficiency- and welfare-reducing features. The problem is illustrated in figure 2.1, in which the horizontal axis represents quantity of agricultural commodities produced and the vertical axis the quantity of non-agricultural goods produced. Curve AB is the production possibility frontier given an economy's resource endowment. Curves II and $I'I'$ are the economy's indifference curves – the further the curve from the origin, O, the higher the level of welfare. Straight lines PP and $P'P'$ represent the relative prices of agricultural and non-agricultural commodities – the steeper the line, the higher the relative price of the agricultural goods. To begin with, no inefficiency in production is assumed and, therefore, production always occurs on the frontier. Under a free trade regime, domestic relative prices are the same as those in the world market, PP. Further, assuming profit maximisation for producers and utility maximisation for consumers, production occurs at $C(g, h)$ and consumption at $D(i, j)$. The economy has to be involved in international trade because of differences in the composition of production and consumption, although total values measured at world prices are equal (both points are on the same relative price line). The economy exports $(g-i)$ of agricultural goods, and imports $(j-h)$ of non-agricultural commodities. Welfare achieved is represented by II.

In a closed economy every component of domestic consumption has to be met by domestic production. This results in a change in relative price from PP to $P'P'$. Both production and consumption are on the same point E – no trade occurs. The welfare reduction resulting from the inward-looking policy is represented by the shift from indifference curve II to curve $I'I'$.

The dynamic impact of the inward-looking approach is even more

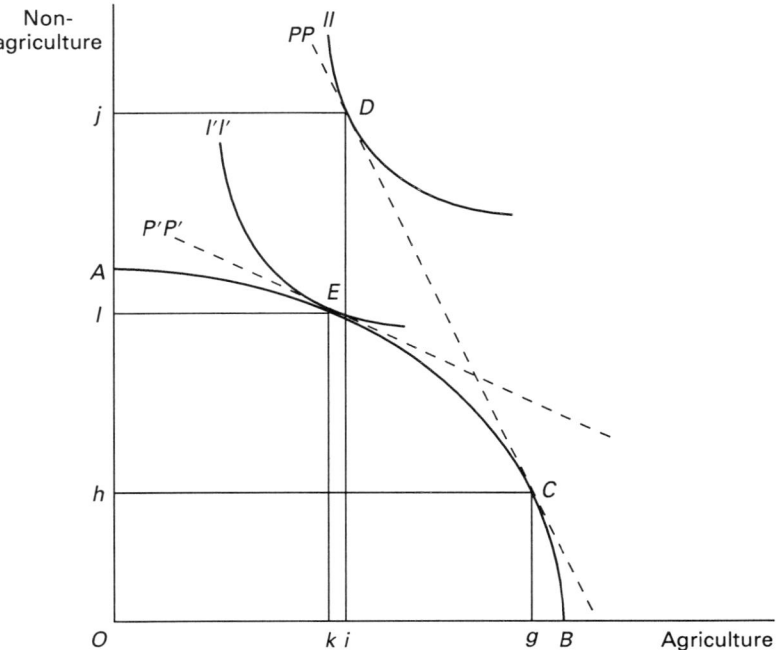

Fig. 2.1. Inward-looking versus outward-looking policies

important for economic development. By precluding an economy from participating in the international division of labour and exploiting its comparative advantage, the inward-looking policy generates adverse effects for productivity improvement and growth potential. An outward-looking economy is more conscious of world best practice and under greater pressure to adopt it.

The UPMS instituted an extreme case of the above. Under the UPMS, agriculture was disadvantaged in its terms of trade but was required to produce unusually high output given the relative prices and resource availability. The unbalanced nature of economic plans during the pre-reform period not only depressed agricultural prices (so that the relative price was even flatter than $P'P'$), but also demanded agricultural supply higher than k (agricultural equilibrium output level associated with E in a closed economy).

Plans requiring production beyond the frontier were unattainable, not to mention the serious output losses which accrued because of allocative inefficiency. Heavy administrative intervention and strong political

34 *Agricultural reform in China*

pressure enforced plans in agriculture for a short period. But over time economic factors were to become important and dominate production and consumption decisions.

Under the UPMS, the government transferred about 510 billion yuan through the distorted price system, amounting to about one-third of total net agricultural output (total output less the value of material inputs), on top of the 98 billion yuan extracted in the form of agricultural taxes (Guo et al. 1993).[13]

The problems of the commune system have been discussed widely in the literature (Chinn 1980; Perkins and Yusuf 1984; Putterman 1987, 1990; Lin 1988). A major problem with the commune system, according to Lin (1988) and others (such as Putterman 1987), lay in the trade-off between the benefit of scale economies and the costs of monitoring. The benefits from collectivisation in other sectors, such as industry, are usually large because monitoring can be carried out relatively easily and cheaply. Each member's effort can be measured accurately and income distribution is fair. But agricultural production has its special characteristics. Its production sites are often scattered and the result of efforts by individuals cannot be measured directly in a collective. Because it was costly, there was virtually no monitoring in China's production teams. Shirking became a widespread phenomenon. Most team members presented themselves in the field, accrued the working points, but made no serious effort to work (Lin 1988). This led to a scenario Chinn (1980) termed the 'universal laziness'.

In one major study on China's collectivisation, Lin (1991c) compared the performance of collectivisation before and after 1958. He argued that the cause of the agricultural crisis in 1959–61 was the change from voluntary to compulsory collectivisation in 1958, rather than alternatives frequently advanced, such as bad weather, bad management and incentive problems associated with the unwieldy size of collectives.

The egalitarian component of the production team distribution system further worsened the situation (Chinn 1980; Putterman 1987, 1990). Because a proportion of agricultural output, mainly grain and crop residues, was distributed on a per capita basis, returns to working points and farmers' efforts were further reduced. Putterman (1990), using a 1970 panel data-set, empirically tested and accepted (mildly) the hypothesis that team members worked harder the more revenue generated they expected to be distributed as income (in contrast to distribution on per capita basis), and the more income they expected to be distributed in the form of cash.

Incentive problems led to further losses in production efficiency. In a production possibility frontier diagram (figure 2.1), production inefficiency is represented by a production point located in the interior of the feasible production set with the distance between the point and the frontier measuring the inefficiencies caused by inappropriate institutional settings.

The whole set of agricultural institutions created significant adverse effects within agriculture. Although agriculture supplied huge quantities of resources for industrial development, farmers' income stagnated. The per capita income of farmers was 133 yuan in 1978, having increased by 1.8 per cent per annum between 1952 and 1978. Per capita grain output in 1977 was roughly the same as in 1957 and total cotton output remained at the 1965 level (Xue 1981). Farmers often failed to feed themselves adequately during the pre-reform period, in part because state purchases were excessive. Famine was widespread in provinces like Anhui, Guizhou, Henan and Ganshu. Agriculture became a severe bottleneck constraining economic development and industrialisation. By the end of the 1970s these problems had grown to an unbearable level.

Notes

1 Lenin proposed two alternative hypotheses as it is possible for the proletariat to triumph first in a country representing the weakest link in the capitalist world: should the proletariat seize power first and then develop the economy and culture of the country, or should it refrain from doing so until after a full economic and cultural development (Xue 1981)? Lenin chose the first course and led the October Revolution. And Mao Zedong followed in China.
2 Official statistics report an average growth rate of 12.5 per cent for the Soviet Union's industrial production during 1928–39. Western sources adjust this growth rate downward to 5 per cent but this is still much higher than the world average in the 1930s (Easterly and Fischer 1987).
3 The fact that the rapid development of its (defence-related) heavy industry also helped the Soviet Union significantly in international politics perhaps made this development strategy more appealing to the Chinese leaders.
4 Most of them, however, were policy slogans without careful evaluation and planning.
5 The Chinese economy is sometimes divided into three broad categories (industries): 'primary' industry includes agriculture and mining; 'secondary' industry is the industrial processing sector; and 'tertiary' industry is the service sector. The proportion of workers in secondary industry is used to illustrate labour force growth in heavy industry because light industry accounted for a declining share before the mid-1960s.
6 Gao and Xiang (1992) identified three reasons for this rising consumption of

grain by farmers. First, demand for grain increased because of higher incomes. Farmers received more income from the increased agricultural output and, at the same time, acquired the rents for land they used to pass on to landlords. The latter part can be regarded as income redistribution. But as income was transferred from relatively high-income households (landlords) to low-income households (previously landless households), it generated a significant and positive impact on rural grain demand. Second, many farmers failed to acquire enough food before liberation. It was natural for these farm households to increase grain consumption after they produced more on their own land. Third, some farmers held grain to sell at higher prices in the expectation of rising agricultural prices.

7 Japan is regarded as an example of an economy which used heavy agricultural taxes to accumulate resources for industrialisation. Around 1870, the share of land taxes in total government revenue was as high as 70–80 per cent. It was still above 20 per cent in 1910. In China, on the contrary, this share was 10 per cent in the 1950s and further decreased to about 6 per cent in the 1960s and 3 per cent in the 1970s (Song 1987).

8 The holding down of raw material and agricultural product prices was said to reduce the costs of industrial production and to generate more profits for reinvestment. From 1953 to 1957, the number of raw materials and industrial products covered by the material control system increased from about 110 to more than 300 and accounted for more than 60 per cent of total industrial output in 1957 (Lin, Cai and Li 1994b).

9 After fulfilment of the state purchase plan, farmers in theory were free to choose what to do with their surplus grain. They could hold grain in storage or sell to the state grain department or the co-operatives, and small-scale exchange between farmers was permitted.

10 Mao Zedong argued that 'Among the peasants masses a system of individual economy has prevailed for thousands of years, with each family or household forming a productive unit. The scattered, individual form of production is the economic foundation of feudal rule and keeps the peasants in perpetual poverty. The only way to change it is gradual collectivisation' (Mao Zedong 1977: 156).

11 There were many cases in which a brigade or a commune was made the basic production and accounting unit. In 1958, there were examples of production and income distribution management at county level (which usually covered a population of half to one million). This was corrected in 1961, partly in response to crop failures, by a national policy stressing production teams as the basic management units. During the Cultural Revolution, however, many communes again tried to enlarge their basic units. In 1977, the communes accepted brigades as the basic management units (S. Guo *et al.* 1989).

12 There were various methods used to determine the number of working points a member was allocated. One was to fix numbers of working points for each piece of agricultural production activity before it was assigned to a team member. Another was to simply record the number of days each member presented to work. At the end of the year, per day working points (usually in

the range between 1–10) were determined through a democratic process among all team members (Lin 1988).
13 The Comprehensive Research Group of the Development Institute (CRGDI) estimated the transfer through price distortion from agriculture to industry as 600 billion yuan (CRGDI 1987).

3

Getting farmers back to work

Early institutional experiments

Returning the responsibility for production decisions to farmers is now regarded as one of the most successful moves made during China's whole reform experience. The government did not intentionally set out to do this at the beginning of the reforms. But by 1978 the government had recognised that solving managerial problems within the production team system in agriculture was the key to improving productivity by raising farmers' incentives. In fact the subdivision of collectively owned land and delegation of production management to individual households were both considered violations of socialist principles and were formerly unthinkable (Lin 1994). The introduction of the household responsibility system and other forms of household-based systems began spontaneously with farmers taking production decisions into their own hands in remote areas within the pre-reform agricultural regime. The speed with which the household responsibility system became widespread at the beginning of the 1980s is astonishing. Individual systemic changes became a revolution that was built on several decades' experiments and learning by Chinese farmers.

The first experiments with the contract system in agriculture began as early as collectivisation – roughly the same time as the massive introduction of elementary co-operatives. In 1956, various forms of production responsibility systems, including management responsibility systems and contracting of output and cost, were created and operated experimentally within Yongjia county and Ruian county of Zhejiang province, Fengyang county of Anhui province, Yuci county of Shanxi province and Jiangjing county of Sichuan province. 'Contracting everything to the household' (*Baogan Daohu*) was widespread in Henan province in 1959 and in the southwest and northwest areas in 1964. In 1961, about 85 per cent of production teams had adopted various forms of production responsibility systems.

While most of these early experiments are not very well documented, Li Yunhe's influential article published in *Zhejiang Daily* provided some detailed information about the experiment of the Liaoyuan Co-operative in Yongjia county.[1] From mid-1956, Liaoyuan Co-operative introduced two forms of contract system – one 'the special management system' and the other the 'contracting of production down to the household'. All the properties of a co-operative continued – public ownership, unified planning and management, collective labour and a distribution system based on working points. Under the 'special management system', the Liaoyuan Co-operative contracted a fixed piece of farm work not suitable for collective labour to individual farmers. Under the system 'contracting of production down to the household', the Liaoyuan Co-operative divided its total land area into plots and assigned the plots to households. Most farm work was still carried out by collective labour. Collectively members worked for a certain number of quota days on the plot and the household with contracted responsibility for the plot (instead of the team leader) would monitor the quality of the work done. The household would also work the plot (for the farm work not suitable for collective labour) and the output of the plot was directly related to the responsible household's income at the end of the year. In fact, the contracting of production to individual households was an 'output responsibility system' which put responsibility for monitoring quality on a household basis. Li Yunhe (1957) specified the four characteristics of the system: contracting output to the team (from the co-operative); responsibility to rest with households; quotas to be fixed for each plot; and unified management. With this system, everybody on the team, rather than just the team leader, had responsibility for monitoring quality of work and achieving yield improvement.

Although still adhering to the superiority of collectivisation, Li Yunhe (1957) argued that 'people did not like having "everyday collective" and "everything collective", often "collectivising" all their time and energy in one place'. The two systems created within Liaoyuan Co-operative, according to Li Yunhe, 'can be adopted as a very good complement to "collective labour" and provide an important way to remedy the defects of "collective production"'. Furthermore, he pointed out that individual farmers' initiative and budgeting care and skills are merits 'once adopted in socialist production and combined with the superiority of collective labour'.

According to Li Yunhe, by January 1957, the experiments that had been ongoing in Liaoyuan Co-operative had produced positive results.

Productivity had improved, lifting enthusiasm for technology improvements that were expected to increase grain yields.

The institutional learning and experiment undertaken in Liaoyuan Co-operative and many other places were, of course, illegal at the time and were phased out forcefully by the government quickly after their introduction. They, nonetheless, provided experience for reforms that were subsequently introduced several decades later.

The end of the 1970s was marked by another round of spontaneous experiments in basing responsibility in individual households. Toward the end of 1978, a small number of production teams, especially those in Fengyang and Feixi counties of Anhui province, began secretly to experiment with a system of dividing the team's land and the obligatory procurement quotas among the individual households that made up the team. Early success, although still illegal, attracted many other teams to experiment as well. Xiaogang village is known as one of the production teams whose experience provided another good case study of institutional learning and innovation.

Xiaogang is a small village in Fengyang county, with thirty-four households and 73 hectares of arable land. In 1955, individual farmers in Xiaogang were organised, by a working group sent by the government, into one advanced co-operative without passing through the stages of a mutual-aid team and an elementary co-operative. In 1958, the advanced co-operative was transformed by the government into a production team of a people's commune. During the agricultural crisis in 1959–62, of a total population of 175, 60 died of hunger and another 76 were forced to leave their homes for survival. During the Cultural Revolution (1966–76), per capita income was only about 30 yuan and per capita grain production was 100 kilograms. In 1978, Xiaogang had a very serious drought and many people had to leave the village to look for work elsewhere. In February 1979, eighteen families of the Xiaogang team made a secret agreement amongst themselves to divide their land among individual households.[2] The household that accepted responsibility for a plot of land was also responsible for the associated agricultural tax, procurement quotas and collective welfare fund. As a result of the responsibility system, the Xiaogang team has had the highest output levels for grain and oil for the past twenty years. Per capita grain output rose to 300 kilograms, enough for them not only to be self-sufficient but also to meet procurement quotas for the government.

This extraordinary success caused a rapid spread of the responsibility systems among neighbouring production teams within a very short period. At the end of 1979, 83 per cent of production teams in Fengyang

Table 3.1. *Adoption of different responsibility systems, 1979 to 1983*

	1979	1980	1981	1982	1983
			per cent		
Special management system	55.7	39.0	16.5	5.1	–
Contracting of output to group	24.9	23.6	10.8	2.1	–
Contracting of output to labour	3.1	8.6	15.8	12.6	–
Contracting of output to household	1.0	9.4	7.1	4.9	–
Contracting all functions to household	–	5.0	38.0	67.0	97.8

Note: The proportion of teams experimenting with contracting everything to individual households was 0.02 per cent in 1979.
Sources: Guo et al., 1993.

county that joined Xiaogang adopted this system of 'contracting everything to the household' (Guo et al. 1993). At the same time, about 85 per cent of China's production teams were involved in various experiments with changing responsibility for monitoring production.

In their early stages of development the responsibility systems depended on what was contracted and how output was related to rewards. The usual grouping included 'special management system' (the term is borrowed from Li Yunhe), 'contracting of output to group', 'contracting of output to labour', 'contracting of output to household', and 'contracting all functions to household' (table 3.1).

Under the special management system (*Dinger Baogan*), team members were still involved in collective labour. But they could contract part or fixed pieces of farm work from the team and would be awarded working points depending on the quality of their work. Income distribution remained the same as that in the traditional production team.

There were systems where the group, individual or household accepted a contract for a plot from the team. They were responsible for output which determined the amount of working points they would receive from the team.

'Contracting all functions to the household' was the system that we call the household responsibility system today. Arable land was divided and contracted to individual households in the team giving them responsibility for meeting obligatory procurement quotas. The household then made production decisions depending on production plans (in the early years). The household retained all output after taking away agricultural taxes and collective levies and fulfilling procurement quotas. The working-point system was thus abolished, while the public ownership of land was maintained.

About 56 per cent of production teams had adopted 'the special management system' in 1979 (table 3.1). Reform spread quickly, becoming more comprehensive. Over the next ten years the number of teams that adopted contracted output to groups and households started to rise. From 1981, the household responsibility system was the most common way in which production was organised. By the end of 1983, about 98 per cent of production teams had adopted the system.

This transition between different forms of responsibility systems was an interesting process of farmers' institutional learning and innovation, given the policy constraints. At the beginning, the majority simply tried to improve the internal management of the commune system. Because of the experience gained from their own experiments and more political freedom from the government explicitly or implicitly, they gradually moved to systems relating reward more directly to efforts. Growth of output and productivity as a result of the new systems developed their confidence in learning and innovation.

Why is the household responsibility system superior?

The demise of the commune system and the adoption of household responsibility in China was not a forced process. But why did farmers tirelessly experiment with various kinds of responsibility systems and why did reform spread so rapidly within two or three years across the country? These questions can only be answered by comparing the household responsibility system (HRS) with the commune system to see if the transition from the latter to the former produced a superior institution. An institutional change is said to be institutionally efficient if (1) it reduces transaction costs, and (2) it promotes productivity growth.

Both of these criteria have been explicitly or implicitly discussed in the literature that analyses the household responsibility system, especially in comparisons with the commune system (Chinn 1980; Perkins and Yusuf 1984; Lin 1988; Perkins 1988).

The core difference between the household system and the production team system relates to incentives. Some also argue that the main problem with the production team system lay in its distributional mechanism (Chinn 1980; Putterman 1987, 1990). Incentives were low because of the egalitarian component of the distribution system. Team members were entitled to certain necessities even if they did not work. On the other hand, the marginal return to work was reduced assuming that the production technology exhibited decreasing marginal returns. Under a pure working-points distribution system, as suggested by Chinn (1980), there might be circumstances leading to 'universal diligence'. The problem of 'laziness' does not exist under the HRS as long as households are actually treated as individuals for production, income, consumption and welfare purposes. Some others point to the potential problems of management, especially when a production team was too large (Chinn 1980; Perkins and Yusuf 1984).

Lin's monitoring theory also explains why incentives are usually low in an agricultural collective (Lin 1988). His central argument is that monitoring agricultural work is costly. By constructing a theoretical model of an agricultural collective including an individual's maximisation of utility over income and effort, the collective's production and its choice of optimal monitoring, Lin establishes that the marginal return to an individual's effort can be described as

$$\frac{\partial I_i}{\partial e_i} = (1 - s_i) * A_i * (Y/E) + s_i Y_E \tag{3.1}$$

where I_i is individual i's income, e_i effort, and so $\partial I_i / \partial e_i$ is individual i's marginal income from his/her effort which represents the incentive to work. Y is the collective's total output, E total efforts and Y_E the marginal output of effort in the collective. A_i is an adjustment factor, ranging from 0 to 1, which makes the marginal return of total average output (Y/E) to individual's effort decrease with the degree of monitoring, and s_i is individual i's share in the collective's working points.

If there is perfect monitoring, the incentive to work in the collective is

$$\frac{\partial I_i}{\partial e_i} = (1 - s_i) * (Y/E) + s_i Y_E \tag{3.2}$$

which is a simple weighted average of the average output and the marginal output. When there is no monitoring, the marginal return to individual's effort becomes

$$\frac{\partial I_i}{\partial e_i} = \frac{1}{N} Y_E \tag{3.3}$$

where N is the number of collective members.

Lin suggests that there was not much monitoring in China's agricultural production teams because it was both difficult and costly, so the incentive to work, or the marginal income of effort, was very close to the case represented by equation (3.3). On the other hand, the incentive to work in an individual farm can be simplified as

$$\frac{\partial I_i}{\partial e_i} = Y_E \qquad (3.4)$$

It is not difficult to establish that the HRS is superior to the commune system by comparing incentives to work under the two systems as specified in equations (3.3) and (3.4). The scenario is complicated by incorporating imperfect monitoring and the scale economies of production. But the speed of the HRS reform indicated that, at least in the case of China, the benefit derived from collectivisation could not offset its efficiency losses. The empirical work of McMillan, Whalley and Zhu (1989) suggests that assuming peasants received their full marginal value of product under the responsibility system in 1984, they only received a little over 30 per cent of their marginal value of product under the earlier production team system.

In his theoretical model, Lin assumes that the team leader maximised the per capita (or total) output of his team (Lin 1988). But in many cases team leaders did not necessarily follow this principle, especially in cases where they were not elected democratically by team members. It was more usual for team leaders to be appointed by the commune authority. Monitoring was insufficient in production teams because of its difficulties. Monitoring was also related to the team leader's behaviour. These problems relate to the earlier discussion of the different aspirations of a household head and a team leader (see chapter 2). Because a household head usually regarded the household as a unit for production and consumption, household income levels related directly to his utility function. Under the HRS, the head would more actively monitor production to maximise the household's income. Within production teams, team leaders were usually allocated fixed working points for managing (as compensation for the leader's time spent on meetings, organisation, planning and management) plus the working points associated with his work. Assuming that the team leader was the only monitor, he would not be able to capture all the increased output resulting from his extra efforts in monitoring. The team leader would get only a proportion (equal to the share of his working points in the team's total points) of the increased output.

Other factors behind the success of household responsibility system reform

From an institutional perspective the success of the HRS reform in China was also facilitated by a number of other factors.

Table 3.2. *Changes in private plot policy, 1955 to 1980*

	The share of private plots in total land-holdings (per cent)	Main uses
1955–56	<=5	Vegetables
1957	<=10	Vegetables; feedgrain
1958	—	(Policy abolished)
1959–61	5–7	Vegetables; fruits; feedgrain; other grain
1962	<=20	Free plantation
1980	5–15	Free plantation

Source: Guo et al. 1993.

Farmers' persistence and the role of the private plot policy

One of the most important influences leading to the successful outcome of the reform was farmers' persistence with institutional experiments. Since the beginning of agricultural collectivisation Chinese farmers had never really stopped trying to improve their commitment by experimenting with various kinds of responsibility systems, even though most of the experiments were politically risky. These farmers may not have understood the sophisticated theoretical models developed later in the literature, but they could see clearly how their willingness to work (either for contracted work or on contracted land plots) was related to their rewards. They observed that output was raised by large margins whenever production activities or land plots were contracted to individuals or households. All aspects of production and distribution were exercised properly when the effort–reward relationship was clearly specified.

Farmers' practical understanding of the institutional differences between a production team and a household-based system came from their memories of individual farming in the pre-collectivisation period, from their experiments and their observations, and also from the co-existence of a private plot system with collective farming during the commune period.

By 1978, China had experienced about twenty-five years of central planning. Most farmers still had clear memories of fully operating markets. This contrasted with the historical background to economic reform in the former Soviet Union, from the end of the 1980s, when most of the current generation had never seen a real free market.

In China the private plot system continued to exist throughout most of the commune years. Production teams usually left out about 5 per cent of arable land and allocated it equitably among individual households for their own use (table 3.2). These plots were still owned by the collective, but households made their own decisions about what crops to grow. Before the 1960s the range of crops was restricted.

Economists have not always taken into account the importance of these private plots. The issue tended to be raised when the question of whether private plots competed with collective farming for resources was asked. Liu (1991) suggests that the role of the private sector was complementary to commune farming, basing this conclusion on his own observations. The private plot system, whether competing with or complementary to collective farming, made two important contributions – one to the commune system and the other to the HRS system. Because farm households could freely manage their private plots and the production teams did not collect from them, these small pieces of land gave farmers tremendous incentives to produce. This leverage helped millions of farmers to survive through crop and management crises, in turn helping the commune system to be maintained. On the other hand, as farmers worked on their private plots through the years, they understood the advantages of household farming, practising and developing farm entrepreneurship on their small plots. This laid the foundation for the successful introduction of the household responsibility system.

A learning process for the government

The experience of household reform suggests that it was not a simple outcome of the government's reform policy; rather it was a gradual process of retreat from the government's original political position. By observing the spread of the household system and its effects on raising output, the government also went through an important process of learning and understanding about institutions.

Local governments in poor areas were the first to permit and even support HRS reform. The central government changed its position gradually in response. At the party's Third Plenum in December 1978, the official position was still that production teams were to remain the basic unit of production management and accounting. Any change to this was strictly prohibited. Despite this stance, in September 1979 the government started to allow experiments with 'special management systems'. In September 1980, it further permitted the adoption of various forms of output contracting (to groups, labour and households). The HRS, however, was only allowed as an experiment in poor areas. It was not until January 1982 and the first 'No. 1 Document' that the HRS was officially adopted as a policy and implemented across the nation.[3] The document confirmed that the HRS as well as the public ownership of basic agricultural means, mainly land, would be maintained as long-term policies. This led directly to an increase in the adoption of the HRS from 38 per cent in 1981 to 67 per cent in 1982 and 98 per cent in 1983.

Why didn't the government learn these lessons and adjust its policies to encourage commitment in the agricultural system in the pre-reform period? The key to the delay lay in the redirection of government strategies at the end of the 1970s. The Chinese government was then wrestling with large economy-wide policy changes: first, to put aside the class struggle and to assign top priority to economic development; second, to abandon the heavy-industry oriented development strategy and to replace it with a strategy for development that related production more to China's comparative advantage. In the pre-reform period any slight deviation from central planning and the commune system was regarded as a violation of the principles of socialism; economic efficiency was only considered after that. After economic development was lifted to the top policy objective during the reform period, economic efficiency, productivity improvement, output growth and raising living standards become more important measures in comparing different production institutions.

Impact of the reforms

Agricultural growth, 1978 to 1984

By any measure the HRS reforms brought about rapid growth in China's agricultural production through the years 1978 to 1984, but especially in comparison with the growth performance in the pre-reform period. First, agricultural yields rose sharply during this period for all major crops (figure 3.1). Average grain yield increased by 43 per cent from 2,535 kg/hectare in 1978 to 3,615 kg/hectare in 1984, almost three times that in 1952. The growth in yields was even more pronounced for cotton, which recorded growth of 13 per cent per annum during 1978–84, compared to 2.6 per cent from 1952 to 1978. Yield growth rates also rose significantly for both oil crops and jute – from around 1 per cent from 1952 to 1978 to above 9 per cent from 1978 to 1984.

Second, as a result of increases in yield, agricultural output rose significantly (table 3.3). The growth rate of total grain output increased from 2.4 per cent per annum over the period 1952–78 to 5 per cent from 1978 to 1984. In 1984, total grain output reached a historical record level of 407 million tonnes. Among various grain crops, the average growth rate from 1978 to 1984 was 8.5 per cent for wheat, negative for potatoes

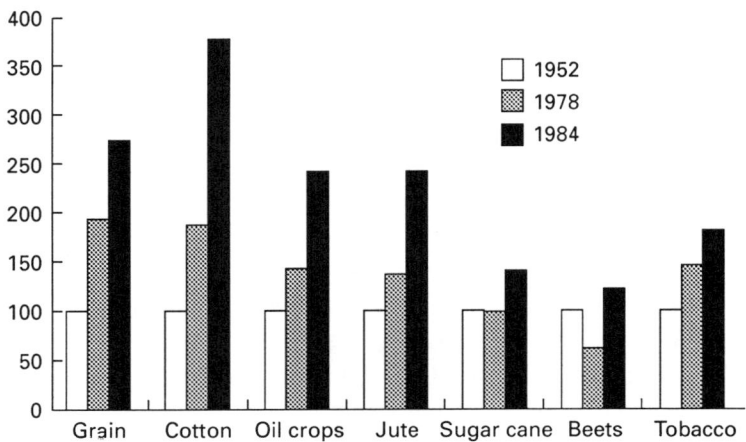

Fig. 3.1. Agricultural yields, 1952, 1978 and 1984 (1952 = 100). The actual 1952 yields (kg/hectare) were: grain, 1,320; cotton, 240; oil crops, 510; jute, 975; sugar cane, 38,955; beets, 13,650; tobacco, 1,200. (*Source:* SSB, *China Statistical Yearbook 1991.*)

(−1.8 per cent), and above 4 per cent for maize, soybean and rice. The reduction of potato output, from 32 million tonnes in 1978 to 29 million tonnes in 1984, reflected an upgrading of consumption. Potatoes, a major foodgrain for many farmers in the pre-reform period, gradually disappeared from dinner tables in the rural areas during the reform period. Output growth for non-grain crops was even more astonishing, partly reflecting the adjustment of production away from that of single grain crops in the pre-reform period. Output of cotton and beets grew at around 20 per cent per annum from 1978 to 1984, while meat output, sugar cane, oil crops and seawater aquatic crops all increased by more than 10 per cent per annum.

As a result, the average growth rate of agriculture rocketed from 1.9 per cent over the period 1952–78 to 7.4 per cent during the period 1978–84. Farmers' per capita income increased from 133 yuan in 1978 to 355 yuan in 1984, in nominal terms. The real growth rate of farmers' per capita income was 15 per cent per annum between 1978 and 1984. Increasing incomes not only lifted the absolute living standards of rural people significantly, but also narrowed the rural–urban income gap. In 1978, the per capita urban income was 136 per cent above the rural income. This gap was reduced to 69 per cent in 1983 and 71 per cent in 1984.

Table 3.3. *Agricultural output growth before and after the reform, 1952 to 1984*

	Agricultural output (million tonnes)			Annual growth rate (per cent)	
	1952	1978	1984	1952–78	1978–84
Grain	163.9	304.8	407.3	2.4	5.0
Paddy rice	68.4	136.9	178.3	2.7	4.5
Wheat	18.1	53.8	87.8	4.3	8.5
Maize	16.7	56.0	73.4	4.8	4.6
Soybean	9.5	7.6	9.7	−0.9	4.2
Potatoes	16.3	31.7	28.5	2.6	−1.8
Cotton	1.3	2.2	6.3	2.0	19.2
Oil crops	4.2	5.2	11.9	0.8	14.8
Jute	0.3	1.1	1.5	5.0	5.4
Sugar crops	7.6	23.8	47.8	4.5	12.3
Sugar cane	7.1	21.1	39.5	4.3	11.0
Beets	0.5	2.7	8.3	6.7	20.5
Tea	0.1	0.3	0.4	4.3	4.9
Tobacco	0.2	1.1	1.5	6.8	5.3
Fruits	2.4	6.6	9.8	4.0	6.8
Meat	3.4	8.6	15.4	3.6	10.2
Aquatic crops	1.7	4.7	6.2	4.0	4.8
Freshwater	1.1	3.6	3.9	4.8	1.5
Seawater	0.6	1.1	2.3	2.1	13.4

Source: SSB, *China Statistical Yearbook 1991*.

By the mid-1980s, the daily nutritional intake of the Chinese population had moved close to the world average, surpassing that of India and of many other developing countries.

Quantifying the contributions of the household reform

How important, then, was the HRS reform in this agricultural 'miracle' during 1978–84? Other reform measures and policy changes were also introduced at this time. State purchase prices of agricultural products were increased and so was government investment in agriculture. Agricultural inputs also increased dramatically at the same time. Empirical studies to identify the effects of different policy reforms on agricultural growth during that period, however, conclude that HRS reform made a significant contribution (table 3.4).[4]

In an attempt to decompose the effects of price increases and the HRS reform for the period 1978–84, McMillan, Whalley and Zhu (1989) apply Solow–Denison type growth-accounting techniques, incorporating the

Table 3.4. *Quantitative assessments of the household responsibility system reform, 1965 to 1985*

Study	Period covered	Findings
McMillan, Whalley and Zhu (1989)	1978–84	Total productivity growth was 41 per cent from 1978, HRS reform accounted for 78 per cent of this
Fan (1991)	1965–85	Annual output growth was 5 per cent, 1965–85, the HRS reform accounted for 26.6 per cent of total output growth or 63 per cent of productivity growth
Lin (1992a)	1978–84	The HRS reform accounted for 46.9 per cent of total output growth from 1978 to 1984 or 96.4 per cent of productivity growth

Note: Lin's study covers the period 1978–87 divided into two sub-periods, 1978–84 and 1984–87. His results for 1978–84 are summarised in this table.

behavioural responses of agricultural workers. Of the total factor productivity increase of 41 per cent between 1978 and 1984 they find that 78 per cent can be attributed to the HRS reform and another 22 per cent to increases in agricultural prices.

Fan's study covers a longer period, from 1965 to 1985 (Fan 1991). He uses an accounting approach to separate the relative contribution of increases in factor inputs, technological change and the HRS reform. He suggests that the average growth of agricultural output was 5 per cent and of productivity was 2.1 per cent during the period under study. HRS reform contributed about 27 per cent of output growth and 63 per cent of productivity growth. He further points out that regional differences were large with land-scarce regions gaining more from the reforms.

Lin (1992a) employs province-level panel data to assess the contributions of HRS reform and other changes to China's agricultural growth in the reform period. The production-function approach proposed by Zvi Griliches is applied. Lin finds that agricultural output increased by 42.2 per cent between 1978 and 1984 and productivity grew by 20.5 per cent. The HRS reform accounted for 46.9 per cent of total output growth and 96.4 per cent of productivity growth.

But the gains that HRS reform brought did not end in 1984, nor were they restricted to the agricultural sector. The most significant change brought by the HRS reform was the re-establishment of the household system. It provided farm households with autonomy in decisionmaking, with incentives to work hard and with room for farmers to use their entrepreneurial abilities. 'Careful calculation', 'strict budgeting' and 'work initiatives' (Li 1957) brought technological progress and the development of non-agricultural production, particularly the rapid expansion of the township, village and private enterprise sector (TVP). Individual farming also increased farmers' bargaining power with the state and other interest groups on issues such as state purchase prices. These secondary effects mostly happened in the post-1985 period and may prove to be more important than the direct effects felt during 1978–84, although they are quantitatively difficult to measure.

Problems and further reform

The HRS has now become a 'model' of successful economic reform. Collective land was contracted to farmers at the beginning of the HRS reform for a term of fifteen years. As this term came to an end, the government announced a new policy in 1995 extending the existing contracts for a further fifteen years. It has been made clear that the HRS will be maintained as a long-term policy.

But it is not without problems. The nature of the HRS can be characterised by two phrases: 'collective ownership' and 'household farming'. The publicly owned land was contracted to individual households on egalitarian principles. According to one recent survey of 274 villages about 75.9 per cent of the total land area was evenly divided up and contracted amongst households on the basis of population, a further 17.6 per cent went to the labour force, and 2.1 per cent was contracted out through a bidding process in 1984. These shares had changed to 78.4, 14.5 and 3 per cent by 1990 (Luo 1994).[5] In theory, the government's attempts to establish a new two-level system – with households as the basic production units and collective services – were strengthened (or at least not weakened). But in reality, effective supply of social services by collectives does not exist in most of rural China except in a number of villages where the collective economy (the TVP sector) is developing rapidly.

One phenomenon that followed the implementation of the HRS was the decay of agricultural infrastructure and the decline in farmers' long-term investment on land. Under the commune system, massive labour forces were mobilised for the construction of agricultural infrastructure. Such work, though very inefficient, significantly improved production infrastructure in the pre-reform period. The demise of the commune system was not accompanied by the development of new mechanisms for organising and encouraging (labour and capital) investment in agricultural infrastructure. Collective investment in agriculture had been 5.2 billion yuan in 1982, but had decreased dramatically to 2.1 billion yuan by 1985. At the beginning of the reform, this did not alarm policymakers and policy analysts as there was an expectation that farmers, now under the HRS, would look after agricultural investment themselves. Farmers, however, did not invest heavily in agriculture. They, instead, invested heavily in housing. Housing investment accounted for 85 per cent of farmers' total investment in 1982. This share decreased slowly in the following years, but was still as high as 70 per cent in 1992 (in fact it increased to 85.5 per cent in 1986 and near 88 per cent in 1987).

Low agricultural investment by farmers in this period can be explained by the competition for investment uses such as agriculture, housing and non-agricultural activities. It can also be explained by the nature of land contracts. According to the law, farmers do not own the land. They are therefore reluctant to make any significant long-term investment in land because of the expectation that the land will one day be taken away from them.

The equal division of land between households also prevented scale economies in agricultural production. Modernisation (which should not simply be understood as mechanisation) becomes very difficult when land is so widely distributed. Farmers with non-agricultural employment keep their small land-holdings, not willing to return them to the collective or to hand them over to other households. Most of them regard their small pieces of land as an employment insurance and as food security.

If not solved quickly and effectively, these property issues will threaten the growth potential of China's agricultural sector. One solution is seen by some theoreticians and policymakers as the privatisation of agricultural land. Others, maintaining the principles of socialist public ownership, try to design complementary institutions. An example is to divide the total land areas into two parts, one contracted according to population for the production of foodgrain and the other contracted through a competition process.

Notes

1 *Zhejiang Daily* is the official newspaper of the Zhejiang province's Party Committee and the government. The fact that Li Yunhe's article was published in an official newspaper indicated some degree of freedom for discussion of these issues at that time. At the time of publication of the article, Li Yunhe was Yongjia county's Deputy Party Secretary. He was, however, purged from the party soon after that. He was later appointed the Deputy Director of the Rural Policy Research Office of the Zhejiang provincial government in the 1980s.

2 The decision was very risky at that time and the team leader was prepared to go to jail for making it.
3 Between 1982 and 1986, the central government issued 'No. 1 Document' at the beginning of every year outlining policies on rural reforms for the year. All the 'No. 1 Documents' had good reputations because of all the new policies. The one in 1982, focusing particularly on the HRS reform, was the first of these.
4 In a broader study, Yang, Wang and Wills (1990) tested the relationship between per capita real income, the degree of commercialisation, efficiencies and property rights using Chinese rural data for 1979–87. The results suggest that the contribution of the reform of the property structure in rural China during this period to economic growth via its effects on organisational efficiency accounts for 48 per cent of total growth and the contribution of the reform to growth via its effects on allocative efficiency accounts for 52 per cent.
5 According to the survey, about 2–3 per cent of land, in both 1984 and 1990, was operated through different mechanisms, such as unified management by the collectives (Luo 1994: 179).

4

Getting prices right

Reform of agricultural prices policy

There were two important policies that contributed to agriculture's success from 1978 to 1984. The HRS was only one, though it was the more important. The other was the increase in state purchase prices for agricultural products. McMillan, Whalley and Zhu's (1989) study, for instance, suggests that 22 per cent of agricultural productivity growth was attributable to price increases.

Looking back at changes in state purchase prices over the past forty years, both the magnitude and frequency of price adjustments increased significantly in the post-reform period (table 4.1). In the pre-reform period, state prices for agricultural products were unchanged for many years. Prices for cotton, for instance, remained almost constant in the periods 1955–62, 1963–70 and, again, 1972–76. Oil crop prices exhibited a similar pattern. Prices for meat, sugar crops, poultry, eggs and tobacco were stagnant for twelve years after 1965, until economic reform. The story for grain prices was largely the same in the pre-reform period (figure 4.1).

Changes in state prices became more frequent and pronounced during the reform period. The first increases in purchase prices for agricultural products in 1979 marked the starting point of China's agricultural reform. Quota prices were increased by 20.9 per cent for grain, 23.9 per cent for oil crops, 17 per cent for cotton, 21.9 per cent for sugar crops and 24.3 per cent for hog meat (Huang 1993a). The average increase for the quota prices was 17.1 per cent. Premiums paid on above-quota delivery of grain and oil crops were raised from 30 per cent to 50 per cent above quota prices, and a 30 per cent bonus was introduced for above-quota delivery of cotton. The average increase in state procurement prices was 22.1 per cent. The weighted average procurement price, which includes both quota and non-quota procurement, increased 21.5 per cent for wheat in 1979, 20.7 per cent for paddy rice, 20.5 per cent for corn and

Table 4.1. Indices of state purchase prices for agricultural products, 1952 to 1990

	Agricultural total	All grain	Wheat	Rice	Maize	Oil crops	Cotton	Jute	Tobacco	Sugar	Meat	Poultry	Eggs	Fruits	Vegetables	Aquatic crops
1952	55.9	54.1	57.3	56.1	49.6	33.7	82.3	69.7	66.0	57.6	51.3	48.2	44.7	63.7	69.0	57.5
1955	62.1	61.2	66.7	62.0	57.3	38.1	80.0	71.8	69.3	60.5	60.1	60.7	58.8	72.8	82.6	65.4
1960	72.4	67.6	68.2	67.2	65.6	64.8	80.1	77.4	72.8	75.8	76.3	93.5	89.5	89.9	109.3	87.7
1961	92.6	85.5	87.3	85.8	81.6	76.0	80.2	82.3	88.6	85.7	91.8	126.7	124.0	103.0	134.1	110.7
1965	86.4	85.1	87.0	86.8	84.3	76.8	88.5	90.6	98.5	89.3	96.5	86.7	85.5	89.3	90.6	95.9
1970	89.7	98.5	100.0	99.0	100.0	76.8	88.5	92.9	98.5	89.3	96.5	93.6	93.0	84.4	91.6	92.5
1975	96.0	99.3	100.0	100.0	100.0	95.8	91.4	98.0	99.5	99.9	99.6	98.3	99.2	88.6	97.0	97.6
1978	100.0	100.0	100.0	100.0	100.0	100.0	100.0	100.0	100.0	100.0	100.0	100.0	100.0	100.0	100.0	100.0
1979	122.1	130.5	131.1	130.2	130.0	132.7	125.3	112.3	100.3	121.9	124.2	120.3	123.2	102.2	109.1	118.2
1980	130.8	140.8	141.3	140.4	140.1	140.0	145.6	125.9	104.6	125.0	127.5	120.7	124.5	107.3	116.7	120.3
1981	138.5	154.5	148.7	147.8	147.4	146.9	152.6	131.6	122.3	130.1	127.9	128.8	132.7	109.1	122.3	122.3
1982	141.6	160.3	154.3	148.8	153.0	149.1	154.9	132.9	122.0	131.6	128.3	130.9	133.7	111.4	121.6	126.2
1983	147.8	176.9	170.1	164.0	168.6	150.0	155.2	130.7	122.4	131.6	128.2	140.5	133.5	106.0	129.1	138.5
1984	153.7	198.1	171.1	164.0	168.6	151.8	156.9	135.3	122.6	137.6	131.1	144.7	135.6	142.8	127.8	209.6
1985	166.9	201.6	171.3	167.3	171.8	158.3	153.3	148.2	125.6	142.7	163.9	169.4	157.1	186.0	157.6	231.4
1986	177.6	221.6	178.6	177.8	198.5	165.6	152.5	174.5	125.8	149.6	171.3	189.9	173.9	156.2	165.2	284.2
1987	198.9	239.3	184.4	201.3	206.6	175.5	159.7	129.3	133.2	165.0	203.8	235.0	220.1	221.1	197.4	376.0
1988	244.7	274.3	212.8	241.2	216.3	210.1	173.4	100.0	142.7	191.5	303.9	278.9	256.4	308.6	241.2	504.9
1989	281.4	348.1	259.4	315.2	285.1	251.7	212.8	115.1	136.3	258.7	333.1	322.4	288.2	278.4	244.3	503.9
1990	274.1	324.4	238.6	291.9	278.3	254.4	274.7	115.3	154.9	277.3	310.1	322.1	296.6	271.4	229.9	497.9

Source: SSB, *China Price Statistical Yearbook*, various issues.

17 per cent for cotton. Alongside the price increases, the procurement quota for grain was reduced by 5.9 per cent to 35 million tonnes. This was further reduced to 34 million tonnes in 1980, and to 30 million tonnes in 1981 (Huang 1993a).

The 1985 reform liberalised the state's purchasing policies for most agricultural products.[1] The post-1985 state procurement policy concentrated on grain, oil and cotton, though some other products, such as pork, were brought back into the planning system when market conditions were not stable. Following several years of difficulties in agricultural production, the government increased state purchase prices for major agricultural products in 1989, alongside the other policies. The purchase price for grain was raised by 27 per cent. Prices for wheat rose by 22 per cent, rice 31 per cent and maize 32 per cent. At the same time, the government also raised prices for oil crops, cotton and jute between 15 and 25 per cent. From the beginning of the 1990s, the government's reform focused on state marketing prices for grain.

State prices in the pre-reform period did not necessarily move in the same direction as the market prices (figure 4.1). In the mid-1970s, when market prices continued to rise, state prices did not respond to this change at all and stayed at exactly the same level. In the post-reform period, however, state prices moved closely with market prices, although the gap was still significant and some time lag in government response to changing market prices was sometimes evident.

It is clear that the increases in state prices have been accelerating. Price adjustments in both the pre- and post-reform periods contributed directly to the growth of agricultural output and increases in farmers' income. There are different views about how state prices affected producers' production decisions and their income. When the state price is the only prevailing price (when no secondary market exists), it serves as the marginal price. By raising purchase prices and holding other conditions, output levels and farmers' income would increase. But in most years of the reform period, parallel markets existed alongside the state purchase plan. The role of state prices became controversial. Lin (1993) suggests that state prices directly affected production and consumption decisions where the state procurement quotas were endogenously set (either as a function of the output level or as a function of the quota in the previous period). On the other hand, Sicular (1988b) argues that, in a dual market, the policies implemented in the state market do not directly affect production and consumption decisions but do have an income effect. The significance of this income effect depends on the levels of quotas, and the gap between state prices and market prices.

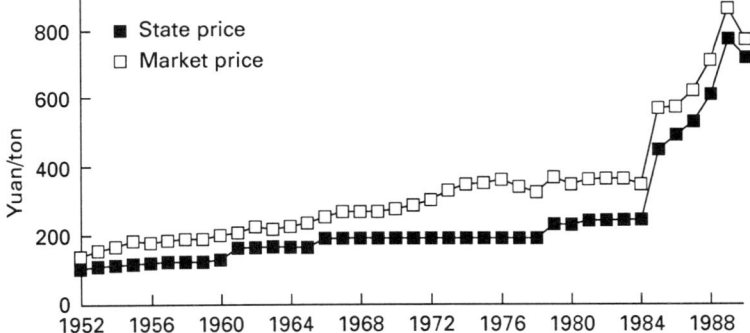

Fig. 4.1. State and market prices for grain, 1952 to 1990. Rural retail prices are only proxies. Grains are measured by tradable units (*Maoyi Liang*) and all prices are mixed average prices.

Ignoring this second-round income effect, a low state price is similar to a lump-sum income tax on producers which equals the gap between the state and market prices multiplied by procurement quotas. Increases in state prices, in this case, are equivalent to a reduction of income taxes on farmers in another instance.

Whichever is the case, there is no doubt that an increase in state prices generates direct benefits to farmers. It is then interesting to ask why the government changed its purchase prices. The answer to this question depends, to some extent, on what approaches are applied to analysing the effects of government policy decisions. Usually, in economic studies, policy decisions are treated as exogenously determined, or as outputs from a black box. The reason lies in the distinction between the private and social valuation of economic activities (Stenvens and Jabara 1988). Economic efficiency in agricultural production is, in many respects, inconsistent with welfare maximisation (Schultz 1978).

Divergence between private and social valuations may occur in various ways (Abel 1978). It may also be argued that, in the case of agricultural prices in China in the reform period, state prices were adjusted simply to eliminate price distortions. This exogenous treatment of government policy offers insufficient explanation in that it neglects interactions between the government and the private sector, particularly in the long run (Rausser, Lichtenberg and Lattimore 1982).[2]

The hypothesis made here is that changes in state purchase prices also relate to an institutional innovation of continuing dialogue between the government and individual interest groups such as farmers and consumers. The government has its own objectives, but these objectives only become important when support for them is strong and opposition is weak. There were only a few price adjustments before the reform because farmers had relatively little bargaining power. Farmers became increasingly powerful through the process of reform. Frequent increases in purchase prices for agricultural products may demonstrate the government's intentions to reduce agricultural distortion.

In this chapter we establish a framework within which the dynamics of state prices can be analysed as a process of interaction between the government and farmers. A co-operative game approach is applied although there is no formal bargaining framework. Changes in grain prices are selected as the subject of an important case study. This particular choice has a number of advantages. Grain is an important agricultural product that was very strictly controlled by the government both before and after the reform. Grain production accounted for a large proportion of farmers' total production and income. More importantly, marketing policies for grain had not changed significantly by 1991. If consumers are not included as an interest group in this game, the analysis is simplified. The empirical work covers the period 1953–90. Marketing policies changed significantly after that period and this changed the structure of the game. A structural variable is incorporated to test changes in the game brought about by economic reform.

Theories on endogenous government policy

Endogenous government intervention in agriculture has been a persistent area of interest in economic studies in the past decades. A number of alternative paradigms addressing the fundamentals of endogenous government behaviour have been developed.

The first is the liberal-pluralist framework which identifies the relationship between policymakers and voters as the central issue. Several classes of models have been developed within this group. Many of these models assume that individuals have a potential demand for redistribution of income toward themselves (Stigler 1970). The self-interest coalition models argue that politicians are motivated by votes and thus attempt to satisfy such demand in order to increase their probability of re-election (Buchanan and Tullock 1962). The prediction made by this type of model is that, over the long run, society continually moves in the direction of greater equality of income distribution. The median model of self-interest, however, argues that, presuming that preferences for distribution toward oneself are single-peaked with respect to income, the median voter predominates and preferences for such redistribution are satisfied through the political process. This model predicts income redistribution from high-income and low-income families toward middle-income families (Stigler 1971). The Pareto-optimal income redistribution formulation transforms issues of distribution into questions of efficiency (Hochman and Rodgers 1969). One variant of this formulation specifies that donors of taxes derive utility from the income levels of transfer recipients. This framework predicts redistribution of income from high-income to low-income individuals.

The second paradigm is the theory of the state. It challenges the liberal-pluralist formulation by arguing that government institutions emerge because one dominant interest group has significant monopoly power (O'Connor 1973; Jessop 1977; Roemer 1978). This theory is based on groups of agents called classes rather than individual economic agents. The dominant class, usually the capitalist class, makes use of its monopoly power to direct or control the resources of the state. Over time, income becomes increasingly concentrated and as the observed income distribution becomes more unequal, the non-dominant classes, usually the working class, the unemployed and farmers, threaten to remove their support of the state and to delegitimise the government. In the face of extreme social discontent, vocal opposition to the state and the threat of possible revolution, the government is presumed to respond by providing a range of social services and income supplements.

The third paradigm is the theory of economic regulation. Political leaders adopt policies with the aim of maximising their chances of remaining in office (Stigler 1971; Peltzman 1976; Tyers and Anderson 1992). The regulator, therefore, desires to maximise the 'majority', defined as the number of potential voters in the beneficiary group times the probability that a beneficiary will grant support less the number of potential voters in opposing groups times the probability those who are 'taxed' will oppose. Interest groups that expect to gain from a potential policy change seek its adoption by investing in lobbying, while those opposed to the policy, lobby against it. Both parties invest until the expected marginal return is zero (Tyers and Anderson 1992).

Anderson (1989) outlines three reasons why the government in a poor country is unlikely to raise the incomes of the farm majority by taxing the non-farm minority. First, the fiscal problems of collecting tax revenue from the non-farm minority to pay even a small subsidy to each farmer would be enormous given the high costs of tax collection and revenue dispersion. Second, the often better-educated, politically more articulate minority is located in urban areas and so is likely to be able to lobby the government at a much lower cost than could farmers. Third, the non-farm minority includes employers of unskilled labour, the wages for whom depend both directly and indirectly on food prices. These ideas have been developed and rationalised through application of computable general equilibrium models incorporating representative parameters to demonstrate the income distribution effects of different patterns of price distortions. The results show that, on a per capita basis, the losers lose little relative to the benefits to gainers (Anderson 1989; Tyers and Anderson 1992).[3]

The fourth paradigm is known as the theory of rent-seeking interest groups and conflict resolution. This formulation explicitly incorporates both economic and political markets, and includes a process for resolving conflicting goals (Krueger 1974; Zusman 1976). Brock and Magee (1978, 1979) present a general equilibrium framework which assumes an economy consisting of individual agents, politicians, firms and goods which are produced and either consumed or used as inputs. In this framework, government intervention generates losses for some agents who would be willing to pay up to a certain amount to prevent the intervention, while the gainers would be willing to offer a certain amount in order to secure the intervention. Brock and Magee (1978, 1979) employed a non-cooperative game-theoretic framework with politicians acting as Stackelberg leaders. Competing politicians attempt to maximise their probability of re-election. These probabilities are functions of campaign contributions from lobby groups and the politician's intervention position.[4]

The setting of policy and its instruments can be divided into two stages: the first involves the legislative choice process and the second, the bureaucratic choice process. Although the concept of an interest group is extremely important in analysing agricultural policy, few studies have empirically investigated the legislative choice process of government intervention in agriculture. Agricultural interests are too specialised to affect the election of all politicians and are probably insufficient to make most electoral frameworks coherent with respect to agricultural policy (Rausser, Lichtenberg and Lattimore 1982).[5]

While the general objectives of agricultural policy might be determined by the legislative choice process (Brock and Magee 1978, 1979; Tyers and Anderson 1992), the bureaucratic choice process is more important in determining the particular policy instruments adopted and the ways in which they are implemented (Zusman and Amiad 1977; Beghin 1990; Beghin and Karp 1991).

A co-operative game-theoretic framework is employed by Zusman

(1976) and Zusman and Amiad (1977) in their studies of Israeli sugar and dairy policies, respectively, and by Beghin (1990) and Beghin and Karp (1991) in examining Senegalese agricultural price policy.

Zusman (1976) assumes an additive utility function for each interest group: the government; the Israeli Labour Federation (representing consumers); and sugar producers. Each of these three groups is assumed to have a utility function which is separable in the benefits and costs imposed by the sugar subsidy and in the cost of exerting effort to influence the level of this subsidy. The concept of equilibrium employed in this game is Harsanyi's generalisation of the Nash co-operative game solution to an n-person game (Harsanyi 1963). The solution concept implies that the entire co-operative game is broken down into two distinct components. The first is a non-cooperative sub-game in which agents bargain to arrive at a division of the final payoff. The division arrived at is determined by the relative bargaining strengths of the agents and the coalitions they form. These, in turn, arise out of the pressure which can then potentially be brought to bear on competing agents and coalitions. In the second co-operative sub-game, all agents jointly strive to maximise the size of the total payoff as this will maximise each agent's and/or coalition's share. At equilibrium, the payoff is divided according to the results of the first sub-game.[6]

Beghin (1990) and Beghin and Karp (1991), in examining Senegalese agricultural price policy, also apply an n-person co-operative game framework by using a reference point solution (Thomson 1981). Reference points are payoffs which players refer to when they evaluate payoff proposals.[7] The Nash conflict point (d) and the point of minimum expectation (mex) are examples of reference payoffs.

For a two-player game, u_d^* and u_{mex}^* are two corresponding solutions on the frontier (H) of the payoff set (P). Any convex combination of these two reference points can be another reference point, the solution of which lies on the frontier between u_d^* and u_{mex}^*. Once the conflict point is known, the original Nash solution is unique, whereas many reference point solutions are possible. This approach avoids the imposition of unnecessary rigidity in the model. It is also assumed that the payoff set and its frontier change with the economic environment. Hence players' payoffs, their bargaining power and their equilibrium strategies are influenced by exogenous shocks (for instance, changes in world prices and exchange rates) (Beghin 1990).

62 *Agricultural reform in China*

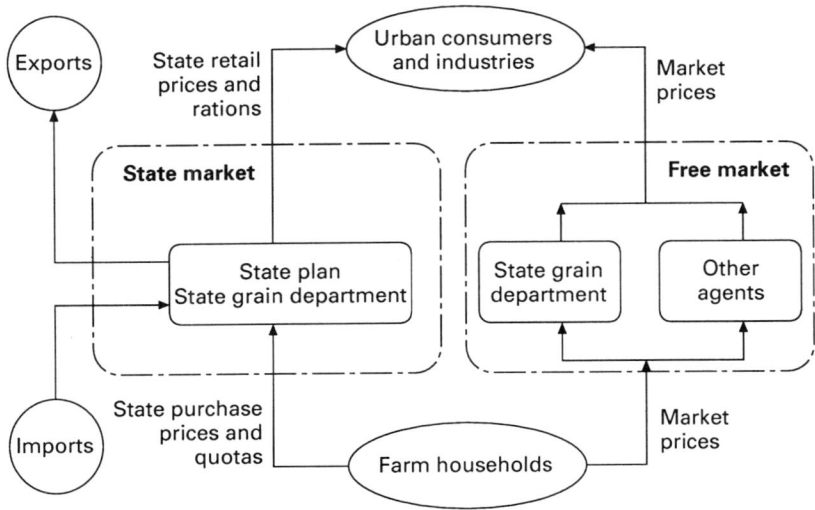

Fig. 4.2. The dual-market system for grain. Exchange of grain between farmers is ignored for simplicity. 'Other agents' refers to newly emerged non-state organisations doing business in grain. The term also covers the case where farmers sell grain directly to urban consumers or industrial enterprises.

State-farmer framework for grain policy

State monopsony in grain transactions

Grain transactions in China operate in a dual-market system (figure 4.2). This system existed before economic reform and was officially recognised at the beginning of 1985 as a part of the rural marketisation scheme. Within the state plan, government agents (the State Grain Department) purchase grain from farmers according to state prices and quotas that are set, and then sell the grain to urban consumers and industries according to state retail prices and retail rationing systems. The State Grain Department is subsidised if losses occur due to price differences, processing and transportation costs or inefficient management. Limited volumes of exports (of rice and coarse grains) and imports (of wheat) are incorporated into the economic plan. Farmers may sell their surpluses at market prices on the free market to either the State Grain Department or to other agents. As the counterpart of the free market, grain transactions managed by the state are defined as the state market.

The state-farmer framework developed in this study focuses on interactions between farmers and the government in China over grain policy. Because retail prices are fixed, the level of the purchase price has budgetary implications. As the government has to finance the gap between purchase and retail prices, the higher the purchase price, the heavier the pressure on the state budget. The government thus has an incentive to depress procurement prices or to minimise the total cost of grain purchases. This objective is constrained by another policy goal, that of grain self-sufficiency. The farmers' objective, however, is to maximise total revenue from grain production or to minimise losses from the state grain purchasing system.

Demand and supply in the state grain market

Grain transactions in the state market can also be characterised by demand and supply behaviour (figure 4.3). The demand curve reflects government's marginal valuation of grain purchases (DD). In the extreme case, if the constraint that the government faces in grain procurement is complete grain self-sufficiency, the demand curve is vertical. That is, the government has to buy a fixed amount of grain which equals a part of the estimated domestic demand by urban consumers and industries.[8] In the case of China, however, the demand curve is downward-sloping. Though estimated domestic demand is fixed, government's demand for grain in the state market is price-elastic as China also trades in the international grain market. The Chinese government pursues basic self-sufficiency, requiring that a dominant part of domestic demand be met by domestic supply. It also has limited flexibility, however, to switch between domestic and international supply sources. When domestic supply is short or the domestic purchase price becomes too high (because domestic demand becomes fully reliant on domestic sources), the government may substitute international trade for domestic procurement. The demand curve on the state market is therefore downward-sloping but very steep (figure 4.3).

Farmers' supply curve of grain is given by the segment of the marginal cost curve above its intersection with the average cost curve (SM in figure 4.3). The supply curve for the state market is slightly different from that of the free market. The special characteristics of the buyer – the government – must be taken into account. There are two ways for the government to depress the farmers' grain supply curve in the state market. First, it can restrict farmers' non-grain production opportunities (or narrow the farmers' feasible choice-set). By controlling farmers'

64 Agricultural reform in China

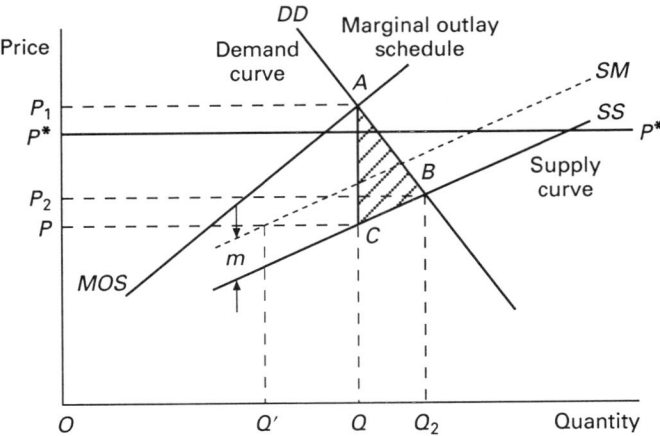

Fig. 4.3. Government monopsony in state grain transactions.

production factors (labour, capital and land) in grain production, the government is able to depress factor prices. The marginal cost of grain production can thus be lowered. This was one of the policies adopted by the Chinese government to enforce low prices for agricultural products.

Second, the government can impose penalties on farmers who fail or refuse to fulfil state procurement quotas (at low state prices). It can close down free markets for grain and other products – as it did many times – whenever there is difficulty in fulfilling the state purchase quota. The government can also create difficulties for troublesome farmers with their children's education, purchase of agricultural inputs, access to other public goods and employment opportunities in township and village enterprises, and in other ways. Through levying these penalties, the government is able to reduce all or some of farm households' income and welfare. From the farmers' point of view, these penalties can be converted into a monetary value, m, for each unit of grain supplied to the state.[9]

Armed with these potential penalties, the government is able to depress farmers' grain supply curve in the state market. Suppose that the marginal cost to produce one unit of grain is ΔC, a farmer will only supply this unit of grain if the market price P is at least as high as the marginal cost ($P = \Delta C$). Further, assuming that the government assigns this farmer a quota of one unit of grain, the farmer has two choices: either to sell the unit of grain to the state at a low state price ($\bar{P}_s$) or to sell it instead to the market at market price (P_m, $P_m > \bar{P}_s$), but incur penalties of m. The two choices are equivalent if $P_m - m = \bar{P}_s$. In other words, farmers would be happy to supply grain to the state as long as the state price is at least as high as $(P_m - m)$. The supply curve in the state market (SS) is therefore normally lower than its counterpart in free markets (SM).

Given supply (SS) and demand (DD) curves, equilibrium would occur at their intersection (B) in a competitive market, with price P_2 and quantity Q_2 (figure 4.3).

In the state market, however, the State Grain Department is the only grain buyer as other agents are prohibited. The government therefore possesses monopsony power. The more the state buys the higher the price it has to pay. Curve MOS is the government's marginal outlay schedule (Carlton and Perloff 1990). The amount the government buys is determined by the supply curve and MOS. The new equilibrium is at $C(P,Q)$. Compared with the equilibrium point B, the introduction of monopsony power into the market reduces both equilibrium quantity and price. The area P_1PCA represents rent captured by the government from its monopsony power and the shaded area ABC is the deadweight loss.

The essence of this game between the state and farmers is how the gap between market and state retail grain prices is shared. The state-farmer formulation presented in this study is obviously a state-dominant framework. A low grain supply price to urban consumers and industries was a preset policy condition (Lin 1991c). Nonetheless, the extent to which government can distort the farmers' supply curve and how much rent it can extract depend on the relative strengths of the two parties to the game.[10] The relative strengths, in turn, are determined by the destructive power each party possesses and the cost to the other in using it. The government punishes farmers who refuse to deliver grain to the state by reducing their income and welfare, although to impose these punishments involves a cost. Farmers, for their part, are not purely passive within this framework. They can choose not to plant grain at all, so that they will not be affected much should the government close the grain market. Exercising this option depends on their ability to survive otherwise. This would be an extremely costly strategy for the government, particularly if farmers adopted it collectively.

The dynamics of the game

In the early stages of economic development under a repressive and vindictive central state system, farmers tend to be weak in the state-farmer policy game, particularly when infrastructure is poorly developed. As agriculture is the major industry of the economy, and farmers are the dominant group of the population, farmers cannot be subsidised in their transactions with government. Any marginal benefit to farmers could entail a significant loss to the other members of society, and a severe burden on the state budget (Brock and Magee 1980).[11] The government is therefore willing to give up relatively large amounts of resources to implement its policies, as the opportunity benefit tends to be large. Farmers are unable to exercise any significant destructive strategy on the government collectively because of isolation and poor communication and transportation conditions. It is impossible to inform every farmer about new policy developments and lobbying. The destructive power of a few farmers refusing to deliver grain is very limited, and adopting this strategy could have significant consequences for the farmers involved.

As the economy develops, these relationships change. Economic development is sometimes characterised by diversification in the structure of economic activity and a fall in the population involved in agriculture (Timmer 1988; Tyers and Anderson 1992). Sources of government revenue become more diverse and revenue from grain production becomes a very small part of total revenue collected. The government, therefore, has a declining interest in agricultural revenue; it is only willing to incur a smaller cost to prevent the rise of state purchase prices or the fall of budget revenue from agriculture.[12] Even if the government contemplates punitive action, the significance of its destructive power has decreased dramatically and the costs of implementation have risen sharply. In a grain-dominant rural economy, the government would have to close the free market for grain as one penalty; now it has to close hundreds of free markets.

As the number of farmers falls and rural infrastructure (transportation and communications) improves, it becomes cheaper for farmers to lobby for a favoured policy. Their destructive power rises accordingly, particularly if the government is still stuck with a grain self-sufficiency constraint. The negative consequences of the government's potential penalties are reduced. If farmers are unhappy with the state purchase policy, they can choose to quit grain production, as many more non-grain and non-agricultural opportunities are available to them. If farmers are restricted from entering the township and village enterprises, they still have the choice of joining rural private firms or establishing one themselves.

All these factors cause the relative bargaining strengths of players in the state-farmer game to change. Farmers may become relatively stronger and the state relatively weaker as economic development progresses. This has two types of consequence for the state grain market.

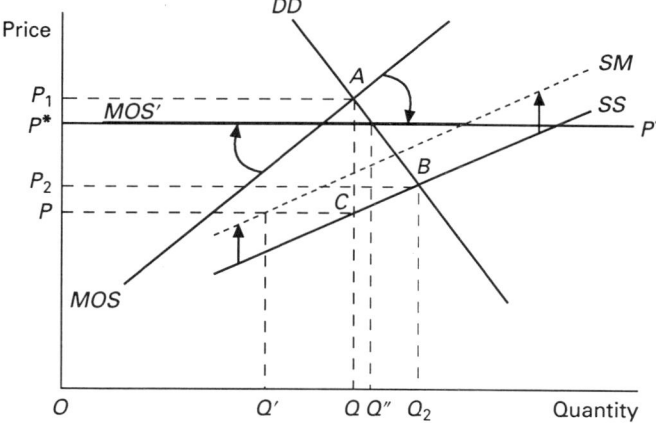

Fig. 4.4. The state and free markets for grain.

The first effect is that the potential penalty consequences (m) will decrease. Farmers thus tend not to accept even small gaps between the state price and the marginal cost of grain production (as $m \to 0$). This change results in upward shift in the supply curve in the state market and this continues during the process of economic development until state and free market supply curves coincide, i.e. farmers operate on their actual marginal cost schedule (figure 4.4).[13]

The second type of effect is that the government finds it increasingly difficult to exercise monopsony power in the procurement of grain. Lower state prices encounter stronger resistance from farmers who demand a market price for the grain they deliver to the state. Owing to the loss of monopsony power in the state market, the government gradually becomes a common buyer in the free grain market. As a competitive buyer, it can no longer affect the market equilibrium price. In figure 4.4, this is captured by the clockwise rotation of the MOS curve to a horizontal position (MOS', which is the same line as the market equilibrium price P^*P^*). The government will now purchase an amount of grain OQ'' and pay the market price, P^*.

A co-operative game-theoretic model

Deriving the model

As each party in the state-farmer formulation has destructive powers over the other's welfare or income, and these relative powers change over time, state purchase policy for grain has to be adjusted frequently. This formulation can be well accommodated by a co-operative game-theoretic model. Actual policy can thus be thought of as an equilibrium outcome of a bargaining process between the government and farmers.

There are two players, the government and the representative farmer, and two policy instruments, state purchase price and procurement quotas. The players bargain over the policy instrument setting with the aim of maximising their own utility. The government tries to minimise total expenditure on state grain purchases, constrained by the basic self-sufficiency condition. The farmer tries to maximise total revenue or minimise total losses from selling grain to the state.

From the possible solution concepts, the reference point solution is used (Thomson 1981) following Beghin (1990) and Beghin and Karp (1991). Reference points are the payoffs to which players refer when they evaluate payoff proposals. The Nash conflict point, d, is an example of a reference payoff, which is on the frontier (H) of the payoff set (P). This approach avoids imposing unnecessary rigidity on the model. It is also assumed that the payoff set and its frontier change with the economic environment. Players' payoffs, their bargaining powers and equilibrium strategies are influenced by exogenous shocks (Beghin 1990).

Thomson (1981) and Friedman (1986) present the four axioms underlying the game. These are analogous to the axioms underlying the Nash game (Nash 1953) but are defined with respect to a reference point rather than a conflict point. The axiom of joint efficiency, or strong rationality, requires that the solution to the game, $U^* = (U_1^*, U_2^*, \ldots, U_n^*)$, lies on the upper boundary, H, of the payoff space, P; U_i^* is defined as the utility of player i in equilibrium. The axiom of linear invariance states that the solution to the game obtained by a positive affine transformation of players' utility functions is the positive affine transformation of the solution to the original game. The axiom of symmetry ensures that indistinguishable players receive the same payoff. The last axiom, the independence of irrelevant alternatives, says that excluding a point from P other than the solution or the reference point, does not alter the solution to the game.

If the reference point, $g(P,d)$, satisfies certain regularity conditions (Thomson 1981), the solution to the co-operative game maximises the modified Nash product

$$\Pi_{i=G,F}(U_i - g(P,d)_i) \tag{4.1}$$

where $U = (U_G, U_F)$ is an element of the set $P(z)$, subscripts G and F

Getting prices right 69

represent the government and the farmer, respectively. If P is compact and convex, the solution, U^*, is on the frontier, H, and satisfies

$$a(z)_G(U_G^* - g(P,d)_G) = a(z)_F(U_F^* - g(P,d)_F) \tag{4.2}$$

where $a(z)_i = \delta H(U^*,z)/\delta U_i$. The functions $a(z)_i$ denote the bargaining-power coefficients of the players. They are usually normalised to sum to one.

If the payoff set, P, is convex, maximising the Nash product is equivalent to maximising the weighted sum of utilities, W,

$$W = a(z)_G U_G + a(z)_F U_F. \tag{4.3}$$

First-order conditions in the strategy space can be derived by maximising either the welfare function (4.3) or the Nash product (4.1). Defining as the kth strategy available to the players, then the necessary conditions for a solution are

$$\sum_{i=G,F} a(z)_i \frac{\delta U_i}{\delta s_k} = 0 \tag{4.4}$$

for all k ($k=1$, state price, and $k=2$, procurement quota).

In the grain policy game, both the government and the farmer seek to maximise their utility. The indirect utility function of the representative farmer is

$$U_F = U_F[\bar{q},p_s,m_F(\bar{q},p_s,z_F) - C_F] \tag{4.5}$$

where $\bar{q}$ is the procurement quota and p_s is the state purchase price. The restricted income function, $m_F(\bar{q},p_s,z_F)$, minus the cost of implementing conflict strategies, C_F, constitutes the net income of the farmer. At the co-operative solution, C_F is equal to zero since conflict strategies are not used (Beghin and Karp 1991). The co-operative strategy involves political support, but no monetary reward is given to the policymaker. The vector z_F, a subset of z, contains exogenous variables affecting the income function. Similarly, the indirect utility function for the government is

$$U_G = U_G[\bar{q},p_s,m_G(\bar{q},p_s,z_G) - C_G]. \tag{4.6}$$

Measuring the welfare effects of policy changes on the government and the farmer is the difficult part of this empirical study. To avoid specifying the utility function explicitly, the study adopts the shares of the gains or losses resulting from state grain purchases in the total revenue of the government and the farmer as approximations to changes in their welfare. As an approximation, this measure appropriately captures welfare change, and has the additional advantage of being easy to use.[14] The gain or loss is calculated from the state and market prices. The underlying rationale is that the government would have to buy grain at the market price if there were no state market. The gap between the market and state prices is the gain that the government can extract from the policy game, which equates to the loss incurred by the farmer. The frontier, H, represents the welfare trade between the two players. A lower state price increases the welfare of the government but leaves the farmer worse off.

The necessary and sufficient conditions for a solution can be empirically estimated. As the payoff functions and their derivatives are endogenous variables, and both are determined by the equilibrium outcome of the game, they are simultaneously estimated using an instrumental variable technique.

The bargaining coefficients are, in turn, determined by many exogenous variables, such as the share of agricultural population, the share of agricultural output, economic growth and market prices. A linear functional form is adopted for the relationship between exogenous variables and the ratio of bargaining coefficients:

$$\frac{a(z)_F}{a(z)_G} = a_0 + a_1 S_A + a_2 S_L + a_3 p_m + a_4 M + a_1^\# HRS^* S_A + a_2^\# HRS^* S_L$$
$$+ a_3^\# HRS^* p_m + a_4^\# HRS^* M \quad (4.7)$$

where S_A is the share of income from agriculture in farmers' total income, S_L is the proportion of the population reliant on agriculture, p_m is the market price of grain and M is income per capita. HRS is the adoption rate of the HRS reform in total production teams.

Furthermore, the bargaining coefficients are normalised so that their sum equals one:

$$a(z)_F + a(z)_G = 1. \quad (4.8)$$

Combining equations (4.7) and (4.8), we have

$$a(z)_F = \frac{\frac{a(z)_F}{a(z)_G}}{1 + \frac{a(z)_F}{a(z)_G}} \quad (4.9)$$

$$a(z)_G = \frac{1}{1 + \frac{a(z)_F}{a(z)_G}}$$

where $\frac{a(z)_F}{a(z)_G}$ is specified in equation (4.7).

Equations (4.9) are substituted into equations (4.2) and (4.4) to form the estimated system (equations (4.10) and (4.11))

$$U_G = \left(\frac{a(z)_F}{a(z)_G}\right)(U_F + b_0) \tag{4.10}$$

$$\frac{dU_G}{ds_k} = -\left(\frac{a(z)_F}{a(z)_G}\right)\frac{dU_F}{ds_k}, \quad s_k = p_s, \bar{q}. \tag{4.11}$$

The intercept term $a_0 b_0$ includes the reference payoffs which are not explicitly identified. The bargaining-power structure (the bargaining coefficients), which can be revealed without the reference point, is the major interest.

Empirical results

Equations (4.10) and (4.11) (with the detailed variables and coefficients specified in equation (4.7) substituted in) were empirically estimated for the case of grain policy in China. The data used were for the period 1953–90. Market prices for grain were derived from the price index for grain in the rural free market. The price levels were calculated by setting the market price in 1952 equal to the purchase price in that year. Estimation results obtained using the iterative two-stage least squares method are presented in table 4.2.

Bargaining coefficients predicted using the estimation results are presented for both government and farmers, together with the partial derivative of the farmers' bargaining coefficient with respect to changes in specific variables (table 4.3).

There are some interesting findings. The results suggest that, in general, the state-farmer framework did not work well in the pre-reform period: most of the variables for that period are not significant. After the introduction of the HRS reform, however, variables like income share and market price became important factors influencing the determination of state price levels. This further indicates the contribution of the HRS reform to agricultural production, beyond its normally identified direct effects. The following discussion focuses on the game structure in this reform period.

Even in the reform period, two variables usually suggested in the literature, the share of agricultural labour and per capita income, did not impact significantly on the game structure. First, the higher the farmers' bargaining power, the lower the share of income from agriculture in total income. This income share also portrays negative changes in the feasible choice-set of farmers. The larger the farmers' feasible choice-set, the higher the part of income earned from non-agricultural productivity. The negative relationship here is consistent with the theoretical analysis.

72 *Agricultural reform in China*

Table 4.2. *Coefficient estimates of the system equations*

Parameter	Estimate	Asymptotic t ratio
a_0	0.6756	9.89
a_1	−0.00003	0.52
a_2	0.0034	0.33
a_3	0.00005	0.63
a_4	0.0004	1.27
$a_1^\#$	−0.0001	−1.22
$a_2^\#$	0.4846	−5.32
$a_3^\#$	0.00004	0.76
$a_4^\#$	0.0012	19.16

Table 4.3. *Predicted bargaining coefficients and their derivatives, 1979 to 1990*

Variable	Mean
a_F	0.29
a_G	0.71
$\delta a_F / \delta S_L$	−2.0E−4
$\delta a_F / \delta p_m$	2.2E−5

When farmers' non-agricultural production opportunities expanded, punitive action by the government offered less threat to them. Second, changes in market prices for grain had a positive effect on farmers' bargaining power. When the market price is higher, government tends to be willing to offer a higher price for grain.

Overall, farmers were relatively weak in the period under study compared to consumers. Farmers' power coefficient is only 0.3 while that for the consumer is 0.7. The difference in the coefficients reflects farmers' relative weakness in the process of bargaining for grain policy settings. This is further evidenced by the unfavourable grain policy faced by farmers throughout the 1970s and the 1980s. According to this framework, it is not difficult to predict that farmers' bargaining power will be enhanced as market prices continue to rise and agricultural income continues to fall.

Toward a better understanding of agricultural policy

In most economic studies, policy changes are treated as exogenous shocks to the system. Such treatment, while adequate when only policy impact is of interest, is insufficient for exploring the full impact of policy mechanisms. Taking policies as exogenously set prevents a fuller understanding of the policy regime and reduces the predictability of policy change.

Through the process of economic reform in China, all economic agents including farmers gradually regained their autonomy in decisionmaking and found ways to express their own interests. It is inevitable that different interest groups attempt to influence the policymaking process, within either the co-operative or non-cooperative game frameworks. Introduction of policy endogeny helps to reveal interactions between the government and different interest groups in the economy. As China is neither a typical capitalist democratic country nor a centrally controlled country, some of the existing paradigms proposed in the literature may not be directly applicable. It is necessary, therefore, to establish some new frameworks that are suitable for China, either through a new formulation, or through modification of the existing models by developing a state-farmer policy game framework

The exercise in this chapter represents only a first attempt in this direction. Because the two parties have reciprocal impacts, the game is a co-operative one, and changes in grain practice are the outcome of an interactive process between the two parties. Given the constraints, the game is set to maximise the joint benefits (or minimise the joint losses), with distribution of the benefits between the two being dependent on their relative bargaining powers, again determined by a set of exogenous variables.

The hypothesis-testing confirmed that farmers' relative strength was negatively correlated with the proportion of labour in agriculture in the country and with average per capita income. The share of agricultural output was not significant for the whole period. The testing also confirmed that economic reform improved farmers' relative bargaining power and that the grain policy game before 1990 was a state-dominated one.

This is only a preliminary effort to understand the way that grain policy was formulated in China and to predict the likely directions of policy change. Within this framework, it can be predicted that farmers will become increasingly powerful, eventually turning the game into a farmer-dominated one.

The framework developed here is still only a partial equilibrium approach. It has not considered, for instance, the distribution of a budget deficit among different interest groups. Again, the consumer group is excluded from the game. While appropriate for the pre-1990 period, it now requires modification as the consumer group has become an important player in China's grain policy since retail price liberalisation in 1992. These developments necessitate further refinement of the model.

A more difficult task would be to develop further the theoretical framework and to carry out additional empirical work on China's policy mechanisms. In the case of grain policy, it is likely that with further liberalisation, consumers will enter directly into the game on agricultural policy.

Appendix: the data-set

State purchase price for grain: Weighted average state purchase prices (yuan/tonne), from SSB, *China Price Statistical Yearbook*, various issues.

Market price for grain: Weighted average rural market prices (yuan/tonne), calculated from price indices in the rural market, from SSB, *China Price Statistical Yearbook*, various issues, by assuming market price equal to the state purchase price in 1950.

State procurement quota: Tonnes of all grain purchased by the state, from the Ministry of Domestic Trade of the People's Republic of China.

Utility measure of the government (U_G): The share of benefits (or losses) from state grain procurement (calculated by multiplying the procurement quotas by gaps between market and state prices) in total government revenue. The share is indexed by setting the highest value between 1953 and 1990 to one. Total government revenue each year is from SSB, *China Statistical Yearbook*, various issues.

Utility measure of the farmer (U_F): The share of the actual sale revenue from grain in the total grain output measured by market prices. The share is also indexed by setting the value of the highest year to one. Total grain output each year is from SSB, *China Statistical Yearbook*, various issues.

Share of agricultural output in the economy (S_A): The share of agricultural output in GDP, both measured in current price values and from SSB, *China Statistical Yearbook*, various issues.

Proportion of agricultural labour (S_L): The share of agricultural labour in the total labour force, both measured in persons and from SSB, *China Statistical Yearbook*, various issues.

Per capita income (M): Total GDP (yuan) at 1980 prices divided by total population, from SSB, *China Statistical Yearbook*, various issues.

Notes

1 The procurement plan and the prices of grain, cotton and edible oil were also liberalised in 1985. Price controls over these products were quickly resumed, however, as a result of significant falls in production in 1985.

2 By treating intervention as given, the results obtained from these analyses represent the conditional response of the private sector.
3 This idea was first demonstrated by Peltzman's result, that losers must be taxed less than the interest of the winners would dictate (Peltzman 1976).
4 In Brock and Magee's analysis, tariffs are used as the exemplary redistribution policy (Brock and Magee 1978, 1979).
5 There are some exceptions in the world such as Japan and France.
6 For a summary of the approach employed by Zusman (1976), see Rausser, Lichtenberg and Lattimore (1982).
7 The reference point, however, is not explicitly identified in the empirical work by Beghin (1990) and Beghin and Karp (1991).
8 The extent to which urban grain demand is satisfied by the government through the state system is another policy issue which is implicitly incorporated in the determination of the demand curve on the state market.
9 If the government denies troublesome farmers employment by the township and village enterprises, the money measure of this penalty (m) is defined as the difference between farmers' potential wage rates in the rural industry and their current income levels.
10 The rent that the government extracts from grain purchases can also be negative – farmers are thus subsidised, as is also the case in Western Europe and the United States.
11 The minority of the population is able to demand a policy favourable to it, as the larger benefit to this minority imposes only a small loss on other groups in the economy.
12 This does not necessarily mean that the cost the government is willing to incur is smaller than before in absolute terms. It is, however, always true on a relative measure.
13 In the extreme, the supply curve in the state market may move above the actual marginal cost schedule. This study, however, will not consider this situation.
14 Income is sometimes used as the simplest measure of welfare (Tyers and Anderson 1992). The share of gains or losses more accurately reflects welfare change, since people with different income levels would of course value a certain amount of gain or loss quite differently.

5

Adjustments in rural markets bring structural change

Liberalisation in an imperfect market

Agricultural performance in the wake of reforms from 1979 to 1984 was not all good news. The Chinese economy was still largely closed to international trade in the first half of the 1980s and sectors other than agriculture had not yet been reformed. Agricultural growth was not matched by growth elsewhere in the economy. Between 1982 and 1984, grain output increased by 27 million tonnes per year and cotton by 3.3 million tonnes. In contrast, over the same period, grain demand increased by only 10–12.5 million tonnes a year and annual domestic demand for cotton was roughly 3.5 million tonnes (compared to total output of 6.3 million tonnes in 1984). Temporary agricultural surpluses presented a major policy challenge and caused a number of other economic problems in the early years of agricultural reform. Because the government had traditionally committed itself to buy all grain and cotton output from farmers as long as they wished to sell, large amounts of agricultural output were added to government stocks. In 1983, state grain stocks increased by 37 per cent. And by the end of 1984, total grain stocks had reached a level that was 50 per cent above storage capacity. Huge amounts of grain, roughly 30 million tonnes in 1984, were stored in open areas (Gao and Xiang 1992). Rising stocks of grain and other agricultural products meant heavy burdens on the state budget.

From 1979 to 1984, grain subsidies increased by 35.5 per cent per year. In turn, huge surpluses discouraged agricultural production. Farmers often found it very difficult to sell surplus products, as the state commercial department was not enthusiastic about buying from farmers because of its storage and financial constraints. Market prices fell significantly during these years and were at times even lower than the state quota prices. From the autumn of 1984, farmers began to readjust production.

The Chinese government took the opportunity to pursue reform in the rural economy, letting prices and quantities be determined by markets. At the beginning of 1985, the 'No. 1 Document' announced a new set of policies that encouraged structural change and introduced market reforms. It was the beginning of a long period of policy debate and frequent adjustment of agricultural policies (sometimes moving toward, but sometimes pulling back from market reform). The debate was particularly acrimonious in the second half of the 1980s when the rate of growth of agricultural production fell and in the first half of the 1990s when agricultural price increases had an impact on inflation, thereby causing macroeconomic problems.

Why was agricultural performance so different in the two periods before and after 1985, when agricultural reform was being persistently pursued? If we compare reform measures in the two periods, we find that, in the first, agricultural reform was concentrated on microeconomic aspects of the agricultural system while, in the second, reform was extended to macroeconomic factors that influenced agriculture. When the HRS reform was introduced, government controls over quantities and prices of production and procurement of agricultural products remained. More importantly, the rest of the economy was still operating under a strict central planning system. Energies released by agricultural reform, therefore, were directly channelled back to agricultural production, mainly of a number of grain crops. Increased inputs, including labour, capital and modern agricultural techniques, and improved productivity had a significant impact on the output of a number of agricultural products.

From 1985, however, market reform increasingly integrated formerly sectoral agricultural policies into the macroeconomy. As controls on prices and resource flows were gradually removed, structural adjustment was inevitable – not only between different agricultural products but also between agriculture and other sectors. Agricultural production was influenced by policies directed toward the agricultural sector, but it was also affected by policies targeted at other parts of the economy. Developments in the agricultural sector thus have to be analysed in a wider framework, both then and now.

What further complicates the story is that market reform in agriculture has been far from complete. This incompleteness is mainly reflected in (1) asymmetry of price control, (2) the segmentation of regional agricultural markets, and (3) isolation of domestic agricultural markets from international markets.

Agricultural performance after 1984

Liberalisation of rural markets from 1985 greatly promoted the growth of the rural economy. Total rural output grew by 13.3 per cent per annum from 1984 to 1994, much higher than average GDP growth (about 10 per cent per annum in the same period). Per capita rural output, at current prices, increased from 631 yuan in 1984 to 1,522 yuan in 1988 and 5,303 yuan in 1994 (figure 5.1). The per capita output in real terms grew between 12 and 17 per cent per annum from 1984 to 1988. Per capita real output experienced a significant drop in 1989 (by −4 per cent) and then recovered in 1990 (with a 10 per cent increase). From 1991, rural China entered another period of rapid growth.

While the rural economy as a whole continued to grow rapidly in the post-1985 period, the growth of agricultural production took a surprising turn (figure 5.2). From the end of 1984, farmers significantly reduced agricultural production. Lin (1992a) finds that the growth rate of chemical fertiliser inputs dropped from 8.9 per cent per year in 1978–84 to 3.7 per cent in 1984–87 and the annual growth rate of the agricultural labour force declined from 2.3 per cent to −8.6 per cent between the same periods. Niu (1988) also points out that the availability of physical inputs did not increase and that some were even cut back. There was also a widespread decline in agricultural yields, reversing the rapidly increasing trend of 1978–84. Yields of most crops dropped significantly in 1985 and did not recover to their 1984 levels until 1987–89.

Falls in agricultural inputs, and therefore yields, created some supply problems for the Chinese economy from 1985 to 1988. Per capita agricultural production decreased for most agricultural commodities during that period. Per capita grain production fell from 393 kilograms in 1984 to 361 kilograms in 1985, remained at around 360 to 370 kilograms during 1986–89, and did not rise again to the 1984 record level (on a per capita basis) until 1990. It declined again thereafter (table 5.1). Per capita cotton production reached 6 kilograms in 1984. This level has not been achieved since and the normal per capita output was between 3 and 4 kilograms per annum during 1985–94. In the post-1985 period per capita output of other agricultural products experienced steady growth. Per capita output of pork, beef and mutton increased from 14.9 kilograms in 1984 to 16.8 kilograms in 1985 and 27.4 kilograms in 1993. Production of aquatic products, fruits and many other products also showed consistently increasing trends.

For agriculture as a whole, however, growth slowed from an annual rate of 7.6 per cent during 1978–84 to 4 per cent in 1984–88 (figure 5.2).

Adjustments in rural markets bring structural change   79

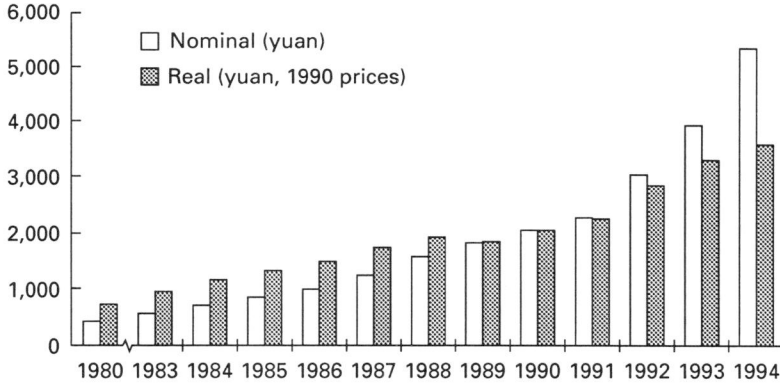

Fig. 5.1. Per capita rural output, 1980 to 1994. (*Source:* SSB, *China Statistical Yearbook 1995.*)

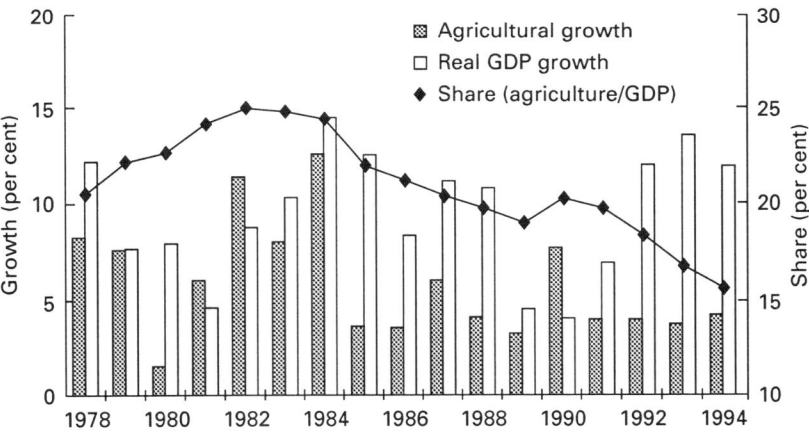

Fig. 5.2. Relative growth of agriculture in the economy, 1978 to 1994. (*Source:* SSB, *China Statistical Yearbook 1995.*)

The growth rate of 4.2 per cent for the period 1984–94 was not an insignificant achievement. Some economists argue that the period 1978–84 was a period of abnormal growth and the year 1985 re-established a period of normal growth (Gao and Xiang 1992).

The rest of the economy, especially the rest of the rural economy, continued to grow rapidly from 1985 to 1988 at 10.5 per cent per annum. As a result, the share of agriculture in the economy, which had risen in

Table 5.1. *Per capita agricultural production, 1952 to 1994 (kilograms)*

	Grain	Cotton	Oil crops	Sugar crops	Tea	Fruit	Pork, beef and mutton	Aquatic products
1952	288.1	2.3	7.4	13.4	0.1	4.3	6.0	2.9
1957	306.0	2.6	6.6	18.7	0.2	5.1	6.3	4.9
1962	240.3	1.1	3.0	5.7	0.1	4.1	2.9	3.4
1965	272.0	2.9	5.1	21.5	0.1	4.5	7.7	4.2
1970	293.2	2.8	4.6	19.0	0.2	4.6	7.3	3.9
1975	310.5	2.6	1.9	20.9	0.2	5.9	8.7	4.8
1978	318.7	2.3	5.5	24.9	0.3	6.9	9.0	4.9
1980	326.7	2.8	7.8	29.7	0.3	6.9	12.3	4.6
1983	378.5	4.5	10.3	39.4	0.4	9.3	13.7	5.3
1984	392.8	6.0	11.5	46.1	0.4	9.5	14.9	6.0
1985	360.7	4.0	14.1	57.5	0.4	11.1	16.8	6.7
1986	367.0	3.3	13.8	54.9	0.4	12.6	18.0	7.7
1987	371.7	3.9	14.1	51.2	0.5	15.4	18.3	8.8
1988	357.7	3.8	12.0	56.2	0.5	15.1	19.9	9.6
1989	364.3	3.4	11.6	51.9	0.5	16.4	20.8	10.3
1990	393.1	4.0	14.2	63.6	0.5	16.5	22.1	10.9
1991	378.3	4.9	14.2	73.2	0.5	18.9	23.7	11.7
1992	380.0	3.9	14.1	75.6	0.5	21.0	25.2	13.4
1993	387.4	3.2	15.3	64.7	0.5	25.6	27.4	15.5
1994	373.5	3.6	16.7	61.6	0.5	29.4	31.0	18.0

Source: SSB, *China Statistical Yearbook*, various issues.

the early 1980s, began to decline quite dramatically (figure 5.2). This trend was continued in the whole post-1985 period except for a small recovery in 1990. Structural changes were also observed in the rural economy. The share of agriculture in total rural output decreased from 63 per cent in 1984 to 57.1 per cent in 1985 and 35.8 per cent in 1992. Declines in the share of cropping were the most pronounced, from over 40 per cent in 1984 to around 20 per cent in 1992 (figure 5.3). On the other hand, the share of rural industry rose significantly, from a little above 20 per cent in 1984 to about 50 per cent in 1992.

Why did agricultural growth slow down?

Stagnation of agricultural production, especially cropping, over the years 1985–88 caused great interest among Chinese economists and led to a heated policy debate. Various hypotheses have been advanced to explain the downturn. The important ones include:

(1) the worsening agricultural terms of trade (Niu 1988; Gunasekera *et al.* 1991);

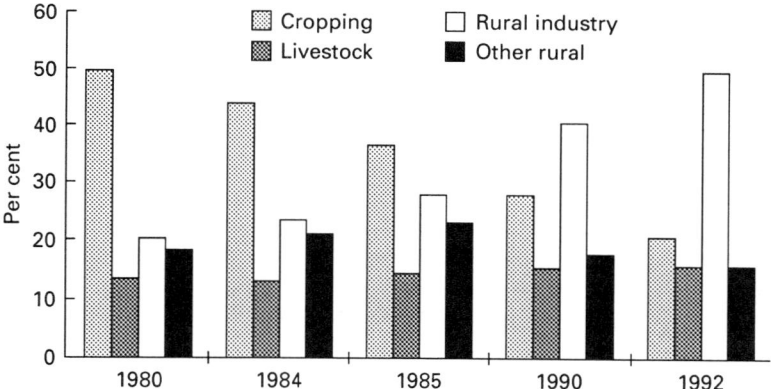

Fig. 5.3. Composition of rural output, 1980 to 1992. (*Source:* SSB, *China Statistical Yearbook 1995.*)

(2) the completion of the household responsibility system reform in 1983 (Gunasekera *et al.* 1991; Lin 1992a);
(3) adverse weather (Chai 1991; Gunasekera *et al.* 1991);
(4) differential changes in technologies in agricultural and non-agricultural sectors, and changes in relative factor endowments (Ma and Garnaut 1992).

The worsening agricultural terms of trade

Changes in relative prices dominate the literature on the causes of agricultural stagnation after 1985 (Niu 1988; Chai 1991; Gunasekera *et al.* 1991). Of the five reasons for agricultural stagnation given in Niu's analysis, three are related to the worsening agricultural terms of trade (Niu 1988). Niu's arguments have been echoed by other economists (Chai 1991; Gunasekera *et al.* 1991).

The statistics, however, suggest a different story. Figure 5.4 plots prices for agriculture relative to the prices of rural industrial products and agricultural inputs.[1] Before 1989, both ratios were increasing apart from a small drop in 1984. Agriculture's share in the national economy and its growth rate, however, fell significantly from 1985 to 1989 (see figure 5.2). Considering that farmers, in making production decisions, usually take market prices in the previous year as the expected prices for the following year, the drop in the relative price of agricultural products in 1984 may offer a possible reason for agricultural contraction in 1985. However, the agricultural growth rate dropped substantially from

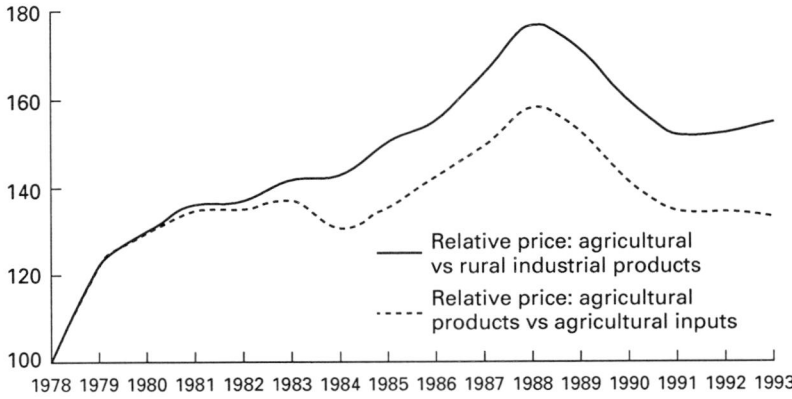

Fig. 5.4. Relative market prices of agricultural products, 1979 to 1993. (*Sources:* Lin 1992a; SSB, *China Statistical Yearbook 1994.*)

12.3 per cent in 1984 to 3.4 per cent in 1985, while agricultural product prices fell 3 per cent relative to prices of rural industrial products and 8 per cent relative to prices of agricultural inputs. The price elasticities are unreasonably large. In particular, it is hard to explain the opposing movements during 1985–90 of relative prices and agricultural growth rates and of the relative prices and the share of agriculture in the national economy (see figures 5.2 and 5.4).[2]

This is reinforced by an investigation of the relationship between the variation of relative prices and the movement of resources within the farming sector. Standard theory predicts that the rise or decline of land allocated to one crop must be positively related to the changes in the relative price of this crop to other prices. A positive relationship between the share of sown areas devoted to grain and the relative price of grain is hypothesised.

Regression results are presented in table 5.2. In the first regression, only relative price was included to explain the variation in the share of arable land which is sown to grain. Considering the potential argument that, since agricultural production has long-run characteristics, the relative price in previous years may be more important in making production decisions than the current price, a second regression was run on the lagged relative price. In both regressions, the relative prices seemed to play a significant and negative role in determining resource movements within the farming sector. The third regression was run on both the relative price and the time trend. The time trend used is a proxy

Table 5.2. *Resource allocation and relative prices in the farming sector, 1978 to 1990*

Explanatory variables	Dependent variable: share of arable land area sown to grain		
	Regression 1	Regression 2	Regression 3
Constant	87.10	86.25	705.74
	(54.7)	(58.3)	(2.49)
Relative price	−0.072		−0.016
	(−5.8)		(−0.6)
Lagged relative price (−1)		−0.067	
		(−5.8)	
Time trend			−0.315
			(−2.2)
Adjusted R^2	0.73	0.75	0.80

Note: The numbers in parentheses under the coefficient estimates are the related t ratios.
Source: SSB, *China Statistical Yearbook 1991*.

variable for technological change or other factors that change over time. These appear to have a very significant and negative impact. The impact of the relative price, though still negative, proved insignificant. Combining the results of the three simple regressions, the minimum implication we may draw is that there is no evidence of a positive relationship between resource movement and variation of the relative price. So we have to reject the hypothesis of a positive relationship.

The completion of the household responsibility system

Economists have argued that the more immediate productivity gains from the introduction of the household responsibility system were likely to have been fully exploited by 1983 when the new system had been implemented (Gunasekera *et al.* 1991; Lin 1992a). Studies by Lin (1992a) and McMillan, Whalley and Zhu (1989) reveal significant contributions by HRS reform to rising agricultural output and productivity during 1979–84. However, if technologies used in agricultural and industrial production were relatively stable, the completion of the HRS reform might have slowed down the growth rate of agriculture but should not have significantly changed agriculture's share in the rural economy.[3] In fact, output of many agricultural products, including grain and cotton, dropped in 1985. In particular, this hypothesis cannot explain why from 1985 to 1988 the labour force shifted from agriculture to industry while agriculture's relative price was increasing and why from 1989 to 1990 the

Table 5.3. *Variables affecting agricultural performance, 1978 to 1994*

	Adoption rate of the HRS (per cent)	Growth of fertiliser application (per cent)	Non-TVP rural labour (million)	Deviation from mean affected by natural disasters (1978–94 mean = 1)
1978	—	9.0	278.1	1.16
1979	1	22.9	281.7	0.90
1980	14	16.9	288.4	1.02
1981	45	5.2	297.0	0.91
1982	80	13.4	307.5	0.75
1983	98	9.7	314.6	0.79
1984	99	4.8	307.6	0.73
1985	99	2.1	300.9	1.01
1986	99	8.7	300.5	1.08
1987	99	3.6	302.0	0.96
1988	99	7.1	305.2	1.16
1989	99	10.1	315.7	1.07
1990	99	9.9	327.5	0.88
1991	99	8.3	334.8	1.27
1992	99	4.5	332.2	1.17
1993	99	7.6	319.1	1.12
1994	99	5.3	311.4	1.19

Sources: Lin 1992a; SSB, *China Statistical Yearbook 1995*.

labour force returned from industry to agriculture when agriculture's relative price was declining (see column (3) in table 5.3).

Adverse weather

A run of unfavourable seasons has also been frequently cited as contributing to the slowdown of agricultural development in the mid-1980s, as weather conditions had correlated significantly with agricultural performance for the preceding decade in China (Chai 1991; Gunasekera *et al.* 1991). From 1979 to 1984 the weather was reported to be very good (except for 1980). This was also a period of rapid agricultural growth. During the period of agricultural stagnation from 1985 to 1988, the weather was reported as unfavourable for agricultural production. The deviation from the mean of arable land area affected by natural disasters, for the period 1978–90, followed the pattern of agricultural growth (see column (4) in table 5.3).

However, the role that the weather plays in agricultural production is only to affect actual output levels. Since weather is an ongoing process, significant resource reallocation can hardly be explained by changes in weather conditions. For cross-sectional data this kind of linkage might be detected, since the weather pattern may affect the optimal mix of inputs. For instance, because of extensive rainfall, southeast China may use more labour and fertiliser input than the dry northwest region. Over time, however, a strong relationship between significant resource movements and temporary weather patterns has hardly been evident. On the other hand, Lin (1990) found that weather seems often to be used by Chinese authorities as an excuse for crop failures occurring for other reasons.

The relative rates of technological change and the Rybczynski effect

In the long run, changes in technologies in different sectors and changes in relative factor endowments can result in the reallocation of resources regardless of changes in relative prices. Suppose there were much faster improvements in non-agricultural technology than in agricultural technology, marginal productivities in the non-agricultural sectors would therefore be higher than in agriculture. Even if there is no change, or there was a small increase in the price of agricultural products relative to non-agricultural ones, factors would move from agricultural to non-agricultural sectors. In the period 1985–90, however, there was no evidence to support significant technology change in the Chinese economy. The Rybczynski theorem, on the other hand, describes the relationship between changes in output structure and relative factor endowment regardless of changes in relative prices. It is suggested that a rise in the endowment of one factor relative to the other will increase the output of the good using that factor intensively relative to output of the other good (Rybczynski 1955; Jones 1956). In applying this to the Chinese rural economy, two arguments should be made. First, while the Rybczynski theorem refers to long-term changes, it is a short-term phenomenon that is being discussed here. Second, the marked increase in investment and capital stock in the rural industries around the mid-1980s and the increase in the industrial output in the rural economy from 1984 to 1987 were consistent with the Rybczynski hypothesis. However, the hypothesis fails to explain the increase in agriculture's share in 1990, when the capital–labour ratio was still rising.

It is clear that these various hypotheses in the literature suggest to some reasons for the slow growth of agricultural production after 1985. But these explanations are far from satisfactory.

The truncated production frontier: an alternative explanation

The efficient functioning of any price structure in guiding an agricultural household's resource allocation depends on two assumptions apart from rationality. First, global equilibrium exists before relative prices change; and second, production activities are not constrained by non-economic forces (such as government intervention), so resources can move freely between different sectors. The argument is best demonstrated by the following model. Suppose, with given quantities of endowments $\bar{X}$, a household can produce either agricultural goods (good 1) or industrial goods (good 2). The prices for agricultural products and industrial products, P_1 and P_2, are given to the household.

The optimal resource allocation between these two sectors can be obtained by solving the following equation:

$$\underset{X_1}{Max} \Pi = P_1 f_1(X_1) + P_2 f_2(\bar{X} - X_1) \qquad (5.1)$$

where f_i is the production function for good i and X_i is the resources allocated to the production of good i ($X_1 + X_2 = \bar{X}$). The production functions are assumed to be well-behaved. The first-order condition for optimality requires

$$P_i(\partial f_1/\partial X_1) = P_2(\partial f_2/\partial X_2). \qquad (5.2)$$

That is, the resources are allocated to the production of the two goods to the point where the marginal products of good 1 and good 2 are equalised. Condition (5.2) can also be expressed in the following way:

$$(\partial f_1/\partial X_1)/(\partial f_2/\partial X_2) = P_2/P_1. \qquad (5.2')$$

This condition can be shown diagrammatically as point A in figure 5.5, where the production possibility frontier is tangential to the relative price line (P).

If no restrictions exist on the production of good 1 and good 2, then changes in production will result in the reallocation of resources from the good with the declining relative price to the good with the increasing relative price along the curve of the production frontier. For example, the change of relative prices from line P to P' will result in the shift of the equilibrium production point from A to B. Therefore, the change in the relative prices will indicate both the direction of resource movement and the relative growth of these two goods.

Under the traditional heavy-industry oriented development strategy,

Adjustments in rural markets bring structural change 87

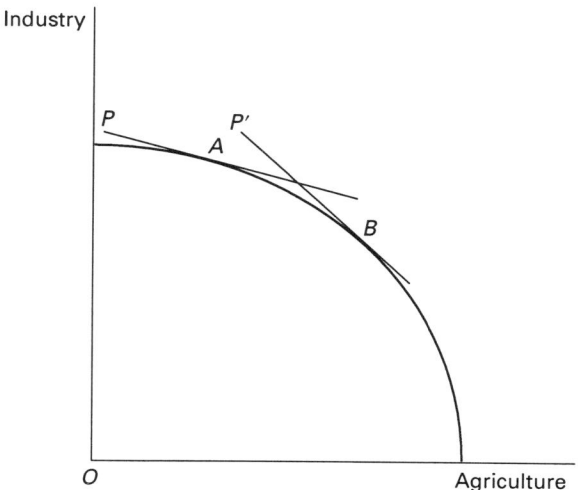

Fig. 5.5. Relative price and production decisions.

however, production in rural areas was largely confined to agriculture, especially grain (Lardy 1983; Lin, Cai and Li 1994b). Production activity in the industrial sector was limited owing to government restrictions. In other words, the production frontier the farmers faced was truncated (figure 5.6). Industry production is restricted to a level no larger than I_r. With the relative prices represented by the line P, production will locate at C, a corner solution.[4] At this point, the necessary condition for optimality will not hold. Instead of the equality of condition (5.2), the following inequality may exist:

$$P_1(\partial f_1/\partial X_1) < P_2(\partial f_2/\partial X_2) \tag{5.3}$$

That is, the marginal value of agricultural product is lower than that of industrial product. A reallocation of resources from agricultural production to industrial production will increase the agricultural household's income. Such a reallocation is prohibited by policy restrictions on industrial production. In this instance, as long as the change in relative prices does not upset the inequality (5.3), it will not cause a reallocation of resources between these two activities. If the production constraint is changed, some abnormal reallocation of resources and sectoral growth may accompany a change in relative prices. Suppose, for example, relative prices are changed from P to P' (figure 5.6). In an unconstrained situation, relative price changes will signal the growth of the agricultural

88 *Agricultural reform in China*

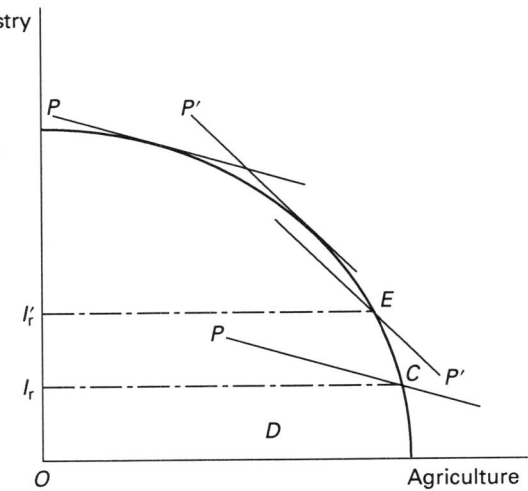

Fig. 5.6. Policy restrictions and a truncated production possibility frontier.

sector and the decline of the industrial sector, with resources flowing from industry to agriculture. In the truncated production frontier case, if constraints on industrial production shift from I_r to I'_r, the production point will be changed from C to E. This is the opposite result to what one would expect from the relative price changes. The opposite scenario, the expansion of agricultural production with the worsening of terms of trade for agriculture, can be derived from the shift in the policy constraint from I_r back to I'_r.

It is this change in policy constraints on industrial production within a truncated production frontier that was the main cause for the puzzling pattern of agricultural growth in China after 1984. As shown in figure 5.6, the trend of agriculture's relative prices and the trend of agriculture's relative share were negatively correlated. This hypothesis is further confirmed by the numbers in the labour force in rural township and village enterprises. In 1989 and 1990, the prices of industrial products relative to those of agricultural ones were increasing, but employment in rural industry declined absolutely (see column (2) in table 5.4).

Policy change and resource allocation

Farmers' feasible production choices in the truncated production frontier have been changed dramatically by the process of economic reform (table 5.5).

Table 5.4. *Development of the TVP sector, 1984 to 1994*

	Number of enterprises (million)	Number of employees (million)	Rural industry price index (1985=100)	Real value of total output (1985 price)	Growth of output value (per cent)
1984	6.06	52.08	96.9	176.5	—
1985	12.22	69.79	100.0	272.8	54.56
1986	15.15	79.37	103.1	343.4	25.88
1987	17.50	88.05	108.1	440.7	28.33
1988	18.88	95.45	124.5	521.7	18.38
1989	18.68	93.67	147.9	502.3	−3.72
1990	18.50	92.65	154.6	547.3	8.96
1991	19.09	96.09	159.3	729.5	33.29
1992	20.79	105.81	164.2	1094.7	50.06
1993	24.53	123.45	183.6	1717.9	56.93
1994	24.95	120.18	215.2	1979.0	15.20

Source: SSB, *China Statistical Yearbook 1995.*

Before economic reform began at the end of 1978, Chinese farmers were largely restricted in the crops that they grew to grain and cotton. Production of cash crops and livestock products was not allowed except for areas arranged by the state plan. Non-agricultural production activities were prohibited, in general, at that time.

There were a few commune and brigade industrial enterprises which received encouragement under specific policies for short periods. During the second half of the 1950s, to achieve the national steel output target (which had been set too high), small steel plants were established all over the countryside. Labour was diverted to very inefficient steel production. Later, in the mid-1970s, for the purpose of realising agricultural mechanisation, small factories producing and repairing farm machines were again established everywhere. Since both targets were inappropriate and inefficient, most of these small enterprises were shut down shortly after their establishment.

The initial reforms were mainly aimed at raising agricultural output. Local experiments with the HRS and, later, its nationwide implementation gave households more freedom to make their own production decisions. Farmers' feasible production choice-set expanded. Production of cash crops and livestock increasingly became an important part of the agricultural economy. But, to begin with, government restrictions on rural industries remained unchanged. The relative prices of agriculture and industry were therefore irrelevant to the allocation of resources between agriculture and industry.[5] The energies released and created by reform could only be allocated to agriculture.

Table 5.5. *Changes in farmers' truncated production frontier, 1978 to 1995*

	Government policy and objectives	Farmer's feasible economic activities[a]			
		Grain crops	Cash crops	Animal husbandry	Rural industry[b]
before 1978	Industrialisation and self-sufficiency in grain	compulsory[b]	restricted	restricted	no
1979–80	Purchase price increases for agricultural products	yes	restriction loosened	restriction loosened	no
1981–84	Household responsibility system and price reform	yes	yes	yes	restriction loosened[c]
1985–87	Use of market and rural industrial development	yes	yes	yes	encouraged
1988–90	Austerity programme and policies favouring agriculture	yes	yes	yes	partly restricted
1991–94	Economic growth and grain policy liberalisation	yes	yes	yes	yes
1994–95	Economic growth and grain market re-control resumed	control	yes	yes	yes

Notes: [a] Economic activities are classified according to their accessibility to farmers. 'Compulsory' implies that the production activity was assigned by the government; 'yes' means farmers can freely decide whether or not to be involved in that production activity; 'restricted' means that farmers can sometimes be involved subject to various policy restrictions; 'no' implies that farmers cannot enter that production activity; and 'encouraged' for rural industry in 1985–87 refers to a period when different policies favouring rural industry were implemented to facilitate rural industrialisation.
[b] The classification of rural industry here does not include some necessary supporting industries such as grain mills.
[c] In some areas, at a later stage, it was actually encouraged by (local) government.

Profound policy changes were experienced in the Chinese economy from the mid-1980s. The following are the major policy changes which expanded farmers' truncated production frontier (or produced an upward movement of line I_r in figure 5.6): the adoption of a fiscal responsibility system (Blejer et al. 1991); banking system reform at the end of 1984 (Wulf and Goldsbrough 1986; Peebles 1990); liberalisation of rural product and factor markets at the beginning of 1985; encouragement of rural industries through the introduction of low taxes and subsidised bank loans.

The adoption of a fiscal responsibility system gave strong incentives to local government to find ways to increase its tax basis. Because of the distorted price structure, industry enjoyed a much higher profit margin than agriculture. Instead of suppressing industrial production, many local governments adopted policies such as low taxes and subsidised bank loans to encourage the development of rural industries. Restrictions on industrial production were removed. One consequence of the banking system reform was the relaxation of credit control in the fourth quarter of 1984 and at the beginning of 1985 (Wulf and Goldsbrough 1986; Kojima 1989; Blejer et al. 1991). A large part of the credit that became available went to rural industries. Bank loans for township, village and private enterprises (TVP) rose by 97.9 per cent in 1984. The TVPs' share in total state capital application increased from 2.2 per cent in 1983 to 3.8 per cent in 1985 (table 5.6). Liberalisation of factor and product markets made the reallocation of resources between different sectors and between different regions easier to realise. A large number of TVPs were established in the second half of 1984 and at the beginning of 1985. The number of TVP enterprises increased by 38.4 per cent in 1984, and doubled in 1985 (SSB, *China Statistical Yearbook 1991*; see also column (1) in table 5.4).[6] At the same time, employment increased 23.1 per cent in 1984 and 34.0 per cent in 1985 (see column (2) in table 5.4).

The experiences of 1989 and 1990 in China showed an opposite movement in the farmers' truncated production frontier. To overcome the overheating of the economy, a package of adjustment policies was implemented from the second half of 1988. A credit squeeze was an important part of these policies, targeted in particular at the rural industries (World Bank 1990b). The growth rate of bank loans to the TVP sector dropped from 17.7 per cent in 1988 to 3.2 per cent in 1989 and 14.5 per cent in 1990, compared to 97.9 per cent in 1984 and 52.2 per cent in 1986 (see column (1) in table 5.6). Inflation was 18.5 per cent in 1988 and 17.8 per cent in 1989, so the real growth of loans to the TVP sector was negative, particularly in 1989. Though the government did not

Table 5.6. *State bank loans to TVP and agricultural sectors, 1978 to 1989*

	TVP loans volume (bn yuan)	TVP loans annual growth (per cent)	Agricultural loans volume (bn yuan)	Agricultural loans annual growth (per cent)	Total state bank loans volume (bn yuan)	Total state bank loans annual growth (per cent)
1978	2.12	—	9.44	—	187.65	—
1979	3.80	79.25	9.87	4.56	216.26	15.25
1980	5.30	39.47	12.29	24.52	262.43	21.35
1981	6.22	17.36	12.75	3.74	307.51	17.18
1982	7.34	18.01	13.91	9.10	361.84	14.12
1983	8.00	8.99	15.12	8.70	412.49	14.00
1984	15.83	97.87	20.90	38.23	537.03	30.19
1985	18.90	19.39	22.76	8.90	637.45	18.70
1986	28.77	52.22	28.27	24.21	811.14	27.25
1987	34.89	21.12	33.67	19.10	987.04	21.69
1988	41.06	17.68	40.26	19.90	1148.53	16.36
1989	42.38	3.21	47.13	16.77	1356.20	18.08

Source: SSB, *China Statistical Yearbook 1991*.

restore administrative restrictions on farmers' economic opportunities in rural industries, the truncated production frontier, at least for some farmers, contracted (described graphically by a downward movement of line I_r in figure 5.6). The number of both enterprises and employees in the TVP sector decreased in 1989 and 1990 (see table 5.4). Real output of the TVP sector declined in 1989 by 2.9 per cent. At the same time, total profits of the TVP sector in nominal terms dropped from 25.9 billion yuan in 1988 to 24.0 billion in 1989, and to 23.3 billion in 1990.

The contraction in the TVP sector forced some farmers to retreat to agricultural activities. Given that there was a minimum scale of investment,[7] monetary contraction resulted in a loss of job opportunities in the TVP sector. Resources moved back to agriculture. The number of employees in the TVP sector dropped by 1.9 per cent in 1989, and declined further by 1.1 per cent in 1990. At the same time, the total rural labour force increased by 2.2 per cent in 1989, and 2.6 per cent in 1990 (SSB, *China Statistical Yearbook 1991*: 95). There was a substantial increase in the agricultural labour force over the two years. Starting from 1988, more investment was directed to agricultural production. In particular, investment in non-agricultural production dropped in 1989.[8]

In short, the monetary and other contractionary policies of the austerity programme from 1988 restricted the expansion of rural industry. The farmers' production possibility frontier was again truncated. The relative increases in factors for agricultural production eventually led to the recovery of agricultural growth and agriculture's share in the national economy in 1990.

Institutional progress and slow agricultural growth

The previous analysis shows that because of market reform in the rural economy, interactions between agricultural and non-agricultural activities became increasingly important after 1985 in the Chinese countryside. Agricultural performance, therefore, is not only affected by agricultural policies, but also by macroeconomic policies (such as the austerity programme in 1988) and policies targeted at rural industrial sectors. The slowdown of agricultural growth in 1985–88 was accompanied by large outflows of resources from agriculture and a rapid expansion of rural industry. Simply observing changes in relative prices before and after this major policy switch in 1985 does not make much sense because non-agricultural activities were largely not available to farmers before 1985 (although the relative price of industrial output was even higher then). Resources moved out of agriculture in the pursuit of higher returns (though the relative price of industrial output started to fall, its absolute profit per unit of input was still much higher than agricultural output). This is illustrated by income data for the rural economy. In 1985, the average wage in agriculture was 4.7 yuan per day, while that in non-agricultural production was 10.7 yuan per day.[9] The return to a day's work in agriculture was only about 44 per cent of the non-agricultural wage.[10] Therefore, farmers moved off their farms to non-agricultural employment when the market reforms opened up the opportunity to them after 1985, although the ratio of the return to a day's labour in agriculture relative to that outside agriculture was already rising (from even lower ratios in previous years).

This hypothesis is further supported by changes in farmers' real income throughout the period. Farmers' real per capita income increased significantly in 1985 by 4.6 per cent, when the agricultural sector stagnated. Real income continued to rise, with growth rates at 1.7 per cent in 1986 and 2.7 per cent in 1987. In 1989, real income dropped by 6.8 per cent, and though it increased slightly in 1990, it was still 5.4 per cent lower than that in 1988 (Jiang and Luo 1989; SSB, *China Statistical Yearbook 1991*: 295).

The reallocation of resources from agriculture to non-agriculture during 1985–88 was largely a result of farmers' profit (income) maximisation behaviour following the introduction of markets to the rural economy and the expansion of farmers' feasible choice-set. Again, in

1989–90, factors moved toward the agricultural sector where both marginal productivities and returns to factors were low. These movements indicate that the growth and decline of the agricultural sector is not the sole criterion of the success of reforms. The relative contraction of the agricultural sector during 1985–88 was actually a successful outcome, considering that it established a more optimal allocation of the limited resources and returned higher incomes to farmers. On the contrary, the agricultural boom in 1989–90 was a forced result. Farmers' economic opportunities in the non-agricultural sector contracted and the agricultural boom occurred at the cost of a recession in rural industry.

Notes

1 Market prices of agricultural products are calculated following Lin. For detailed explanation and method, see Lin (1992a).
2 By simply regressing agriculture's share on its price relative to industry, the relationship is shown to be significantly positive in 1978–84 and significantly negative in 1985–90.
3 One possible cause for the swift outflow of agricultural resources being induced by the completion of the HRS reform is differential changes in productivity between non-agriculture and agriculture. Suppose that the completion of the HRS reform resulted in a cessation of agricultural productivity improvement but that industrial productivity continued to increase rapidly. In this situation the ratio of marginal product in the two sectors would change markedly. Because marginal productivity in the industrial sector would be rising relative to that in agriculture, factors would move quickly from agriculture to industry to achieve a new economy-wide equilibrium. This possibility, however, can be ruled out for this case.
4 The actual production may locate at some point *within* the frontier, such as D, because of incentive issues, which are discussed in Lin (1988). However, we will ignore this complication and assume that production locates on the frontier.
5 Farmers with only one feasible economic opportunity, such as grain production, might choose to consume leisure if the profitability of grain production was too low. The increase in purchase prices could induce them to convert time from leisure to labour input over a period.
6 In *China Statistical Yearbook 1991*, the numbers up to 1983 are enterprises at the township and village levels (excluding private enterprises) while the numbers from 1984 are *all* township and village enterprises. The latter, apart from the enterprises at the township and village levels, also include rural co-operative and private enterprises.
7 This minimum scale can vary across sectors and regions. However, as the TVP sector grows and technology develops, the likely trend is that the minimum scale will rise.

Adjustments in rural markets bring structural change 95

8 Since most rural investment is realised in the short term, newly increased capital stock can proxy the investment in a particular year. The newly formed capital stock per farm household for agricultural production, from 1986 to 1990, was annually 7.0, 32.9, 63.4, 55.7 and 65.0 yuan; while that for non-agricultural production was 42.5, 44.2, 60.6, 37.3 and 66.4 yuan (SSB, *China Statistical Yearbook 1991*). More investment was directed to agriculture by farm households at the end of the 1980s because of the minimum scale of industrial investment. Possibilities for obtaining bank loans decreased significantly, and farmers' own funds could not reach the minimum scale for industrial investment. As an alternative, they had their own funds to invest in agriculture.

9 These average wage rates are calculated from the data in the *China Agricultural Yearbook 1986* quoted by Wakashiro (1990). According to the statistics, in 1985 the daily wage was 4.9 yuan for growing crops, 4.4 yuan for livestock farming, 8.4 yuan for processing agricultural products, 8.6 yuan for commercial services and restaurants, and 15.0 yuan for transportation and industrial processing.

10 The two possible reasons for the gap between the suggested ratios are: (1) the average wage calculated is a simple mathematical average rather than a weighted average; and (2), as the capital in the agricultural sector is not appropriately priced, labour might be priced at average productivity instead of marginal productivity.

6

An agricultural economy without freedom to trade

The 'third revolution' and preparing for institutional change

Despite the successes of the 1985 reform, the decline in agricultural production that followed presented serious questions for China's overall economic development. At the same time as the government was implementing an austerity programme in the second half of the 1980s, it was stressing the importance of improving agricultural production, particularly of grain. Both agricultural investment and purchase prices were increased by large margins. Some planning measures to control both production and distribution were also resumed. Agricultural production recovered quickly in 1989 and 1990. Grain output reached 1984 levels (about 407 million tonnes) in 1989 and further increased by 9.5 per cent in 1990.

Good harvests, however, did not solve more fundamental problems: rising demand for grain was due to rapid increases in income and declining resources for grain production because of competition from other activities. This led to a continuous rise in domestic prices for grain and other agricultural products. The dilemma for the government was that on the one hand, given farmers' increased bargaining power (see chapter 4), it had to increase its purchase prices to encourage grain production and secure procurement of a certain amount of grain, while on the other, every increase in purchase price had to be financed by a government subsidy that was directly transformed into a burden on the state budget.

To solve this policy dilemma, the government took a substantial step toward the liberalisation of marketing policies in urban areas at the beginning of the 1990s. Changes to policy marked a very important institutional innovation for Chinese agriculture, and was regarded by farmers as the 'third revolution' in the countryside. The 'first revolution' had come at the beginning of the 1950s with significant land reform, while the 'second revolution', in the early 1980s, was the introduction of household responsibility (Garnaut, Guo and Ma 1996). The 'third revolution' did not happen suddenly. It was built on many years of gradual policy reforms and experiments with grain policy, founded in the experiences of reform in non-staple food policy in 1988 and various regional policy experiments from 1987 to 1990. The process began in 1985 when a two-tier price system was established and officially recognised.

The two-tier price system for grain

The two-tier price system was a comprehensive package that included both purchasing and marketing policies. In reality, it was a system that allowed for the co-existence of a state monopoly and a secondary market.

Before 1985, free markets for grain had only a limited role in its production and distribution and the government committed itself to purchasing all surplus grains from farmers. In order to limit government subsidies on grain, a two-tier price system was officially established in 1985. The government set procurement quotas and purchase prices each year, and the system was brought to farm households through several levels of the government.

To facilitate state procurement at low prices, the government instituted compensation policies. For instance, farmers were entitled to buy 3 kilograms of quality fertilisers at subsidised prices and to receive a 15 per cent cash advance for the delivery of 50 kilograms of grain. The benefit from compensation policies went only a little way toward offsetting the losses incurred from state procurement and, in many cases, implementation of the compensation package was problematic.

In 1985, the procurement quota was 79 million tonnes – it was reduced to 61.5 million tonnes in 1986. In 1987, the quota was further reduced to 50 million tonnes. The government announced later that the 1987 quota would remain unchanged for another three years (1988–90). In the event, the procurement quota did not change for yet a further three years (1991–93) (see chapter 4). State purchase prices were consistently lower than market prices in the second half of the 1980s. Fulfilment of the procurement plan was therefore difficult and administrative measures often had to be applied. The grain procured from farmers by the government was mainly sold at subsidised prices to urban consumers and rural residents in grain-deficit regions. In 1987, for instance, 73 per cent of subsidised grain sold went to the urban areas and the remainder to rural areas.

Beyond this state procurement and marketing, grain could be bought and sold on the free market where prices were determined by supply and demand. The major organisations involved in secondary market grain transactions were the State Grain Department, rural supply and marketing co-operatives, private agents and industrial firms using grain. The State Grain Department was the most important trader as it accounted for about 60 per cent of transactions in the secondary market. There were two reasons for the State Grain Department buying from the market: to fill in the gap between state procurement and state marketing set by the plan; and to make profits.

The establishment of a two-tier price system for grain was an important institutional innovation in the recent history of Chinese agriculture. Its main purpose was to introduce the market mechanism to grain transactions while maintaining some direct government control over agricultural products so as to avoid large changes in income distribution. Through the dual system the government removed the link between increased production and consumption of agricultural products and the state budget. Consumers could gradually adapt to the market system as they met their demand beyond the state ration.

There were problems in the implementation of the two-tier system. The government frequently intervened in market transactions and free markets were often closed before state procurement quotas had been fulfilled. Some government policies also magnified fluctuations of the market. The State Grain Department tried to extract extra rent from the two-tier system by reporting a larger volume of products in the free market and less state price procurement or vice versa. Despite these problems, however, farmers started to apply market signals in decision-making after 1985 (see chapter 5). The experiences of the two-tier system for government, farmers and consumers were important preparation for the 'third revolution' that occurred several years later.

Experimenting with institutional change

As early as 1988, the government considered eliminating all price distortions. Comprehensive price reform did not proceed, however, because of large market fluctuations and economic and social discontent. The government was unsure how to implement reform of the price system without significant political and economic consequences. Unlike the household responsibility system reform, where farmers created the new system and the government only permitted and adopted the new institutions, the government was a major designer of the post-1985 reform. The government was now operating in an area where it had few domestic or international examples to follow.

To fill the gap between demand for, and supply of, institutional change, the Chinese government established a number of policy experiment zones. Some of the experiment zones were directly administered by the central government, while others were initiated and administered by local government (but often permitted by the central government). From 1988, experimental reforms in grain purchase and marketing policies were carried out in various regions including Henan, Guangxi, Guizhou and Inner Mongolia. Guangdong and Fujian provinces also pioneered grain policy reform by abolishing consumption rations for grain in 1988. The central government gave these two provinces autonomy to import grain for their own use.

Grain policy experiments took three different avenues. One programme attempted income redistribution for farmers. Grain purchase prices were raised to market levels with the increase financed by agricultural taxes levied according to arable land area. Government compensation policies, sales of agricultural inputs at subsidised prices and cash advances in return for farmers' low prices for agricultural products were abolished. This proposal maintained marketing policies at first but introduced market mechanisms on the production side, while the government budget burden remained constant. Price subsidies on consumers were later converted to lump-sum income subsidies and grain was exchanged freely at market prices. This programme was put into practice in Xinxian municipality of Henan province in 1988. It had the advantage of the gradual introduction of market mechanisms to the existing income distribution patterns. Unfortunately, it received weak support from the public and government departments – even farmers were not initially interested in the reform as they did not directly benefit from it.

Another programme raised both state purchase and marketing prices. It aimed to redistribute income among urban and rural interest groups. The difference between state and market prices was converted to lump-sum subsidies and paid to urban consumers. The subsidy was mainly financed by employers – enterprises in the case of workers and the government budget in the case of government officials. This approach directly increased farmers' income and reduced government expenditure. Free markets were the only mechanism regulating grain production and consumption. Compared to the first approach, this one took only one step to implement a market mechanism. Its weakness, however, was the burden it placed on enterprises. The reform experiments in Guangxi,

Guangdong and Fujian were largely successful where economic development was rapid. There would be difficulties, however, if this approach was introduced to less developed regions, especially where large state enterprises were concentrated.

A final approach was the gradual reduction of quotas for procurement and consumption rations. The proportion of grain handled through the market mechanism was simultaneously expanded. State procurement and marketing eventually would become an insignificant portion of the grain market. This method of reform was adopted by Meitan county of Guizhou province.

In May 1988, the government introduced reforms to the non-staple food policy in urban areas. State marketing and subsidised prices for non-staple foods were abolished and a lump sum paid to urban consumers as compensation (in the range 5–13 yuan per month). This reform was co-ordinated by the central government while detailed reform programmes for the cities were implemented by local governments. Compensation funds usually came from the government budget and enterprises. The reform intended to liberalise non-staple food prices and free the government budget from the burden of them. In reality, however, state prices remained and were set at even higher levels.

The regional policy experiments in the second half of the 1980s and the 1988 non-staple food policy reform made significant contributions to China's reform programme. They tested the various approaches in a real economy and boosted the central government's confidence in pursuing reforms.

The 'third revolution'

Change came quickly. The government initially raised state retail prices significantly at the beginning of 1991 and then unified the two sets of prices (purchase and marketing) by April 1992 (Garnaut and Ma 1992a).[1] By the end of 1993 only 25 out of 2,000 counties, had not introduced complete market reforms to their grain marketing system. Grain coupons were also abolished after being used for forty years in urban areas. A number of other policies were introduced at the same time as the price liberalisation. These included replacing inter-regional grain transfer administered by the central government with a contract system among provincial governments. Supplies for Beijing, Tianjin, Shanghai and military use had been secured through annual state purchases from farmers. The government reformed the input supply system by re-

An agricultural economy without freedom to trade 101

moving subsidies and allowing non-government businesses to supply inputs to producers and establishing ceiling prices. Previous awards of fertilisers, diesel and cash advances paid for deliveries of grain and oil crops to the state were converted to money payments.[2] A Bureau of Grain Stocks was established and market risk funds were to be raised and divided into two parts: a central fund mainly used to stabilise national fluctuations in the grain market; and a local fund for specific uses. Grain support prices were instituted by the government. In 1993, the support price for winter wheat was 650 yuan per tonne in the north and 620 yuan in the south. The support price for maize was 420 yuan inside the Great Wall and 400 yuan outside, while it was 420 yuan for early rice and 560 yuan for late rice.

It was only when this whole package had been completely implemented that it could safely be said that the previous unified purchase and marketing system for agricultural products was over.[3] The 'third revolution' was particularly important because it allowed movements in purchase prices to reflect changes in the markets for the most important agricultural product (Garnaut, Guo and Ma 1996). After the 1992 reform, rises and falls in the prices of grain were absorbed by producers and consumers in the markets, with no implications for the government budget.

Reform and agricultural market prices

Farmers expected prices to rise faster than under the previous system. But in the short run, the government was concerned that domestic grain prices would rise very rapidly after price liberalisation, although, in theory, price fluctuations would be absorbed by producers and consumers and increases in market prices would encourage grain production to meet rapidly increasing domestic demand. The government was aware that significant fluctuations in market prices could cause social problems because of the high proportion of food in consumers' expenditure.

Fortunately, the grain market was smooth during 1992 and most of 1993. Grain prices increased by only 3.4 per cent and food market prices by only 5.8 per cent in 1992, significantly less than in most of the pre-1992 years. Grain prices in most of 1993 were quite stable, with an annual increase of 10 per cent, and grain production reached another historical high (456 million tonnes).

The grain market situation started to change, however, from the end of 1993. Because of small reductions in grain (rice) production in some southern provinces, grain market prices rose significantly within a few days, first in these southern provinces and then in other parts of the country. Market prices increased by as much as 20 per cent in ten days. Price increases were quickly brought down by the government through economic and administrative measures. Price ceilings were announced and the State Grain Department had to sell grain at low prices. Grain stocks were also used to push down prices by increasing supply to the market. These measures were effective, with market prices stabilising within one to two weeks. As a result, the 1993 growth rate was about 10 per cent for grain prices and 7 per cent for food prices.

This price fall was only temporary. Grain prices rose again in early 1994 (table 6.1). The wheat price rose from 1,118 yuan per tonne in December 1993 to 1,583 yuan per tonne in May 1994, rice from 1,479 yuan per tonne in December 1993 to 2,697 yuan per tonne in September 1994, and maize from 722 yuan per tonne in December 1993 to 1,288 yuan per tonne in September 1994. Prices for grain as a whole increased by 50.4 per cent in 1994. Similarly, food prices rose by 32 per cent.

The large rises in the prices of grain and food were used to explain the record inflation rate of 1994. According to the State Statistical Bureau of China (SSB, *China Statistical Yearbook 1995*), food price increases contributed about 55.8 per cent and grain price increases contributed about 12.4 per cent to total inflation, which measured 21.4 per cent.

This sharp rise in grain and food prices caused serious problems for many low-income households, apart from the usual macroeconomic effects of high inflation. In 1994 and 1995, some new policies were introduced to reduce the side-effects of grain policy liberalisation. The major concern was that the nation's food security might be threatened if agriculture failed to deliver sufficient produce. High and unstable food prices also resulted in uncertainty in society. From late 1994, grain coupons were re-introduced and the State Grain Department's subsidised prices resumed.

A more important problem was that there was not a unified domestic grain market and regional development varied widely. Achieving self-sufficiency in grain seemed very difficult at the national level. This was demonstrated by Guangdong and Fujian provinces' experience with grain policy reform. After reforms in 1988, Guangdong and Fujian bought grain from their neighbouring grain-producing provinces. This pushed up market prices in Hunan and Jiangxi and caused difficulties for their local governments as their budgets were still linked with grain prices and because these provinces were relatively poor. After receiving complaints from grain-producing provinces, the

Table 6.1. *Inflation of grain prices, 1993 and 1994 (12 months previously = 100)*

	1993	1994
January	101.4	141.8
February	98.3	139.6
March	104.3	139.3
April	104.0	138.1
May	102.0	138.6
June	100.9	152.2
July	98.9	157.3
August	100.6	159.0
September	101.1	162.8
October	101.2	164.3
November	102.0	161.9
December	113.2	157.1
Annual average	102.3	151.0

Source: Personal communication, Ministry of Agriculture, China.

central government issued a policy prohibiting Guangdong and Fujian from buying grains unless the purchase was arranged through the central government.

In 1994 and 1995, the government adopted a policy that required every province to manage its own supply of grain. This policy was accompanied by further increases in purchase prices. In Prime Minister Li Peng's words, 'provincial governors are responsible for their rice bags, while mayors are responsible for their vegetable baskets'. These recent changes in grain policies mark a significant retreat from the earlier reforms, especially the 'third revolution'.

Causes of high inflation in the early 1990s

The tightening of controls over production and the market for grain products reflected government concern over the possible negative impact of rising food prices on food security and inflation. These issues are being debated in China with two specific questions at the centre of the discussion. First, why did grain and food prices rise so rapidly? Second, what was the true relationship between rising food prices and high inflation? Careful investigation of these issues is critical for both the future of China's agricultural reform and finding a solution to the macroeconomic problems of inflation.

Increasing grain and food prices

Some economists suggest that the root of rapid price increases for grain and food lay in the failure of agricultural production (or failure to increase output sufficiently). Most agricultural economists, however, reject this proposition. Rapid price increases occurred after grain output had reached a historical level in 1993 (456 million tonnes). A mere 2.6 per cent of output reduction in 1994 could hardly explain a 51 per cent increase in prices (Johnson 1995). A group of economists from the Chinese Academy of Social Sciences argue that there has been no significant gap between demand and supply for grain in recent years (Annual Analytical Group on Rural Economy 1995). China constantly had grain surpluses over the period 1989–93, although the size of the surplus fluctuated (table 6.2). Even though total consumption demand rose significantly in 1994, it is unlikely that total demand exceeded output (444.5 million tonnes).

Then what were the causes of the sharp rise in prices? One common explanation is the price liberalisation in 1992 and 1993 and subsequent increases in purchase prices by the government – 20 per cent, on average, in 1994. Price liberalisation had a temporary upward effect on grain market prices. Agricultural economists also point to low relative prices of grain and the imbalance of varieties and regions in grain production as reasons for sharp increases in grain prices (Annual Analytical Group on Rural Economy 1995).

The mixed price for grain was 716 yuan per tonne in 1990, decreased to 677 yuan per tonne in 1991 and rose again, moderately, to 706 yuan per tonne in 1992. During the same period, prices for agricultural inputs increased by 13 per cent. Including the sharp rise of prices in the last quarter of 1993, grain prices rose by 9.8 per cent in 1990–93, while prices for agricultural inputs rose by 28.5 per cent. Agricultural input prices continued to increase in 1994, partly because of foreign exchange reform implemented at the beginning of the year. Rapid increases in grain prices in 1994 were partly a response to more expensive agricultural inputs and higher production costs.

Regional and crop imbalance in grain production became more striking. Because of the difficulties experienced selling rice in 1992 in many southern provinces, farmers in Hunan and Jiangxi provinces reduced the land area allocated to rice production. Rice output decreased by 4.6 per cent in 1993 (7.7 million tonnes). At the same time, however, demand for rice continued to rise rapidly, especially in southern provinces. Rice is the major staple food for many labour migrants in

Table 6.2. *Grain demand and supply, 1989 to 1994*

	Total output (million tonnes)	Total consumption (million tonnes)	Annual surplus (million tonnes)	Farmers' per capita stock (kg)
1989	407.6	400.2	7.4	394.0
1990	446.2	413.3	32.9	428.9
1991	435.3	418.3	17.0	405.9
1992	442.3	427.5	14.8	457.8
1993	456.4	436.0	20.4	533.1
1994	444.5	..	..	541.0

Note: Farmers' per capita grain stock is measured at end of year.
Source: Annual Analytical Group on Rural Economy 1995.

more developed provinces such as Guangdong. World rice output also decreased in 1993, and some provinces which had previously imported rice from other countries were prohibited from doing so later. Some rice-producing provinces, however, increased their exports because of the favourable prices. These changes significantly increased the domestic rice deficit. On a regional basis, those provinces with more rapid economic growth experienced a reduction or stagnation in grain production. While the total grain output increased by 10.2 million tonnes in 1993, the north, northeast and northwest regions increased their output by 14.5 million tonnes. The traditional grain-deficit regions – the southeast coastal and southern regions – experienced a reduction in output of 3.8 million tonnes. China's rapidly rising grain prices started with increases in rice prices in the southern provinces in the last quarter of 1993 which continued into 1994 and 1995. Price fluctuations were further magnified by farmers' reluctance to sell as they expected prices to rise further.

Inflation in 1994 and 1995

Rapidly rising grain and food prices in 1994 were seen as an important source of high inflation. Food prices officially contributed more than half of the overall inflation rate. A high inflation rate must be facilitated by monetary expansion. But in the institutional setting of China, relative scarcity and rising relative prices of food led to pressures for monetary expansion through rural channels.

China has had three periods of high inflation since the mid-1980s. In 1985 inflation peaked at 11.9 per cent and in 1988 it reached 20.7 per cent (Garnaut and Ma 1992a). The inflation rate in 1994 was the highest – at 21.7 per cent – since the Communist Party took control in 1949.

The monetary factors behind each round of high inflation were clear in the post-reform period. The 1985 inflation related to the restructuring of the banking system and decentralisation reforms. The scale of credit exploded in late 1984 and 1985 and similar factors surrounded the high inflation in 1988. The decentralisation programme significantly increased the influence of local government over the scale of credit (Blejer et al. 1991). After a decade-long effort to reform the banking system, there are still serious institutional problems in the management of monetary policy. The central bank is still not an independent monetary authority. Its power depends on specific political interventions, constraining its ability to implement austerity programmes such as the one introduced in mid-1993. The soft-budget problems of the state enterprises and the special interests of local governments further exaggerated inflationary pressure. The investment ratio exceeded 30 per cent of GDP in 1994 for the third successive year – increasing to an extraordinary 38.7 per cent. The government loosened controls over bank loans to the state sector from the middle of the year, leading to rapid expansion of investment. Although the total approved foreign direct investment in 1994 – at US$81 billion – was much lower than the previous year, total realised foreign direct investment increased from US$27 billion in 1993 to US$34 billion in 1994.

If the three periods of inflation are compared, it is found that the 1994 inflation was accompanied by rapid growth of grain and food prices, while in the earlier rounds of inflation increases in prices of producer goods played a greater role. The fluctuation in the grain and food market in China contributed to increases in overall prices in 1994. This happened through the special macroeconomic mechanisms that link food prices to the government budget, and therefore to fiscal and monetary expansion and the soft-budget of the state enterprises.

There were some consumer groups who were worse off because of high inflation. Salaries of state sector employees and government officials stagnated in the face of a 20 per cent inflation rate. Many employees of loss-making state enterprises had, in fact, a reduction in their nominal income because of difficulties in production. Some of them were simply laid off and paid about 100 yuan by the government. The living standard of these people was significantly affected by high food prices. In 1994, the government had to increase payments (salaries) to these government officials and state sector employees as compensation.

The rising grain and food prices presented more problems to state enterprises who were already running at a loss or were operating at the

Table 6.3. *Growth of money and the inflation rate, 1979 to 1994*

	Monetary growth		Year-end money/GNP		Inflation rate (per cent)	GNP growth (per cent)
	M_0 (per cent)	M_2 (per cent)	M_0/GNP	M_2/GNP		
1979	26.3	25.8	6.7	36.5	2.0	7.6
1980	29.3	26.4	7.7	41.2	6.0	7.9
1981	14.5	21.2	8.3	46.8	2.4	4.4
1982	10.8	15.9	8.5	49.9	1.9	8.8
1983	20.7	18.7	9.1	52.9	1.5	10.4
1984	49.5	34.8	11.4	59.6	2.8	14.7
1985	24.7	17.0	11.5	60.8	8.8	12.8
1986	23.3	29.3	15.6	69.3	6.0	8.1
1987	19.4	24.2	12.9	73.9	7.3	10.9
1988	46.7	22.4	15.2	72.1	18.5	11.0
1989	9.8	18.3	14.7	75.1	17.8	4.0
1990	12.8	28.0	15.0	86.5	2.1	5.2
1991	20.2	26.5	16.0	97.5	2.9	7.7
1992	36.5	31.3	18.1	105.9	5.4	13.0
1993	35.3	24.0	18.7	100.4	13.0	13.4
1994	24.3	34.4	16.6	107.2	21.7	11.8

Source: Yi 1995.

margin, especially to those in labour-intensive sectors or those using agricultural products as inputs. This raised their demand for bank loans or government subsidies. Some stopped producing because of difficulties in selling their products; the government then had to pay a living allowance to each redundant worker. Government revenue did not increase in proportion to these payouts. The extra expenditure had to be financed by issuing money or bonds (table 6.3). The inflation rate was thus exaggerated to a high level.

Yi (1995) argues that money supply is still largely endogenous in China – and that this is reflected in the formulation of the monetary base. The main contributing sources are foreign exchange holdings by the central bank and borrowing by the central government. Government borrowing is closely correlated with the soft-budget problems of the state enterprises. In 1994, these factors caused a 43 per cent increase in quasi-money.

The continued growth in the money supply and bank credit in 1993 and 1994, despite the austerity programme, reflected the government's ambition that the 'overheated' economy should land 'softly' as well as the ineffectiveness of monetary controls. By mid-1995, the consumer price inflation index was still above 20 per cent.

Lack of freedom in agricultural trade

An important characteristic of the Chinese agricultural market – the lack of freedom to trade – is often neglected. But has the maintenance of an inward-looking strategy for agriculture been a negligible factor for the rapid growth of grain prices in recent years? The answer is clearly negative. There may be some other temporary factors also contributing to the recent grain price inflation, but as long as the free market operates, it is inevitable that grain prices in a land-scarce country like China will sooner or later shoot off.

The Chinese grain market is segmented by regions, and the domestic market is isolated from international markets. Although price controls over the agricultural economy were removed, there is no freedom to trade between regions or with other countries. Regional grain flows are largely impossible unless arranged and administered by the government. The import and export of grain have been increasingly used as measures for balancing domestic demand and supply, but both are also monopolised by the government.

In an agricultural economy without freedom to trade, the market is vulnerable and unstable. Neither producers nor consumers have confidence in the market. A small change in production and consumption can result in significant price fluctuations especially if consumer expectations are taken into account. When prices rise, consumers tend to buy more and producers tend to sell less in anticipation of even higher prices. When prices fall, consumers tend to buy less and producers tend to sell more in an anticipation of lower prices. Small changes in market prices are therefore turned into large fluctuations.

This was exactly what happened in China in 1993 and 1994. A small reduction of rice output could easily have been smoothed if the economy had had free and timely access to the international market and other regional markets. But because grain could not be moved around the country freely, a reduction in output in one region caused a sharp rise in local grain prices. This in turn provided the wrong market signals to other regions and further magnified the price fluctuations. In this way, grain price inflation easily accelerated.

The proposition that a certain degree of production (or consumption) fluctuation usually leads to larger price changes in a small segmented grain market without freedom to trade than in a large integrated market can be shown through a simple model. Let us assume a country's grain demand (D_1) and supply (S_1) can be specified as

$$D_1 = a_1 + b_1 P_1 + \Omega_1(w) \tag{6.1}$$

$$S_1 = c_1 - d_1 P_1 \tag{6.2}$$

where P_1 is grain market price (ignoring the time lags in production responses), all the parameters a_1, b_1, c_1, d_1 are positive numbers, and $\Omega_1(w)$ is a variable capturing changes in grain production which are assumed to be a function of the weather.

For a closed economy without trade, the market equilibrium will occur when

$$D_1 = S_1 \tag{6.3}$$

which is the same as

$$a_1 + b_1 P_1 + \Omega_1(w) = c_1 - d_1 P_1 \tag{6.4}$$

Rearranging the above equation we obtain the equilibrium grain price as

$$P_1 = \frac{c_1 - a_1 - \Omega_1(w)}{b_1 + d_1} \tag{6.5}$$

From equation (6.5), the impact of a change in output, due to weather variations for instance, on market price can be calculated by taking the partial derivative

$$\frac{\partial P_1}{\partial \Omega_1(w)} = \frac{1}{b_1 + d_1} \tag{6.6}$$

Now, let us assume that there is another economy with a similar grain market structure

$$D_2 = a_2 + b_2 P_2 + \Omega_2(w) \tag{6.7}$$

$$S_2 = c_2 - d_2 P_2 \tag{6.8}$$

If the two economies are well integrated with each other, we have identical grain prices in the two markets, $P_1 = P_2 = P$ and

$$P = \frac{c_1 + c_2 - a_1 - a_2 - \Omega_1(w) - \Omega_2(w)}{b_1 + b_2 + d_1 + d_2} \tag{6.9}$$

The impact of a change in economy 1's output because of weather conditions on equilibrium price is

$$\frac{\partial P}{\partial \Omega_1(w)} = -\frac{1}{b_1 + b_2 + d_1 + d_2} \tag{6.10}$$

Comparing (6.10) with (6.6), it is clear that in an integrated market, the price fluctuation resulting from the same change in output is much smaller than in a segmented market, because

$$\left| -\frac{1}{b_1 + b_2 + d_1 + d_2} \right| < \left| -\frac{1}{b_1 + d_1} \right| \tag{6.11}$$

On the other hand, if a small economy is integrated into the world market, it faces a horizontal supply function. Changes in domestic output alter the quantity of imports or exports, but not the quantity of consumption or the price. As China is a large economy, changes in its output may affect the world market. But the derivation has demonstrated clearly that price fluctuations resulting from changes in domestic production would be much smaller in a world market than in a single market.

The case of increasing grain stocks

Greater instability in a highly segmented domestic grain market without freedom to trade has implications for food security in the domestic economy. Rising peasant grain stocks in the 1980s and 1990s demonstrated farmers' expectations of market instability and a lack of confidence in food security.

China's grain stocks are a controversial issue because data recently released in official Chinese publications indicate very high stock levels (table 6.4). The subject had for so long been a state secret. The figures were probably published to reassure consumers that higher retail grain prices in November and December 1993 were not indicative of any grain shortage, and to forestall panic buying or the excessive retention of supplies by producers (Huang 1995).

Previously, the United States Department of Agriculture estimated that China's grain stocks rose from 40 million tonnes in 1970 to around 60–80 million tonnes in the second half of the 1980s (United States Department of Agriculture 1993). Recently released data based on the State Statistical Bureau's survey results, however, suggest that stocks totalled 491 million tonnes in 1990 (more than annual total consumption), whereas the United States Department of Agriculture's estimate for that year was 82 million tonnes (United States Department of Agriculture 1993). These newly released stock data were vastly different from the earlier United States Department of Agriculture estimates. It has also been revealed that the largest proportion of grain stock was held by farmers.

Grain stocks in China

In a market economy, there are two types of grain stock – commercial stocks and stabilisation reserves. The former are held by commercial organisations or firms for the purpose of marketing if there are supply delays due to transport or processing. The latter are held by government agents for the purpose of market intervention in cases of severe price fluctuation. The necessary levels of these stocks, particularly commercial stocks, are dependent on operating efficiency and infrastructure conditions.

In China, the State Grain Department usually performs both commercial and stabilisation functions. This was especially so during the reform period: when market prices rose rapidly at the end of 1993 in some southern provinces, state grain stores were required by the central government to sell at assigned prices to stabilise the grain market (see chapter 4). Efforts have been made to separate the State Grain Department into two parts relating to the different functions. Special reserves were also to have been established. As of mid-1996, however, the reform had not been accomplished. State grain stocks therefore include both commercial and reserve stocks. Considering the inefficiency of the State Grain Department and poor transportation facilities, it is understandable that both commercial and reserve stocks may be larger than actually required.

Most Chinese farmers grow grain for their own consumption. Even in provinces like Guangdong or Jiangsu where the opportunity costs of grain production are extremely high, many farmers still produce their own food grain. Farmers' grain stocks can therefore be classified into two parts: those held as reserves and those held for consumption later in the same year.

According to the United States Department of Agriculture (1993), grain stocks data for farmers are on a January/December calendar year but grain production is based on an April/March year. The first harvest starts in April in Hainan and Guangdong. Given delays in harvesting, drying, transporting and processing, newly harvested grains would not be delivered to consumers until May or June. Recorded grain stocks should therefore include six months of circulating grain stocks for farmers and two months of commercial stocks for the state. Using this classification, China's grain stocks may not be as high as suggested. Take 1990 as an example. Estimated total grain stocks were 491 million tonnes and the estimated stocks held by farmers were 356 million tonnes. This indicates that grain stocks held by the State Grain Department were 135 million tonnes.

112 *Agricultural reform in China*

Table 6.4. *Grain stocks, 1970 to 1994 (million tonnes)*

	Total grain production (grain equivalent)	USDA estimates of total ending grain stock	Grain reserve data attributed to the SSB	Annual net change in SSB stocks	Estimated grain stock held by farmers
1970	240.0	36.5	40.0	..	..
1974	275.3	65.8	80.0	..	..
1984	407.3	..	..	..	249.9 [a]
1986	391.5	76.8	336.0	..	..
1987	403.0	72.0	363.1	27.1	..
1988	394.1	64.0	380.0	16.9	266.0 [b]
1989	407.6	64.0	417.0	37.0	258.8 [d]
1990	446.2	82.0	490.9	73.9	355.9 [c]
1991	435.3	..	582.8	91.9	345.4 [b]
1992	442.7	..	..	..	433.3 [a]
1993	456.4	..	..	..	465.7 [d]
1994	444.5	..	..	..	478.7 [e]

Notes: Grain in United States Department of Agriculture estimates includes wheat, rice, coarse grains and soybeans. In Chinese statistics, grain includes wheat, rice, corn, sorghum, millet, barley, oats, soybeans, pulses and other grains such as buckwheat and potatoes (converted from a wet to a grain equivalent dry-weight basis on a 5 to 1 ratio).
[a] A State Statistical Bureau rural survey team's random survey of 67,000 rural households in thirty provinces found that per capita grain stocks increased 64.2 per cent, from 311 kilograms in 1984 to 511 kilograms in 1992 (*China Statistical News*, April 1993).
[b] On an April/March 1988 grain year basis, the state held stocks equivalent to 102.5 kilograms per capita (about 114 million tonnes). In 1991, State Statistical Bureau surveys found that per capita peasant grain stocks at the end of the year were 405 kilograms (*China's Rural Economy*, 20 April 1994).
[c] An OECD report noted that the bulk of 1990 grain stocks was in fact held by farmers, as market stocks held in the state cereals network were estimated to be around 135 million tonnes, including 35 million tonnes of centrally controlled special reserves (OECD 1994).
[d] The Chinese Academy of Social Sciences reported that farmers' per capita grain stock was 394 kilograms in 1989 and 533.1 kilograms in 1993 (Annual Analytical Group on Rural Economy, 1995).
[e] The State Statistical Bureau announced in mid-1995 that farmers' per capita grain stock was 540 kilograms in 1994.
Sources: United States Department of Agriculture 1993; OECD 1994; Annual Analytical Group on Rural Economy 1995; SSB, *China Statistical Yearbook*, various issues.

In 1990, total sales were 93 million tonnes of milled grain or 124 million tonnes of unmilled grains (using a conversion ratio of 0.75). Commercial stocks for two months (April–May) were 21 million tonnes. In other words, estimated government reserve stocks were 103 million tonnes (including 35 million tonnes special reserve) in 1990 – close to the original United States Department of Agriculture estimate (82 million tonnes – equivalent to 23 per cent of national total grain consumption or 83 per cent of non-farmers' annual consumption). Similarly, farmers' total grain consumption was 326 million tonnes in 1990 and estimated grain stocks were 356 million tonnes. Farmers' stocks for the next six months were 163 million tonnes. Therefore, estimated reserve stocks held by farm households were 193 million tonnes or 60 per cent of their own yearly consumption. Total grain stocks, even the calculated reserve stocks, are very high in China after taking farmers' grain stocks into account.

Why China's grain stocks rose in the 1980s

The following reasons have been offered to explain the increase in China's grain stocks from the early 1980s to 1994:

- a general rise in the food supply
- a decrease in the direct consumption of grain resulting in relative grain surplus
- scientific and technical advances in other production that indirectly cut grain consumption
- restrictive policies and poor infrastructure
- production unsuited to the changing structure of demand resulting in low-quality grain in stocks
- a physical saving in the face of high inflation.

Food supply increased markedly in the 1980s and consumers were less dependent on grain for daily calorie intake. Direct grain consumption decreased relatively and new hog breeds with a more efficient grain–pork conversion ratio were introduced. These factors suggest that while grain output increased significantly, total grain demand did not rise at the same pace. The gaps between these increases in supply and demand became increments to grain stocks.

These arguments are relatively weak when considering grain stock increases over ten years, especially in the light of grain shortages from 1985 to 1988. If total demand had stagnated or grown more slowly than production, market prices would have fallen. Farmers would have had sufficient time and autonomy to adjust their production structure, particularly after 1985 when a two-tier system for grain was officially instituted. Under these circumstances grain stocks should not have accumulated over two to three years. In fact, in 1989, when grain output reached the 1984 level after several years of decline, grain stock held by farmers was reduced to 259 million tonnes from 266 million tonnes in the previous year (table 6.4).

Poor infrastructure, particularly transportation facilities, may partly explain the high level of grain stocks. Deficit regions kept larger stocks because the transportation network could not be relied upon when grain was desperately needed.

To further understand changes in China's grain stocks, farmers' behaviour must be investigated. Grain stocks held by the state increased only gradually, from less than 100 million tonnes in the mid-1980s to 114 million tonnes in 1988 and 135 million tonnes in 1990. Considering increases in total consumption, this rise in state grain stocks was not surprising.

Japan's post-war protective grain policy largely grew from the memory of starvation immediately after World War II. China also has its own bad memories. Estimates of deaths due to both policy and natural disasters between 1959 and 1961 are in excess of 30 million. In addition, it was not until 1983 that most Chinese exceeded subsistence calorie intake levels. Food security is therefore a top priority for farmers and there is a tendency to internalise food security within the household. This is partly evidenced by the fact that rich farmers with non-agricultural jobs in southern and eastern provinces still prefer to grow their own food grain. Some may produce enough grain in one year to leave the land idle in the following years. It is not uncommon for a farm household to have sufficient grain stocks to meet one to two years' household consumption. This cannot be explained by factors such as increases in production or declines in total demand.

The internalisation of food security explains the high grain stocks held by local governments. Both deficit and surplus-grain regions have high grain stocks because barriers to regional trade are a common problem. Deficit provinces are often restricted from buying grains from neighbouring regions, particularly when there is a grain shortage. This results in duplicated grain stocks at different levels of government (current state grain stocks are about 23 per cent of total annual consumption). The rationale behind this widespread internalisation of food security among farmers and local governments is the lack of confidence in China's grain market. Because there is no integrated domestic market and no freedom to trade, farmers and local governments may have problems in supplying their needs in the presence of grain shortage.

Before farmers and regions can gain confidence in the central government's ability to stabilise the grain market effectively, grain stocks must increase when more market-oriented reforms are introduced. Abolition of central planning might generate greater uncertainty in grain supply. This may in part explain the rapid increases in grain stocks after 1989 and probably in 1991 and 1992.

But why did grain stocks rise only during and after the 1980s? There are two reasons why farmers did not accumulate grain stocks before the 1980s. First, before economic reform farmers' grain was controlled and allocated by communes or production teams. Households did not play a large role in the allocation of grain. Second, grain was constantly in short supply. Furthermore, as agricultural production was planned by the government, all grain in excess of farmers' own consumption in grain-surplus regions was taken away by the government. The amount of grain that farm households received from the communes did not usually cover a year's consumption.

Economic reforms, particularly the introduction of the household responsibility system, provided both necessary and sufficient conditions for farmers to internalise grain security. According to the responsibility system, farmers are allowed to retain all their output, including grain, after fulfilling the assigned state quotas and delivering levies to the collectives. Farmers can decide what to do with the surplus part of household-produced grains – either to sell extra produce in the markets (or to government agents at higher prices) or to hold it as household stocks. The large increases in grain output in the 1980s produced a grain surplus.

Farmers wanted to hold grain stocks for food security. Without any social security system, grain stocks are often farmers' means of protecting themselves against unpredictable weather changes and risks in crop production, and, in some cases, serve as life and health insurance.

Internalising food security is a special phenomenon when memories of food insecurity are still fresh and the government has not yet built a strong market stabilisation capacity. The high levels of grain stocks held by farm households and regions will fall gradually when the market mechanisms begin to work effectively, and when the transportation network and government stabilisation operations are more efficient. Farmers and regions will give up their own grain stocks when they feel their access to food is secure even in the presence of market instability. This will be a gradual process, however, and will probably take over ten years.

An incomplete revolution

There were various factors that contributed to the rapid rise of grain and food prices from 1993 to 1995, including increases in input prices and an adjustment following price liberalisation. A more fundamental factor, however, was a lack of freedom to trade between and within regions, and between countries. Although it is true to say that high inflation is a monetary phenomenon, it was rapidly increasing grain and food prices that triggered the growth of overall prices, given China's fiscal and monetary institutional setting.

The 'third revolution' in 1991 and 1992, although an important step forward, is still largely incomplete. The lack of freedom to trade, especially in domestic regional markets, makes the domestic grain market vulnerable. This was the main source of significant fluctuations in the domestic market in 1993–94. The result was rapidly rising prices for grain and food. Changes in food prices were then transmitted to the macroeconomy through the special mechanisms for monetary and fiscal policies and the soft-budget problems of the state enterprises. The inflation rate was pushed to a higher level.

From 1995, the government again started to tighten controls over prices and quantities in grain purchase and marketing. Prices for food and grains (and overall prices) continued to rise rapidly, however. On one hand, the government only controlled a proportion of grain products, and it did not have the power to influence the level of market prices. On the other hand, the State Grain Department, which was supposed to smooth market fluctuations and bring down high prices, did not operate as expected. In the pursuit of profit, it tended to exaggerate, rather than reduce, market fluctuations. Requiring each province to look after its own grain supply without the option of free regional and international trade, implied that each county and village had to produce its own grain. Such policies were a significant drawback against the background of overall economic liberalisation and reform.

Given the current institutional settings, including the self-sufficiency policy, the soft budget of the state enterprises, the link between the government budget and grain and food prices and the connection between fiscal and monetary policies, large fluctuations in food markets are likely to continue. Another small reduction in grain output will push up market prices significantly and trigger another round of high inflation.

A fundamental means of eliminating the possibility of excessive responses in grain and food prices and associated high inflation is to reform the institutions allowing such a process. Regional blocks in the domestic market must be removed to enable a smooth adjustment and better exercise of regional comparative advantages. Links between domestic and international markets will also significantly reduce fluctuations in grain prices. Elimination of the state enterprise soft-budget problem will be essential to bring down China's high inflation rate. While assistance to some will be necessary in the face of high food prices, the government will need to abandon its current practice of subsidising everyone.

Notes

1 As with the case of food policy reform in 1988, a lump-sum subsidy per month was paid to urban residents as a compensation.
2 Two-thirds of the funds for these payments came from the central government with local government providing the remaining one-third. Farmers have experienced frequent problems in receiving the latter part of the payment.
3 Unfortunately, as it has transpired, the unified purchase and marketing system is far from over. Some of the measures of the system were re-introduced following severe fluctuations in grain markets.

7

China's agricultural policy choices

A turning point in China's agricultural development

Increases in grain and food prices in 1993–95 not only revealed critical deficiencies in the post-liberalisation grain market, but also led to an important turning point in China's agricultural development and policy – the ending of forty years of policies discriminating against agriculture. The government now faces a policy choice which will determine China's future pattern of agricultural production and consumption and will also affect, to some extent, its major trading partners' welfare and world trade patterns.

Pre-reform agricultural institutions created two types of distortion of incentives in agriculture – distortions due to procurement policies and distortions due to border policies. Policy changes during the reform period have focused on eliminating the first type of distortion. In theory, after the liberalisation of grain prices in 1992, state purchase prices should not differ significantly from market prices. Price reforms, the introduction of free markets and trade liberalisation have also gradually reduced the second type of distortion.

Changes in nominal rates of protection

There are many different methods used in economic analysis to measure the degree of protection of domestic markets. The nominal rate of protection is the simplest indicator. It directly compares domestic and border prices and can be expressed in percentage form as

$$ERP_t^i = \frac{eP_t^i - P_t^{i*}}{P_t^{i*}} * 100 \qquad (7.1)$$

where P_t^i is the domestic price of good i at time t in domestic currency, P_t^{i*} is the border price in foreign currency (US dollars), and is the

Table 7.1. *Nominal rate of protection for grain and oil crops, 1978 to 1994 (per cent)*

	Wheat	Rice	Maize	Oil-bearing crops
1978	−51	−6	−45	—
1980	25	−43	18	−3
1984	−11	−39	−27	−45
1985	−13	−43	−21	−44
1988	−12	−53	−10	−43
1989	−5	−42	18	−39
1990	−10	−53	−3	−40
1991	4	−58	−20	−46
1992	−14	−44	−19	−49
1993	−12	−31	−15	−33
1994	10	2	8	11

Note: Domestic market prices (and the above-quota prices before 1984) are converted through the secondary market exchange rate. International prices are average prices reported in Food and Agriculture Organization of the United Nations *Production Yearbook* various issues.
Sources: Personal communication, Ministry of Agriculture, China; International Monetary Fund, *International Financial Statistics*, various issues; Garnaut, Cai and Huang 1996.

exchange rate measured as foreign currency per unit of domestic currency (US dollars/yuan). A score of zero for the nominal rate of protection implies free trade (no protection), while a value greater than zero implies positive protection of the domestic market (domestic price is higher than the border price) and a value less than zero implies negative protection. The nominal rate of protection is a convenient measure to apply because its calculation requires only limited data. Difficulties often occur when choosing an appropriate border price (allowing for quality differences and potential transportation costs) and exchange rate (especially if there is not a free market for foreign exchange).

In the calculation of the nominal rate of protection for China's most important agricultural products in 1978–94, the secondary foreign exchange rate was used (table 7.1). A convincing secondary market exchange rate did not exist before 1986. These figures must therefore be examined with caution, especially for the years before 1986.

The nominal rate of protection for wheat, rice, maize and oil-bearing crops in the second half of the 1980s indicates that all products were heavily and negatively protected, reflecting the continuation of the pre-reform discriminatory agricultural policies. Although positive numbers occurred for some products during this period, the nominal rate of protection normally ranged from around −10 per cent for wheat, about

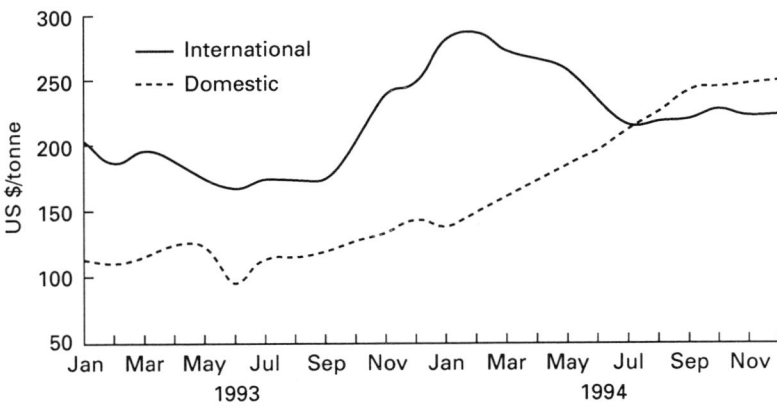

Fig. 7.1 International and Chinese cereal prices, 1993 to 1994. Cereal prices are average prices of wheat, rice and maize weighted by their output shares in China's production. China's domestic prices are market prices in rural and urban fairs converted using the swap exchange rate and international prices are f.o.b. Gulf of No. 1 hard red winter (ordinary protein) for wheat, f.o.b. Bangkok white milled 5 per cent broken for rice and US exports prices are f.o.b. Gulf of No. 2 yellow for maize. (*Sources:* International Monetary Fund, *International Financial Statistics*, Washington, D.C., various issues; State Planning Commission and Ministry of Agriculture, Beijing.)

−40 per cent for rice, −15 per cent for maize and −45 per cent for oil crops.[1] The first year that China's main agricultural products experienced a unified drop in the nominal rate of protection was 1989. It resulted from the rise in domestic prices in the last quarter of that year. Continued and more rapid increases in domestic prices in 1994 pushed the nominal rate of protection nearer to zero with some positive values marking an important historical turning point. By mid-1994, domestic prices exceeded international prices for wheat and maize, and by September this was also so for rice, despite large increases in world rice prices following Japan's entry into the market as an importer (Garnaut, Cai and Huang 1996).

In calculating comparative aggregate cereal prices here in both domestic and international markets, the commodities included are wheat, rice and maize, which together account for 95.5 per cent of China's total cereal production and 84.7 per cent of its grain consumption (figure 7.1). Both international and domestic prices are weighted by the output share of individual commodities in China's production. The movement of international prices may be different from what can be observed from other sources. While a significant upward movement in the price of rice in 1994 had an impact on the international prices calculated for China, rice only accounted for a small share of world grain trade. Even when a larger than usual effect of rice price increase is incorporated into the calculation of international prices, it is still clear that China's domestic cereal prices and international prices converged quickly in 1994. By July 1994, domestic prices were similar to international prices, and they exceeded international prices in the months that followed.

Movements in the producer subsidy equivalent

While the nominal rate of protection is easy to use, it ignores domestic distortions. The producer subsidy equivalent is in this sense a more comprehensive measure of the degree of agricultural protection. The producer subsidy equivalent indicates the value of the transfer from consumers and taxpayers (in terms of both direct subsidies and other indirect benefits) to producers resulting from a given set of policies at a point in time. The base for comparison is the free trade situation. Compared to the nominal rate of protection, the producer subsidy equivalent provides a more complete picture of distortions in agriculture because it incorporates domestic, non-price distortions. It is often difficult, however, to calculate the producer subsidy equivalent owing to the data requirements. There are three ways in which to express a producer subsidy equivalent: total producer subsidy equivalents in money terms, producer subsidy equivalent per unit of product and the proportion of producer subsidy equivalent in total revenue.

There are seven items included in the calculation of the producer subsidy equivalent (table 7.2):

- *Income transfers due to border policy.* Calculation of this item is similar to calculating the nominal rate of protection. Income transfers are the difference between agricultural output evaluated at domestic and international prices. The large negative numbers, ranging between -100 and -400 billion yuan, imply that the border policies in general result in income losses to farmers. This is consistent with the estimates of the nominal rate of protection.
- *Agricultural taxes.* Agricultural taxes are mainly land taxes. Other agricultural taxes include taxes on special agricultural products and special production processes. These represent a negative item and diminish farmers' income.

Table 7.2. *Producer subsidy equivalent estimates for agriculture, 1986 to 1994 (billion yuan)*

	1986	1988	1990	1992	1993	1994[a]
Producer value	401.0	587.0	766.0	909.0	1030.0	280.0
Income transfer due to border policy	−190.6	−414.6	−245.2	−209.9	−251.4	−96.5
(*Exchange rate*)	5.0	6.3	5.8	6.5	8.6	8.7
Agricultural taxes	4.5	7.4	8.8	9.0	9.6	9.6
Budget on agriculture	18.4	21.4	30.8	37.9	44.1	44.1
Disaster subsidy	1.1	1.1	1.3	1.6	1.6	1.6
Welfare subsidy	0.3	0.3	0.3	0.3	0.4	0.4
Input subsidy	1.0	1.2	1.4	1.4	1.5	1.5
Interest difference	7.9	11.3	14.9	20.8	24.7	24.7
Agricultural loans	28.3	40.4	53.1	74.0	87.8	87.8
Producer subsidy equivalent value	−162.0	−379.0	−197.0	−148.0	−179.0	−24.0
Per cent share	−40.0	−65.0	−26.0	−16.0	−17.0	−2.0

Note: International food price is an aggregate international price weighted by value shares in total world trade. The commodities included in the calculation are beef, lamb, pork, eggs, wheat, rice, maize, oranges, apples and tea. Domestic price is based on the rural market food price.
[a] Estimates according to available information.
Sources: China State Planning Commission and Ministry of Agriculture; Garnaut, Cai and Huang 1996.

- *Budget spending on agriculture.* Budget spending includes investment in agricultural infrastructure, expenditure on agricultural scientific research, education and extension. It also includes special assistance to agricultural production.
- *Disaster subsidy.* This subsidy is used to assist farmers with living and production difficulties after a natural disaster. The data are directly from government budget reports.
- *Welfare subsidy.* This is indirectly related to agricultural production and is usually spent on improving farmers' educational, cultural and entertainment facilities.
- *Input subsidy.* The input subsidy is associated with the government's procurement policy for agricultural products. As compensation, the government sells limited agricultural inputs such as fertilisers and pesticides to farmers at subsidised prices in return for certain quantities of agricultural products. The price gap between the subsidised and market prices for agricultural inputs is equivalent to a lump-sum subsidy received by farmers. After 1993, the government abolished its input compensation policy and converted it to lump-sum subsidies paid directly to farmers.

- *Interest difference.* Agricultural loans from the state banks have always enjoyed preferential interest rates, similar to subsidies to farmers. The interest differential is calculated by multiplying total agricultural loans at the end of the year by the gap between interest rates for agricultural loans and those for other industrial and commercial loans.

The estimated producer subsidy equivalents ranged from -40 to -65 per cent in the mid-1980s, reflecting severe discrimination against agriculture. After many years of successful agricultural reform, farmers lost one-third of the product value due to various distortion policies. The producer subsidy equivalent then rose to around -20 per cent in the early 1990s. An estimate of the producer subsidy equivalent close to zero in 1994 implies that farmers' net income from agricultural production would then be similar to that under free trade.

Temporary fluctuation or long-term trend?

Distortions against agriculture introduced in the pre-reform period had been nearly eliminated by 1994. Did this mark another temporary fluctuation or, alternatively, a historical turning point in China's agricultural development? There were some temporary factors behind the rapid rise of grain and food prices in 1993–95 (see chapter 6). Grain price increases also reflected a long-term trend in prices relative to international prices in a densely populated country. If this long-term trend remains in place, it will push domestic prices above international prices.

It has been suggested that world prices for agricultural products, especially grain, will rise following the implementation of the Uruguay Round settlement (Goldin and Knudsen 1990; Brandão and Martin 1993; Huang 1994). Tyers and Anderson (1992), for instance, predicted that a phased 50 per cent reduction in agricultural protection in industrial economies between 1991 and 2000 would lead to a price increase of 19 per cent for wheat in 1995, 6 per cent for rice, 5 per cent for meat and 11 per cent for the weighted average of food products (table 7.3). Most other studies project a similar pattern of price change (Goldin and Knudsen 1990). Wheat prices would rise substantially, reflecting the removal of high average rates of protection in industrial economies, as would rice prices but to a lesser extent because of the role of industrial economies in world rice trade. A simulation based on the Dunkel proposal and using the RUNS model (Brandão and Martin 1993) predicts increases in

124 Agricultural reform in China

Table 7.3. *Effects of agricultural trade liberalisation on international prices (per cent change in international commodity prices)*

	Wheat	Rice	Coarse grain	Meat	Sugar
Liberalisation in industrial economies					
Tyers and Anderson (1992)	19	6	−5	5	6
Zeitz and Valdés	3	2	..	10	15
Cramer, Wailes and Shui (1993)	..	5	..	..	..
OECD/MTMD	−5	..	..	5	9
USDA/SWOPSIM	27	18	..	16	29
IISA	18	21	..	17	..
RUNS (Brandão and Martin 1993)	4	2	3	5	6
Walras	17	..	..	10	..
Global liberalisation					
Tyers and Anderson (1992)	1	−6	..	8	−12
Zeitz and Valdés	−12	−21	..	13	1
Cramer, Wailes and Shui (1993)	..	25	..	..	..
OECD/MTMD	−7	−5	..	−4	7
USDA/SWOPSIM	23	..	..	7	7
IISA	23	..	..	11	..
RUNS (Brandão and Martin 1993)	6	−3	4	5	12
Dunkel proposal					
RUNS (Brandão and Martin 1993)	6	4	4	6	10

Sources: Goldin and Knudsen (eds.) 1990; Tyers and Anderson 1992; Cramer, Wailes and Shui 1993; Brandão and Martin 1993.

international prices resulting from the implementation of the Uruguay Round – 6 per cent for wheat and meat, 4 per cent for rice and coarse grain, and 10 per cent for sugar.

Predicted price increases in the next decade or so would reverse the long-term decline of agricultural prices over the past several decades, although the magnitudes of price increases would not be great.

But price increases for agricultural products in China are likely to be larger and come more quickly than those in international markets if the Chinese agricultural economy continues to be isolated from trade. China is a large country with a limited per capita agricultural resource endowment. Its population density (121 persons per square kilometre) is not high compared to many countries in Western Europe and East Asia, although it is much higher than the world average (table 7.4). China's agricultural area, including arable land, forestry and pastoral areas, however, is very small on a per capita basis. China has about 22 per cent of the world's population, but only 7 per cent of the world's arable land area. China cannot be expected to have a comparative advantage in agricultural production as incomes rise.

Table 7.4. *Population and agricultural resources in selected countries, 1992*

	Total population (millions)	Population density (persons/km^2)	Arable land	Forestry (ha/person)	Pastoral areas
China	1,158.2	121	0.08	0.11	0.19
United States	252.7	27	0.74	1.16	0.96
Canada	27.0	3	1.70	13.28	1.04
Australia	17.3	2	2.81	6.11	24.09
Germany	80.3	226	0.15	0.13	0.07
Britain	57.4	235	0.12	0.04	0.19
France	57.1	103	0.32	0.26	0.20
Japan	123.9	328	0.03	0.20	0.01
Korea	43.3	437	—	—	—
Taiwan	20.4	565	0.04	—	—
Indonesia	187.8	99	0.09	0.60	0.06
India	841.7	283	0.20	0.08	0.01
Philippines	62.9	210	0.07	0.16	0.02
Thailand	56.9	111	0.33	0.25	0.01
Malaysia	18.3	56	0.06	1.05	0.00
Pakistan	115.5	145	0.18	0.03	0.04
Bangladesh	118.7	825	0.07	0.02	0.01
Mexico	87.8	45	0.26	0.48	0.85
Argentina	32.7	12	0.76	1.81	4.35
Brazil	153.3	18	0.33	3.22	1.20
World	5,389.2	40	0.25	0.75	0.63

Sources: SSB, *China Statistical Yearbook 1993*; Food and Agricultural Organization of the United Nations, *Production Yearbook 1992*.

It will be increasingly difficult for Chinese agriculture to meet rapidly rising demands for grain and agricultural products. On one hand, China's economic growth is likely to be high – between 8.5 and 9 per cent per annum for the next two decades. Both income effects and increasing population will push consumption demand steadily upward. On the other hand, as the Chinese economy is, and will be, developing rapidly, it will experience significant structural change. It is inevitable that agricultural production will face tougher competition for rural resources. This process has already begun in China, especially since 1985.

Arable land area decreased from 99.4 million hectares in 1978 to 95.1 million hectares in 1993, a reduction of 4.3 per cent. The largest proportion of changed land use was capital construction by or through the state. The rapid development of township, village and private enterprises also placed demands on arable resources, as did housing construction by farm households. These forces will continue in the future and present further difficulties for agricultural output growth. The convergence of domestic and international prices for grain and food was therefore a reflection of a long-term trend, given China's resource endowment and rapid growth.

While agriculture is one major source of industrialisation in the early stages of an economy's development, there comes a time when such a contribution becomes unnecessary (Timmer 1988). This has already been experienced in industrial economies and the rapidly growing East Asian economies. Economic history further suggests that this will come about sooner the fewer agricultural resources an economy has and the faster the economy grows.

The Chinese economy has already reached a stage of development similar to that when Japan, Korea and Taiwan turned from taxing to subsidising agriculture. China's per capita GNP in 1994, adjusted for international comparison, was around US$1,500[2] – very close to the income levels of Korea and Taiwan in the 1960s and 1970s and similar to Japan's in the pre- and post-war years.[3]

China's policy options

Evidence suggests that China's forty years of policies that discriminated against agriculture are to end. But what future policy directions should the Chinese government pursue? This question is under heated debate in China. There are two possible avenues: follow other East Asian economies and introduce agricultural protection; or go beyond the Uruguay Round agreement to internationalise its agricultural sector.

Why introduce agricultural protection?

There is a powerful lobby for agricultural protection in China, although it does not usually include farmers. Rather, it is the agricultural economists and agricultural bureaucrats who strongly favour protection. It is argued that agricultural protection is necessary because China is already at a stage of economic development similar to that of Japan, Taiwan and Korea when they started to protect their agricultural sectors. These East Asian economies all had very successful experiences in rapid industrialisation and modernisation. To follow the development paths of other East Asian economies, as China is already doing in many ways including labour-intensive manufactured-export led growth, it should also introduce policy measures to protect its agriculture (Cheng 1993).

Looking back at China's own experiences over the past forty years, it is also argued that policies discriminating against agriculture not only adversely affected agricultural production but also hampered overall economic growth. It was often difficult for farmers to feed even themselves. Maintaining balanced development across agriculture, industry and service is essential for achieving sustainable growth. Protection of agriculture is beneficial and necessary if China is to learn anything from its own experience (Chen and Deng 1993).

Food security constitutes one of the most important reasons for introducing agricultural protection policies. China has a population of 1.2 billion, more than one-fifth of the world's population. Relying on international markets to satisfy China's consumption demand for food is claimed to be both inappropriate and dangerous because of potential instability in world agricultural markets, difficulties in raising sufficient foreign exchange for grain imports and the possibility that major agricultural exporters will refuse to sell grain to China if political disputes arise. For domestic agriculture to meet the rapidly rising demand for food and other agricultural products, sufficient incentive must be provided to agricultural producers.

Agricultural protection is also supported by arguments in favour of income equity. Because of the nature of agricultural production and income elasticities of demand for agricultural products, it is likely that farmers' income will rise less rapidly than that of non-farm workers in the course of economic development, thereby presenting a serious social problem. To prevent a widening income gap between farm and non-farm workers, the government believes it must provide monetary assistance to farmers.

Internationalising the agricultural sector

Agricultural protection will, however, impose adverse effects on production, consumption, trade and welfare (Vousden 1990). Distorting the domestic terms of trade by artificially raising agricultural prices draws resources away from more efficient uses, such as labour-intensive manufacturing, and prevents the economy from fully exercising its comparative advantage. Efficiency losses in resource allocation lead to reductions in aggregate output, reducing the economy's income and welfare. An agricultural protection policy is also likely to place heavy burdens on government budgets, as the current experiences of Japan, Korea, Taiwan and many Western European and North American economies show. More importantly, agricultural protection also affects the welfare of a country's trading partners as agricultural protection policies are often a source of trade conflicts.

Introducing agricultural protection in China is likely to exaggerate current economic problems – the rapidly rising grain and food prices, associated high inflation, and unstable domestic markets with significant fluctuations from year-to-year (Cai 1993; Huang 1994, 1995; Garnaut, Cai and Huang 1996).

What is important is that the domestic agricultural market is linked directly with the international market (Huang 1995). The international market will then serve as a discipline for domestic supply and demand behaviour. Agricultural output can only be increased if it is internationally competitive.

A third group of economists suggests an agricultural policy to increase domestic supply to its limits and to utilise the international market as a means of balancing domestic demand and supply. There are various studies indicating that China still has great potential to increase its agricultural yields. Arable land areas are believed to be under-reported. Productivity can be increased significantly through the appropriate re-ordering of agricultural research priorities. Government investment in agricultural infrastructure declined over the past years, leading to large-scale decay of the infrastructure. As a large and densely populated country, China should make significant efforts to improve agricultural productivity.

The real question is whether China can ever achieve basic self-sufficiency in grain cost-effectively? China could achieve self-sufficiency in grain at any point in time if it were willing to incur the necessary cost. While answers might be very different in the short run, a positive answer to this question is unlikely in the longer term. Involvement in international trade is therefore inevitable. But there are two ways to involve the international market. The first would be to buy and sell in the international market but cut the linkage between domestic and international prices. Allowing only small quantities of agricultural trade would be likely to evolve into a protection scenario as the domestic lobby for protection, as well as the cost of agricultural production, would grow. The second would be to directly link domestic and international prices. International prices would therefore serve as 'caps' to the domestic market. If domestic production could not increase at the same rate as domestic consumption at competitive prices, imports would have to increase to balance the market. This would then probably evolve into a free trade scenario. In the end the Chinese government needs to choose between trade protection and free trade.

Misconceptions about agricultural trade policy

'China should adopt agricultural protection to emulate East Asia's success'

This is a widely held belief among most Chinese economists. Rapid economic growth in East Asia in the post-war period amazed the world. To some economists, agricultural protection is an inseparable component of the policy package that contributed to this economic achievement (Cheng 1993).

But how successful were agricultural protection policies in Japan, Korea and Taiwan? This question has already been well addressed in the literature (Anderson and Hayami 1986; Hayami 1988; Tyers and Anderson 1992). There is sufficient evidence to conclude that although economic success was achieved in the past decades in these countries, their adoption of agricultural protection largely failed and became a real policy problem for their whole economies.

Japan, Korea and Taiwan all reached an important turning point in applying agricultural policies and chose to increase agricultural protection significantly in the post-war period. The nominal rate of protection for twelve major agricultural commodities increased from 18 per cent in 1965 to 210 per cent in 1986 in Japan, from -4 per cent in 1965 to 117 per cent in 1986 in Korea, and from -1 per cent in 1965 to around 50 per cent in the mid-1980s in Taiwan (Anderson and Hayami 1986).

These profound changes caused serious problems. In Japan, government expenditure on rice price support increased from less than 2 per cent of total budget spending in 1960 to above 5 per cent in 1970. Policy measures were introduced to control expenditure. The cost, however, was still as high as 700 billion yen in 1985. Heavy budget burdens were not the only problem. It is estimated that about one-half of rice farmers' income in the mid-1980s was redistributed from consumers. Moreover, producers did not receive all the benefits from government spending. Economic welfare loss (the deadweight loss) due to the rice protection policy was about 781 billion yen in 1980.

While domestic prices rose enormously, surplus stock accumulated in the 1960s and again after the 1973–74 food crisis, further enlarging the government deficit. More important consequences lay in the stagnation of Japan's agricultural productivity because of the protection policy. Agricultural protection, moreover, became one of the most frequent sources of trade conflict between Japan and its major trading partners, and increased its difficulties in expanding its export markets (Hayami 1988).

The difficult part is that after fifty years' practice in China, it is hard to remove agricultural protection policies. An interest group in favour of protection, comprised of non-farmers, has been formed and serves as a powerful opponent to any extension of agricultural trade liberalisation. Domestic prices are now many times greater than international prices. A further difficulty is that simply to remove protection policies would bring about major structural adjustments.

The experiences of Japan, Korea and Taiwan lead one to conclude that not only did agricultural protection fail to achieve rapid economic growth and welfare improvements, but also it became a headache for domestic and foreign economic relations. Protectionist policy significantly disadvantaged Japan during the Uruguay Round negotiations and has done so in many other bilateral and multilateral trade negotiations.

'Agricultural protection is necessary to achieve food security'

Food security is perhaps the strongest argument for agricultural protection and is held by many non-agricultural economists and government officials. Any government feels a responsibility for food security in order to maintain social and economic stability. This issue seems more important in China as it has such a large population and because of the political isolation China has felt in the world political economy. But can agricultural protection really deliver food security?

Hayami (1988) analyses the effects of the protection policy in Japan on food security in the face of three potential crises: worldwide crop failure inducing food supply reduction and rising food prices; the termination of food imports because of war or serious natural disasters; the increase of population faster than food supply (the Malthusian scenario).

Hayami (1988) argues that to attempt to increase self-sufficiency in food by ignoring an economy's comparative advantage is not effective. If Japan's self-sufficiency in soybean is raised from the current 4 per cent to 10 per cent in the future, it would not make any significant difference in a crisis. To raise self-sufficiency to a level capable of resisting the significant influences of a worldwide crisis would impose unbearable social costs on society. A more reliable and efficient method, suggested by Hayami, is to diversify import sources and to strengthen co-operation with an international grain stock programme. This argument is relevant to the future of China's food supply. Although China's current grain production still meets demand to a high degree, there are two factors that need to be considered. First, it is possible that grain output would be at a lower level if government interventions were removed. Second, and more importantly, it will become more difficult to deliver self-sufficiency in grain with rapid economic development. China will have to opt for a distorted production pattern with high economic and social costs to maintain the levels of self-sufficiency in grain that it is achieving at the moment. The costs will rise over time.

The degree of self-sufficiency is not relevant to food security in the face of the second kind of crisis. If there were a war – the extreme case – conventional production techniques might not be valid. Supply of energy to agricultural production might be cut off because of more urgent uses. An appropriate strategy is to increase domestic stocks. Hayami further suggests development of a livestock industry as an effective way to protect against such a sudden crisis, as both animals and foodgrain can be turned to staple food in an emergency situation.

The Malthusian scenario bothers many Chinese, especially senior officials. If enough grain could not be produced to feed the population, it would not only be a problem for China but also a serious concern for the world. Production technology, however, is responsive to changes in demand over the longer term (Mitchell, Ingco and Duncan 1997). Even if there is a possibility that the whole world may be short of food, an increase in grain self-sufficiency through agricultural protection would not help at all. Agricultural scientific research and extension is crucial to improving the growth potential of agricultural output. A protection policy, on the other hand, would only slow down the growth of agricultural productivity.

Another scenario that Hayami does not consider is a reduction in domestic output. This scenario suggests not only the irrelevance of a protectionist policy, but also the harm that it inflicts on food security. Japan maintains a protectionist policy for the domestic rice industry because of the arguments for food security. On account of inclement weather, its output experienced a significant reduction in 1993 which resulted in a shortage of rice. Japan had to import rice from the international market to meet domestic demand. This clearly demonstrated that without access to international imports, Japan would not have had food security.

A related concern is that trade liberalisation in agriculture will lead China to rely significantly on grain imports. From an economic point of view, it is not a worry if grain imports conform to an economy's factor endowment and comparative advantage. Rather, by participating more deeply in the international division of labour, an economy can significantly increase its income and improve its welfare.

At the same time, however, free trade does not prevent an economy

132 *Agricultural reform in China*

from making significant efforts to raise its agricultural productivity through investment in agricultural research and extension. The important discipline of a free trade regime is that incentives (both price and non-price ones) must not be distorted. The domestic agricultural sector is therefore integrated into the world economy and competes on the international market. This is not contradictory to investment in higher productivity from a public goods perspective. There are many studies that show the technological potential for further increases in China's grain yields.

'Free trade destabilises the domestic market'

There are some grounds for concern if the movements of prices in China and in the international market are compared over past decades. China's domestic prices were largely stable because of strict government controls while international prices were unstable because of growing protectionism in the late 1970s and 1980s (Tyers and Anderson 1992). All economies trade with each other only at the margin. The world market in the 1980s became a market residue. This not only limited the scale of the market but increased price fluctuations. Any moderate change in demand and supply for a single economy can cause significant changes in world prices.

Market fluctuations are much greater in a small market than in an integrated larger market subject to the same output shock (see chapter 6). It is much easier for larger international markets to accommodate production fluctuations than for smaller, closed domestic markets. Domestic market prices were not stable in the years after policy liberalisation. The international market, on the other hand, will become more and more stable following the implementation of the Uruguay Round settlement. With the integration of the Chinese economy, the stability of the world market will be increased significantly.

'China may not be able to earn enough foreign exchange for grain imports'

Many developing economies have experienced foreign exchange shortages and are reluctant to use scarce foreign exchange to buy grain imports. Can China earn enough foreign exchange to buy grain on the international market? Scarcity of foreign exchange usually results from the mismanagement of macroeconomic policies. The opportunity costs of foreign and domestic moneys should be the same, given an appropriate exchange rate, in an economy without distortion. As long as an economy is integrated into the world economy, it is normal for it to import some goods and, at the same time, to export other goods.

China's recent experience during the reform period has shown its ability to earn foreign exchange through the rapid expansion of labour-intensive manufactured exports. Its total exports increased by about 20 per cent per annum in US dollar terms during 1978–94. Strong export performance has also contributed to China having large foreign exchange reserves (US$50 billion at the end of 1994).

Import of grain will not present any serious problems to foreign exchange earnings. On the other hand, there will be a problem if China continues rapid export growth without buying from others. An accumulated trade imbalance will eventually become a source of conflict between China and its trading partners and constrain expansion of foreign exchange earnings.

'Agricultural protection raises farmers' income and improves equity'

Policies protecting agriculture in China may not have the usual income redistribution function. Maintaining farmers' income has been an important excuse for implementing agricultural protection policies in Western Europe, North America and East Asia. The argument is that because of relatively slow productivity growth in agricultural production and lower income elasticities of demand for agricultural products, agricultural returns may not rise as fast as returns in other sectors (such as manufacturing and services). This will lead to inequality between farmers' and non-farmers' incomes. Through tariffs and subsidies and quantitative restrictions (quotas) on agricultural trade, the government is able to improve the domestic terms of trade for agriculture relative to the international terms of trade. Farmers' income relative to that of non-farmers can be higher than under free trade.

This argument does not seem to be relevant in China. Because of the characteristics of rural industrialisation in China, most farmers derive their income from rural non-agricultural sectors as well as from agriculture. In the early 1990s, agricultural production contributed to about 60 per cent of farmers' total net income. This share is expected to rise steadily as the rural township, village and private enterprises gather momentum. Agricultural protection may raise agricultural income on the one hand, but it may depress other, non-agricultural income on the other. Quantitatively, the net impact on farmers' total income is uncertain. It is certain, however, that agricultural protection is not an effective policy measure to raise farmers' income levels and the total impact of protection policies on farmers' net income will be negative as long as farmers derive an increasingly large proportion of their income from non-agricultural activities. Japan's current situation is a good reference point for the future of China's rural economy. Income derived from agricultural production now accounts for only 20–30 per cent of farmers' total income. Protection in agricultural production is against the interests of farmers as a whole. This argument is further supported by China's own experience of rural development over the past ten years. After 1985, the largest proportion of income increases for farmers came from the development of non-agricultural sectors rather than agricultural production.

'Internationalisation results in unbearable adjustment problems for farmers'

It is argued that internationalisation will result in a flood of foreign imports on domestic markets and will present serious adjustment problems for Chinese farmers. Such an adjustment may be unachievable given that rural China already has a huge pool of surplus labour.

Is adjustment avoidable? The answer is clearly negative given the current worldwide trend of agricultural trade liberalisation following the conclusion of the Uruguay Round negotiation. Even economies like Japan, Korea, Taiwan and those in Western Europe started to accept trade liberalisation in the face of domestic and international pressure. China may be able to delay its adjustment process for a number of years, but by then the situation will be even more challenging. After domestic prices have increased further above international prices and the domestic political base supporting protection policies has become even better established, liberalisation will involve not only higher economic costs but also more difficult political adjustments. This is exactly the problem that Japan, Korea and Taiwan have today.

China's rural development after 1985 is a history of successful adjustment and rapid economic growth. Farmers' income grew because of the relocation of capital, labour and other resources from agricultural to non-agricultural activities (see chapter 5). Some tough adjustments may not be avoidable in the future, but such adjustments can be accommodated smoothly in a dynamic and rapidly growing economy like China's.

China's current comparative advantage lies in labour-intensive manufacturing, with labour-intensive exports crucial to its rapid economic growth. If China integrates with the world economy, with dynamic labour-intensive sectors increasingly producing more employment opportunities to absorb surplus farmers, growth can probably be sustained or even accelerated for another decade or two.

Rural China has already developed a township, village and private sector employing about 100 million rural labourers. If the relative returns to agriculture decline because of trade liberalisation, farmers will move to the rural industrial and service sectors within their township or village.

If the government chooses to liberalise domestic grain markets when China's domestic prices for wheat, rice and maize are very close to international prices, the immediate adjustment costs will be minimal. Since international prices are expected to remain stable or to increase moderately in the next decade, adjustment costs incurred by wheat and maize farmers will be gradual, allowing farmers to pursue alternative crops or to find jobs in non-agricultural sectors.

'The overall impact of agricultural protection is minimal as the economy develops'

This is probably the last thing protectionists would argue. The East Asian experiences suggest that the percentage loss of overall economic growth due to agricultural protection is likely to be very small. Japan, Korea and Taiwan all grew at very high rates for several decades despite the protection policies in place.

But this does not necessarily imply that the protection policy's damage to the economy is small. First, growth records of OECD countries suggest a significant positive correlation between economic growth and the outflow of agricultural labour (Dowrick 1992). Agricultural protection policies tend to keep more labour within the agricultural sector and therefore reduce the overall economic growth.

Second, agricultural protection hampers productivity growth in agriculture. Because of high protection, the agricultural sector is not exposed to international competition and has less pressure for productivity improvement and technological progress. By holding more than an optimal quantity of resources in agriculture, the protection policy also reduces the efficiency of non-agricultural protection.

Third, when agricultural protection becomes a constant source of trade conflict, it adversely affects economic growth by reducing the potential of export growth. Finally, agricultural protection usually involves large government expenditure which further prevents government investment in more productive and efficient uses. The cost of agricultural protection in a general equilibrium perspective – to the whole economy – is by no means small or negligible.

Political economy of agricultural trade liberalisation

Which policy the government eventually adopts will depend on the political economy of China. The government makes policy decisions to maximise its support (if not to maximise its probability of remaining in power). This will apply even more so as China's economic and political systems are decentralised.

Currently, the major group demanding agricultural protection includes agricultural economists and agricultural bureaucrats. Farmers' lack of involvement in this process may be explained by the size of the farm population and undeveloped communication and transportation facilities. According to the theory of political economy, farmers in China are not yet in a position to lobby for a policy. But a more relevant explanation is that agricultural protection may not necessarily bring benefits to farmers. Agriculture was a major source of increase in farmers' income before 1984. This happened because of the elimination of efficiency losses induced by the previous commune system and because in 1978–84 agricultural production was the only activity in which farmers could participate. After 1985, non-agricultural income became increasingly important for farmers, especially for their incremental income. Whenever farmers had non-agricultural employment and investment opportunities, their real income grew rapidly. Whenever their off-farm opportunities were limited by policy, their real income tended to stagnate. This was true for the period 1985–91 (see chapter 5). This suggests that an agricultural protection policy may not be beneficial to farmers. If self-sufficiency policies were pursued together with protection policies, it is likely that state intervention in domestic food markets would be heavy, as is the case in Japan. It would also affect the availability of off-farm opportunities in the economy. Therefore, a protectionist policy would at the minimum constrain the growth of farmers' income, if not keep farmers in perpetual poverty.

Then why are agricultural economists and agricultural bureaucrats so keen for a protection policy? Some of them are seriously concerned with the interests of farmers and have worked on China's agricultural economic issues for decades. A more fundamental reason, however, is the profession's standing in society and its access to resources. In China, the Ministry of Agriculture is only given more attention and resources when there is an agricultural supply problem. When there is a good harvest, agricultural economists and bureaucrats feel forgotten and unheard. Government economic and political interest in agricultural economists and bureaucrats could be retained by maintaining self-sufficiency in grain and the introduction of protection policies. The difficulties for China in achieving self-sufficiency in grain are immense. Trying to attain self-sufficiency would secure permanent attention and increasing resources for agricultural economists and bureaucrats over the long term. Once on track, it is extremely hard for the central government to turn around policies.

A danger is that agricultural economists and bureaucrats are able to mislead farmers to act against their own interests. At times, farmers have felt that their interests have been defended by agricultural economists and bureaucrats. But this can only happen when the farmers' vision is blocked by their short-term interests. It is easier for them to calculate the loss of income from removing import quotas but much harder to perceive the potentially greater returns to structural adjustment over a longer period. This is not only possible in China, but has also recently occurred in Japan and Germany (Hayami 1988).

Currently, there are two major forces opposing an agricultural protection policy – one from consumers and the other from major agricultural exporting countries. Since food still accounts for about 60 per cent of urban consumers' living expenditure, they are sensitive to any increases in food prices. Because consumers have so far been compensated by the government for any price increases, however, consumers' direct opposition to agricultural protection has been weak. This opposition will become stronger if the government completely cuts off the link between food prices and government subsidies, and if all price fluctuations are to be absorbed by consumers or producers.

If an international policy is not put in place in time, the opposition to agricultural protection will become increasingly weak because of higher incomes for workers throughout the economy and a smaller proportion of food in their living expenditures. This is what is happening in Japan today, where it is extremely difficult to turn the direction of policy. There is insufficient political support for such an action even though many economists and officials are fully aware of the costs of maintaining its protectionist policies.

The Chinese government should take action before this happens. Although for the government the final determinant of a policy choice is the political economy, careful analytical work and education about costs and benefits of agricultural protection and free trade will generate a response from the public. The opposition to protection by major agricultural exporters and trade negotiation under bilateral and multilateral trade arrangements can also be utilised to overcome domestic resistance to agricultural trade liberalisation.

Notes

1 Guo *et al.* (1993) suggest that the nominal rate of protection in 1988 was reduced to −48 per cent for rice, −26 per cent for maize, −4 per cent for wheat, −16 per cent for soybean, and between −30 and −50 per cent for pork, beef and lamb. The gap between domestic and international prices narrowed quickly after 1989, with the nominal rate of protection for some agricultural products turning positive in 1989 and 1990.
2 World Bank statistics report China's per capita GNP at US$370 in 1990. This is widely regarded as a significant underestimate. Perkins (1992) estimates it as having passed US$1,000 by 1990. Using purchasing power parity measurement, Summers and Heston (1993) suggest China's per capita GNP was US$2,472 in 1988. Based on evidence from the consumption pattern of food and other commodities, Garnaut and Ma (1993) and Garnaut, Ma and Huang (1996) propose an income level of around US$1,000 in 1990. Using this estimate as a basis, China's per capita GNP can be derived for the following years according to China's real GNP growth rates (this gives US$1,500 in 1994). The advantage of these re-evaluated figures is that they are directly comparable with the income data of the other low-income economies.
3 Not all indicators convey the same message, however. The importance of agriculture in total output and employment was relatively greater in China in the early 1990s than in other East Asian economies at the same turning point. Agriculture's share in the Chinese economy rose in the early stages of economic reform but fell after 1985. Its share of GDP was 35 per cent in China in 1990. This compares with 18 per cent and 21 per cent, respectively, in 1935 and 1955 in Japan, 30 per cent in Korea in 1970 and 32 per cent in Taiwan in 1960. Agricultural labour's share in China's total labour force is high, perhaps reflecting earlier policies restricting labour movements between rural and urban areas, especially in the pre-reform period. At 60 per cent in 1990, it was higher than that in Japan in the years before and after World War II, but was very close to Korea in 1960 (61 per cent).

8

Chinese farmers can adapt

A computable general equilibrium framework

Can the Chinese economy accommodate changes in its agricultural sector resulting from trade liberalisation? The answer is complicated by changes in the world agricultural market, especially since the implementation of the Uruguay Round settlement. The agricultural policy debate is entering a difficult stage. While economists disagree, it is often because they do not have a common baseline. Effects are discussed but not quantified, leaving room for poorly defined dispute. This is a problem when recommended policies contain both positive and negative effects – as is the case with agricultural trade liberalisation. Analysis using a quantitative framework is essential to economists' understanding of the impact of various policy options but also to government decision-making.

Why a computable general equilibrium model?

There are a number of quantitative frameworks available for empirical economic analysis. Partial equilibrium models, such as those utilising flexible profit functions and consumer demand systems, are widely used in economic studies because they are easy to establish, understand and apply. But a comprehensive analysis cannot be made through partial equilibrium models. The scope offered is narrow, with usually only production and/or consumption of one or two commodities being studied. Partial equilibrium models ignore interactions between the sector or commodities and other parts of the economy. They do not capture any feedback effects of policy changes and are unable to consider economy-wide implications.

Macroeconomic models overcome the weaknesses of partial equilibrium models by bringing together the whole economy into a consistent framework. The effect of a change in one part of the economy on other parts is recognised through quantitative relationships between variables specified in the models. The economy adjusts to achieve a new equilibrium (or disequilibrium). Macroeconomic models are inappropriate for the purpose of agricultural policy analysis, however. Macroeconomic models incorporate economic activities at an aggregate level. Without detailed specification for production and consumption of agricultural and non-agricultural products, they can neither accommodate changes in agricultural policy nor capture the effects of structural change. Furthermore, some *ad hoc* specifications of macroeconomic models lack a microeconomic foundation. Unusual specifications such as the inclusion of lagged variables in behavioural equations are often difficult to understand and interpret.

The computable general equilibrium model is the most suitable avenue for examining agricultural policy issues while taking an economywide perspective. Although debate continues on the appropriateness of the model specifications, parameter choice, disaggregation and the representation of policy measures, computable general equilibrium models have become a popular applied quantitative framework in economic analysis (Shoven and Whalley 1992).

Computable general equilibrium models originated in the debate over the feasibility of the centralised computation of a Pareto-optimal allocation of resources within an economy. The operation of a market economy is specified in considerable detail. The structure of production, consumption, government revenue and expenditure, and foreign trade are modelled. Computable general equilibrium models emphasise the interdependence of decisionmaking throughout the economy. Whenever the government intervenes in agriculture or an exogenous shock occurs, resources are reallocated across all sectors of the economy, with efficiency and distributional consequences. A computable general equilibrium model describes where resources come from, what implications policies have for various parts of the economy and to what extent feedback from other sectors affects agriculture.

The model applied in this book – the China model – was developed by Huang (1993a) in a study of the interactions between agriculture and the rest of the economy in China. Some modifications and improvements were made in later applications (Huang 1995).

Characteristics of the China model

The China model is an economywide, comparative-static computable general equilibrium model. The objectives of this study necessitate that the model be capable of capturing the intersectoral features of the Chinese economy. Although a large part of the economy is substantially simplified in specification, the model is comprehensive in that all sectors of economic activity are included. Projections from the model add up in the sense that appropriately weighted sector outcomes are equivalent to outcomes for the relevant macroeconomic variables. Hence, following a change in the incentive structure, the sum of the output changes for each sector equals the change in the economy's aggregate output.

The model provides projections at only one point in time – the solution year. It is a comparative-static model of the Johansen type. This solution contains no information about the time path of adjustment as in dynamic models. Such models work in terms of percentage changes in variables. Model results demonstrate how much levels of economic activity in China, such as an increase in international prices for agricultural products, would increase (or decrease) as a result of a shock. Comparative-static models are not time-specific, although the China model is short-run. The time frame reflects the response elasticity estimates incorporated in the model.

Each simulation of the model results in a state of general equilibrium. All parts of the model are interdependent and reach equilibrium simultaneously.

The general equilibrium conditions can be written as

$$F(X) = 0 \tag{8.1}$$

where X is the vector of variables included in the model and $F(.)$ is the set of excess demand and unit profit functions of the model (Clarete and Warr 1992). Through an appropriate closure, X may be partitioned into a vector of endogenous variables (Y) and a vector of exogenous variables (Z). Total differentiation of equation (8.1) with respect to X yields

$$AY + BZ = 0 \tag{8.2}$$

which can be solved for Y,

$$Y = -A^{-1}BZ \tag{8.3}$$

The percentage-change type model has the disadvantage that results are only linear approximations to the non-linear system and hence is valid only for small changes. The model, however, possesses a number of advantages. The solution algorithm is separated from the model and is unaffected by the model design changes, which are therefore easier to implement. The mechanisms underlying the results are easier to understand and explain to policymakers. When there are several policy changes under study, the separate effect of each can be decomposed (National Centre for Development Studies 1990).

Main assumptions

The China model embodies a number of crucial assumptions usually applied in computable general equilibrium modelling. In its treatment of production and demand, the model incorporates the conventional features of neoclassical microeconomics. It assumes optimising behaviour on the part of producers (profit maximisation and/or cost minimisation) and consumers (cost minimisation and/or utility maximisation) subject to the various constraints in the economy such as the supply of factors (labour, capital and land), the balance of payments and technology. The resultant equations emphasise the responsiveness of economic agents to changes in relative prices, with the degree of presumed responsiveness reflected in the value assigned to substitution elasticities. All markets are assumed to be competitive, so no activity earns pure profits. This requires the assumption of constant returns to scale in production activities. Market clearing is assumed in all commodity and factor markets.

The applicability of perfect-market assumptions raises questions with respect to modelling the Chinese economy. China has a history of nearly thirty years of central planning following a long history of heavy government influence in market exchange. Commodity and factor markets did not operate competitively during this period. After ten years of market-oriented economic reform, the imperfections of the market mechanism still suggest significant differences between the Chinese and market economies.

The operation of state enterprises raises doubts when specifying the optimisation behaviour of industry producers and consumers. Farmers, after the establishment of the household responsibility system, became largely independent producers. Farmers adjusted their resource allocation in pursuit of maximum income or profits in the second half of the 1980s (see chapter 5). Lin (1992b) found that even in nascent factor markets, farmers behave in a rational manner. Another important part of the Chinese economy is the non-state industrial and commercial sectors, which include the township, village and private enterprises in the countryside and the collective sectors in urban areas.

The peculiarity of state enterprises' departure from profit-maximisation behaviour is largely ignored for three reasons. First, the state sector no longer dominates Chinese industry, although the industry share of the state sector varies. Non-state sectors – the rural township, village and private enterprises and urban collective enterprises – operate at the margin and respond to market changes. Second, after ten years of reform, profit is an increasingly important objective of state enterprises. Third, the China model primarily relates to the agricultural sector and its interaction with the rest of the economy. This weakness leaves room for further improvement. In empirically modelling a real economy, especially an economy in transition, there are always doubts about the applicability of stylised neoclassical economic assumptions. There are many areas in the China model waiting for further improvement. This study only indicates the direction and movements following different policy choices with respect to China's agricultural trade. The predictions made should become closer to real change as market reform is pushed forward in China, with actual behaviour and theoretical assumptions converging.

Basic structure of the model

One important feature of the China model is the distinction made between rural and urban economies. Industrial sectors are separated into rural and urban sub-sectors. Capital and land are not mobile across sectors due to the short-run features of the model. There are two labour markets – one rural and one urban. Labour is mobile between the two markets and among different sectors. Labour movements between rural and urban areas follow a partial adjustment mechanism – reflecting the imperfect mobility of labour between the two areas in China today.

The model includes eighteen commodities, seven of which are agricultural products (paddy rice, wheat, other grain, cotton, other crops, wool and livestock products), and twenty-two sectors covering nine urban and nine rural industries in addition to cropping, livestock, forestry and fishing sectors. Consumers sell their factor endowments (labour) in the factor market and buy commodities for consumption to maximise their utility. The producers (industries) maximise profits or minimise costs by buying factors and intermediate inputs and selling outputs in both the domestic and export markets. Government revenue and expenditure are not specified explicitly in the model. Implicitly, however, it is assumed that authorities make adjustments to fiscal policies as needed to keep real absorption at an exogenously determined level. A skeletal monetary sector is incorporated to allow determination of the aggregate price level as a numeraire (Martin 1990). Following Armington (1969), domestically produced and imported goods are assumed differential products. Restrictions to trade are classified as quantitative and non-quantitative. The Hicksian compensating variation is incorporated to allow evaluation and comparison of different policy options.

A more detailed explanation of the model – including its sector detail, theoretical structure, equations, parameters and coefficients – is provided in the Appendix.

The behavioural coefficients for the model are mostly adopted from previous empirical studies, following the usual conventions of computable general equilibrium modelling. Because the agricultural sector is a major concern in this study, the supply elasticities for the agricultural sector are empirically estimated using a panel data-set (containing twenty-eight individual provinces for the years between 1986 and 1990) and applying the generalised McFadden profit function (Huang 1993a, 1993b).

Model closures and design of experiments

Model closures

Definition of the model closure is critical in a computable general equilibrium model. A particular model closure specifies which variables are exogenous and which are endogenous. While the exogenous variables will remain unchanged during the simulation, economic change occurs through the transmission of exogenous shocks between endogenous variables.

Two sets of closure specifications are defined. In the first set, real absorption is defined exogenously by the government, and this determines changes in government demand and demand for investment in fixed capital and stocks. While demand for labour, capital and land by individual sectors is endogenous, total supply of labour, capital and land for individual sectors is exogenous. Prices for these factors are determined through market-clearing conditions. The foreign currency prices of imports are, however, exogenous since the model contains no equations describing foreign supply conditions. Another set of exogenous variables are restrictions to trade including import tariffs, export taxes and quantitative restrictions. Their exogenous settings allow computation of the effects of protection against imports on the domestic economy. Money supply is exogenously determined by the monetary authorities. Finally, all the variables reflecting technological change and preference variations, including neutral and factor- or commodity-augmenting variables, are assumed to be exogenous.

Another closure is defined specifically for the simulation of the self-sufficiency policy in agriculture. Because trade is restricted under this scenario, quantities of agricultural imports, mainly grain, are set exogenously. But to solve the model, the non-quantitative restrictions to trade for these particular commodities are then set endogenously.

Policy choices

In regard to its agricultural trade policy, China could introduce agricultural protection or internationalise its agricultural sector (see chapter 7). The government still has choices, given the broad direction of reform, on the extent of liberalisation of agricultural trade or the degree of self-sufficiency in agriculture to pursue. Quantitative analysis helps an understanding of policy choices by providing more detailed information on the implications of each alternative.

If China fails to join the World Trade Organisation soon, the prospects for agricultural liberalisation will be gloomy. Self-sufficiency policies will probably be restored, at least for grain, thereby reversing China's agricultural reform. Relying on the international market for domestic food demand is dangerous, according to the Chinese government, because China has no influence over foreign supplies, especially when they are related to political issues. Policy changes in many Western countries toward China after the events of 4 June 1989 are a good example. On the fringe of the international community, China will be unable to resolve economic disputes such as those over China's labour-intensive manufactured exports. It may not have the confidence to raise sufficient foreign exchange to import the required amount of food (Anderson 1989).

What if China is able to join the World Trade Organisation in the near future? Will a self-sufficiency policy be the best choice? Here, there is a range of other policy choices that need to be looked at. One alternative arises if China is able to join the World Trade Organisation as a developing economy. It may be able to apply for special articles of the GATT rules that will exempt it from further agricultural internationalisation. China, like other East Asian economies, may pursue free trade in manufactured goods while retaining some protective measures in the agricultural sector. It has been argued that China's agricultural policy is not subject to the agricultural agreement of the Uruguay Round because it is a low-income economy.

A third possibility is that China may follow the trend of the international community and pursue gradual reform toward free trade in agricultural products. This approach is supported by the argument that there are acceptable adjustment costs in the transition phase. As only partial reforms are introduced in most of the other economies, world agricultural markets will expand only gradually. Gradual reforms by China may reduce adjustment costs for the world as well as for itself.

A fourth option is for China to internationalise its agricultural sector completely using the current unique opportunity for policy reform. In fact, China has pursued unilateral trade reforms over the past fifteen years. China has the chance to implement further unilateral reform of agricultural trade, especially if it joins the international trading system and its exports and GDP continue to grow rapidly. More importantly, unilateral trade reform by China may provide the conditions for, and pressures on, other countries to reform further, which may, in turn, produce a more favourable world market environment for China's rising demand for agricultural imports and increasing supply of labour-intensive manufactured goods.

One important factor that should be considered when simulating trade policy effects in China is the implementation of the Uruguay Round settlement in the next decade. The Uruguay Round agreements cover a wide range of issues from the Multifibre Arrangement to intellectual property rights. Here we look only at changes in agricultural trade policy.

The agricultural agreement has two main dimensions – market access and domestic support. Under the agreement, non-tariff import measures are to be replaced by tariffs providing the same level of protection. Existing tariffs, and those resulting from the 'tariffication' process, will be reduced by an average of 36 per cent by industrial economies over six years starting from 1995/96. Developing economies will fulfil these requirements over ten years. Access opportunities must represent at least 4 per cent of domestic consumption of designated products, such as rice in the case of Japan and Korea, in the first year of the implementation period, and rise annually to reach 8 per cent in the sixth year.

The aggregate measurement of support provided on either a product-specific or a non-product-specific basis and not qualifying for exemption is to be reduced during the implementation period by 20 per cent for industrial economies and 13.3 per cent for developing economies, with no reduction requirements for the least developed economies. Over the six-year implementation period, members are required to reduce the value of direct export subsidies to 36 per cent below the 1986–90 base, and the volume of subsidised exports by 21 per cent. Developing economies have to fulfil two-thirds of what is required of industrial economies.[1]

The literature points to a rising trend in agricultural prices in the international markets following the implementation of the Uruguay Round settlement (see table 7.3). The study by Brandão and Martin (1993) simulating the Dunkel proposal suggests a 4 per cent increase in prices for rice and coarse grains and a 6 per cent increase in prices for wheat and meat. This result will be applied in the modelling as the future given conditions for China's agricultural trade.

Scenario 1: pursuing self-sufficiency in grain

The first experiment approximates a scenario where some international prices are raised after the implementation of the Uruguay Round settlement and China adopts a protective strategy for its agricultural policies. This may happen if China is excluded from the World Trade Organisation and therefore from the international community. To implement this simulation, the second closure involves making quantities of imports exogenous and tariff-equivalent non-tariff barriers endogenous for rice, wheat, other grain and wool. A 100 per cent reduction of imports of these products from their base levels (zero imports), together with increases in international prices for grains and livestock products, are introduced as a shock (table 8.1). Because the model is static, it is only asked what would have happened if there were no imports of grain and wool in the base year.

The structure of grain production will experience substantial change if domestic self-sufficiency is to be achieved. The output of paddy rice (currently exported) decreases by 3.5 per cent, while output of wheat increases by 7.4 per cent and other grain by 0.3 per cent. The major commodity in 'other grain' – maize – currently has net exports. Its increase in output reflects the demand for it as a staple food (because of a slight reduction of farmers' income). Output of cotton and other crops declines, largely because of competition from grain production for land and other agricultural resources.

Domestic prices of most agricultural products, with the exception of cotton and livestock, increase within a range of 1–6 per cent. It is at first glance surprising that increases in domestic grain prices simulated by this experiment are generally smaller than changes in international prices (Brandão and Martin 1993). The simulation only captures the likely outcomes of the self-sufficiency policy, with all the other condi-

Table 8.1. *Pursuing self-sufficiency in grain (per cent change)*

Macroeconomic variables	
Real GDP growth	−0.5
Urban economy	−0.2
Rural economy	−0.9
Farmers' real income	−0.9
Export	−3.9
Import	−3.6
Compensating variation	−1.0
Agricultural output	
Paddy rice	−3.5
Wheat	7.4
Other grain	0.3
Cotton	−7.2
Other crops	−2.0
Livestock	0.5
Wool	118.4
Domestic agricultural prices	
Paddy rice	0.6
Wheat	6.2
Other grain	2.4
Cotton	−1.1
Other crops	1.6
Livestock	−5.5
Wool	54.3

tions held steady. From these simulation results, however, it can be concluded that domestic prices will move upward consistently above international prices over time under a number of other influences.

To maintain self-sufficiency in grain and wool, the tariff-equivalent non-tariff barriers to trade will have to rise by 220 per cent for rice, 839 per cent for wheat, 505 per cent for other grain and 994 per cent for wool. These changes raise the tariff-equivalent quantitative restrictions between 60 and 200 per cent.

A self-sufficiency policy also has a negative impact on the macroeconomy. Self-sufficiency now would cause real exports to decrease by 3.9 per cent and imports by 3.6 per cent. Real GDP falls by 0.5 per cent. The welfare loss is significant, at about 1 per cent of the GDP. Adverse effects are also generated in the textile industry – its output falls by 12 per cent and exports by 37 per cent. These results demonstrate the inferiority of an inward-looking agricultural policy.

A more important result of this policy choice is that despite the increase in output of many agricultural products, farmers' real income falls by 0.9 per cent because farmers derive their income from both agricultural and non-agricultural sources. A self-sufficiency policy significantly disadvantages the development of rural and, to a lesser extent, urban industries. Declines in textile output and exports illustrate the effect. Not only do some farmers employed in rural industry come back to agriculture, but also those who work in urban areas lose their temporary jobs (such as in construction). The declining income of farmers refutes the income and equity argument of agricultural protection.

Scenario 2: maintaining existing policy regimes

The second experiment includes only increases in international agricultural prices. This simulation corresponds to the second policy choice, in which the Chinese government does not change its current policy-setting for the agricultural sector.

Consistently with findings by Tyers and Anderson (1992) using a partial equilibrium model of the world food market, the outcome of this experiment suggests that China may gain from trade liberalisation in other economies even if it does not participate, enjoying an increase in real GDP of 0.1 per cent (table 8.2). There are significant rises in the exports of rice, other grain, livestock products and processed food, and, to a lesser extent, cotton. Imports of wheat, cotton and wool decrease. Indeed, China becomes a net exporter of grain because of increases in international prices. This is only valid in the short term. Overall, total export volume increases by 0.5 per cent and imports by 0.3 per cent, thereby improving China's balance of trade.

There are also some important changes to the domestic production and price structure for agricultural products. Output of rice and other grain rises, while output of other agricultural products decreases. Transmitting changes in international markets, agricultural prices increase (except for cotton), notably in the cases of rice, other grain, wool and livestock products.

The welfare measure, compensating variation as a share of GDP, rises by 0.5 per cent (GDP increases by 0.1 per cent), indicating the possible welfare gain for China.[2] The impact on the urban economy is nearly zero given that other non-agricultural agreements of the Uruguay Round settlement are not incorporated into the simulation. The rural economy, however, grows by 0.2 per cent, resulting in a 0.1 per cent increase in farmers' real income.

The comparative-static nature of the model limits its ability to capture the effects over the longer term. The improvement of the agricultural balance of trade in the base year arising from a switch, induced by price

Table 8.2. *Maintaining existing policy regimes (per cent change)*

Macroeconomic variables	
Real GDP growth	0.1
Urban economy	0.0
Rural economy	0.2
Farmers' real income	0.1
Export	0.5
Import	0.3
Compensating variation	0.5
Agricultural output	
Paddy rice	1.7
Wheat	−1.1
Other grain	1.1
Cotton	−3.4
Other crops	−1.0
Livestock	−1.8
Wool	−7.9
Domestic agricultural prices	
Paddy rice	1.6
Wheat	0.4
Other grain	1.2
Cotton	−0.8
Other crops	0.5
Livestock	4.1
Wool	1.6

changes, between being a net importer and a net exporter may not occur in the future in China, because income growth over time is associated with large increases in domestic demand for grain products (Carter and Zhong 1991; Garnaut and Ma 1992; Huang 1995). On the other hand, this diminishing effect may also be offset by the Tyers-Anderson style of endogenous productivity response. The static result, however, is interesting because it rejects the assertion made by many economists about losses in income or welfare from liberalisation and rises in international agricultural prices (Ma 1993).

Scenario 3: implementing the Uruguay Round agreement

The third experiment examines increases in international prices, a 50 per cent uniform tariff reduction for non-agricultural products and a 24 per cent reduction in domestic agricultural supports. This approximates the scenario of China joining the World Trade Organisation. In an effort to join the World Trade Organisation, China made a commitment to reduce

Table 8.3. *Implementing the Uruguay Round agreement (per cent change)*

Macroeconomic variables	
Real GDP growth	1.2
Urban economy	1.1
Rural economy	1.3
Farmers' real income	1.3
Export	9.4
Import	15.3
Compensating variation	1.0
Agricultural output	
Paddy rice	3.7
Wheat	0.9
Other grain	3.9
Cotton	6.6
Other crops	2.4
Livestock	8.1
Wool	6.3
Domestic agricultural prices	
Paddy rice	3.5
Wheat	−1.0
Other grain	−0.3
Cotton	1.8
Other crops	−0.3
Livestock	9.3
Wool	7.8

50 per cent of its tariffs over a 3–5 year period. A 24 per cent reduction in domestic agricultural distortion is designed to capture gradual reform – consistent with the Uruguay Round settlement for developing economies.

Under the simulation, agricultural output increases – 4 per cent for rice and other grain, 1 per cent for wheat and cotton, and 6 and 8 per cent for wool and livestock products (table 8.3). Not all change in agricultural prices is in the same direction: prices fall for wheat, other grain and other crops but rise for rice, cotton, wool and livestock products.

There are significant decreases in the exports of rice (20 per cent) and other grain (32 per cent). Exports of other sectors, especially the textile industry, increase significantly. As a result, total export volume rises by 9.4 per cent, while the increase in import volume is even greater (15.3 per cent) because of a reduction in trade barriers. There is a negative effect on the balance of trade.

Overall, real GDP grows by 1.2 per cent and the welfare gain is also significant (about 1 per cent of GDP). The rural economy grows by

Table 8.4. *Welfare impacts of agricultural trade liberalisation* (US$ million)

	China	Developing	OECD	World
Krissoff et al. (1990)				
Industrial reform	−69	−4,985	33,128	28,133
Global reform	−76	2,060	33,065	35,125
Tyers and Anderson (1992)				
Industrial reform	2,900	16,600	46,500	62,200
Global reform	12,900	33,400	73,300	106,400
Brandão and Martin (1993)				
Conventional				
Industrial reform	−81	629	72,666	78,355
Global reform	24,132	59,152	73,425	139,061
Dunkel proposal	893	19,791	63,304	88,854
Developing economies	23,334	56,464	−18,158	36,789
Productivity response				
Industrial reform	4,304	29,299	71,055	107,779
Global reform	81,457	130,961	64,972	202,941
Dunkel proposal	7,393	44,264	61,636	113,202
Developing economies	74,900	98,282	−22,208	74,196

Sources: Krissoff et al. 1990; Tyers and Anderson 1992; Brandão and Martin 1993.

1.3 per cent and the urban by 1.1 per cent. The reason the rural economy grows faster is that the rural township, village and private sector is dynamic and able to grasp opportunities provided by trade liberalisation. Farmers' real income also increases by 1.3 per cent, demonstrating gains, even for farmers, from trade liberalisation.

It is interesting to compare this scenario with the previous one in which there is no policy reform in China. When China participates more actively in trade liberalisation, it gains in terms of both increases in real GDP and improvements in welfare.

These results can be compared with other simulation results related to the Uruguay Round and China (table 8.4). Most studies, except that of Krissoff *et al.* (1990) and one scenario of Brandão and Martin (1993), find positive gains for China, whether or not China is directly involved in agricultural liberalisation associated with the Uruguay Round trade negotiations.

Scenario 4: liberalisation beyond the Uruguay Round

This simulation is similar to the third except that China phases out all restrictions on agricultural trade (import tariffs, non-tariff import restrictions, export taxes and tax-equivalent export restrictions). The results are

Table 8.5. *Liberalisation beyond the Uruguay Round (per cent change)*

Macroeconomic variables	
Real GDP growth	1.3
Urban economy	1.1
Rural economy	1.6
Farmers' real income	1.4
Export	9.8
Import	15.4
Compensating variation	0.8
Agricultural output	
Paddy rice	4.7
Wheat	0.7
Other grain	3.0
Cotton	8.1
Other crops	0.8
Livestock	10.0
Wool	7.5
Domestic agricultural prices	
Paddy rice	1.3
Wheat	1.3
Other grain	2.7
Cotton	5.1
Other crops	2.0
Livestock	11.0
Wool	8.3

largely the same as the previous scenario but with some changes in magnitudes (table 8.5).

The only surprising outcome is that while the income gain in terms of real GDP increment is larger in the complete internationalisation of the agricultural sector scenario, welfare improvement tends to be greater in the scenario of partial reform of agricultural trade policy. The welfare measure used in this study – the Hicksian compensating variation – takes into account the effects of shocks on consumer and producer welfare, and on revenue from tariffs, export taxes and the trade taxes imposed by licensing and exchange rate overvaluation. A lower welfare gain in the complete internationalisation scenario may simply indicate higher adjustment costs in the short run. This welfare outcome may also be justified by considering the potential adjustment costs to the economy. While the current China model assumes instant factor and commodity flows and achievement of the new equilibrium, it is costly and takes time for the economy to move from one condition to another.

154 *Agricultural reform in China*

Can Chinese agriculture survive trade liberalisation?

The purpose of this chapter was to examine scenarios that the groups who resist trade liberalisation in agriculture say are likely to have detrimental consequences for China. Answers have been sought by applying the China model.

Simulation results show that if China chooses to restore its self-sufficiency policy for grain and wool, not only is its income loss large (0.5 per cent reduction in real GDP), but domestic agricultural prices rise significantly (the rise for grain and wool is greater than that transmitted from a 20 per cent increase in international prices). The fact that urban workers gain more than rural farmers suggests that a self-sufficiency policy or trade restriction is not an efficient measure for protecting farmers' incomes. This effect is additional to the losses of total income and overall welfare.

On the other hand, China may gain from implementation of the agricultural agreement of the Uruguay Round by GATT member-countries even if it stays out of the World Trade Organisation and maintains its current policy regime. Given the rises in international agricultural prices, China may turn from a net importer of grain (1987 base year) to a net exporter.

China's gains can be enlarged if it actively participates in trade reform (through delivering a 50 per cent tariff reduction in line with efforts to join the GATT and removing 24 per cent of agricultural support as required by the Uruguay Round settlement). When China extends its partial agricultural trade reform into complete internationalisation of its agricultural sector, real GDP growth is higher (1.3 per cent compared to 1.2 per cent), but the compensating variation falls significantly (0.8 per cent of GDP compared to 1.4 per cent), primarily because higher adjustment costs may be involved in the short run.

Agricultural protection can in no way help farmers' income in China. Currently, Chinese farmers derive about half or more of their total income from non-agricultural sources. Agricultural protection can only reduce Chinese farmers' real income by adversely affecting the development of the rural and urban industries. On the contrary, agricultural trade liberalisation and consequent structural adjustment enable China to better exercise its comparative advantage, to promote rural development and to raise farmers' income and living standards.

The policy implications of these findings are clear. China should participate actively in agricultural trade reform for its own benefit. The small gap between domestic and international prices for many agricultural products and the low level of agricultural distortion do not suggest that China should switch from taxing to subsidising agriculture. Policies discriminating against agriculture adversely affected the development of the whole economy. The experiences of other East Asian economies have proved that policies favouring the agricultural sector by distorting incentive structures do not help overall economic growth. Considering the adjustment costs involved in the process of trade liberalisation, a gradual reform approach is preferable. China can, for instance, liberalise those products which have less economywide importance, and therefore smaller domestic distortions, and then gradually extend reforms to other products and sectors.

Notes

1 The agreement on export subsidies was later revised between the EU and the United States on the initiative of France. While the end-objectives remain the same, the EU and the United States will be allowed to subsidise another 15 million tonnes of wheat exports during the implementation period (Garnaut and Huang 1994).
2 Compensating variation here measures the maximum amount of income that could be taken from the economy which gains from the exogenous change.

9

Getting reform right in agriculture

Agricultural reform from an institutional perspective

What was wrong with pre-reform agricultural institutions?

In the pre-reform period, the Chinese government adopted a heavy-industry oriented development strategy to catch up with and overtake the major capitalist economies in a short period. Under this strategy, economic institutions were framed to mobilise resources for heavy-industrial development. Control of foreign exchange, depressed interest rates and mandatory resource allocations were examples of policy measures introduced to facilitate this development strategy.

Agriculture was seen as the major supplier of resources required for industrial development. To facilitate resource flows from agriculture to industry, a set of agricultural institutions was established exhibiting three major features – an inward-looking approach, the unified purchase and marketing system and the collectivisation of agricultural production.

An inward-looking approach was the only possible choice for the government at that time. After the Communists took power in 1949 and the Kuomintang were driven to the tiny Taiwan, Western countries led by the United States adopted a policy that economically and politically blockaded mainland China. The Soviet Union and Eastern Europe was the only bloc with which China could trade, and at the time it was pursuing the same development strategy.

The inward-looking approach was also driven by the chosen development strategy. China was a large, densely populated developing country at the beginning of the 1950s. China would never be able, within a short period, to develop its heavy industry so as to participate in the international division of labour, as its comparative advantage clearly lay in labour-intensive manufacturing. To achieve its development objective, the government essentially had to cut off linkages between China and the world economy. The former Soviet Union in the period before 1960 and Japan after 1960 were the only important outside suppliers of machinery and equipment for China's heavy-industrial development.

An inward-looking approach was also an important measure to facilitate domestic resource flows. It eliminated many opportunities (represented by relative prices in the international markets) for domestic producers (especially agricultural producers) and significantly reduced resistance to low agricultural prices.

The unified purchase and marketing system was instituted to transfer resources directly between sectors and regions and to guarantee necessary agricultural supplies. The system was a complete set of policies ranging from agricultural production plans to regulations (and prices) relating to the procurement and marketing of agricultural products.

The key element of the unified purchase and marketing system was a low state price for agricultural products. By supplying food and other agricultural products to the urban industrial and consumer markets at low prices, the government ensured that the industrial sector was able to maintain low production costs (through both cheap raw materials and cheap labour). The extra profits generated by the industrial sector could thus be re-invested, either by the government or by the enterprises themselves.

To secure delivery of the required quantities of agricultural products at low prices, production and procurement quotas were assigned to farm households (before collectivisation) and production teams through the unified purchase and marketing system. In the pre-reform period, several hundred agricultural products were governed by this unified system. To eliminate possible high-return alternatives, not only did the government control the procurement and marketing of important agricultural products, but free markets (rural and urban) were also restricted or not allowed to operate at all.

Collectivisation of agricultural production and the establishment of the commune system were used in an attempt to modernise agriculture. Individual, small-scale household farming was seen as an inefficient farming institution that prevented the adoption of modern production technologies and the growth of productivity. This was incompatible with the government's ambition to industrialise. The commune system would mobilise mass labour in the construction of agricultural infrastructure. It was anticipated that agricultural production would grow as required by the industrialisation programme without the need to make capital investment. According to China's pre-reform development strategy, scarce capital had to be invested in industrial sectors.

A more fundamental motivation for collectivisation, however, was to smooth the implementation of policies discriminating against agriculture and to transfer resources away from agriculture (nested in the unified purchase and marketing system). The differing behaviours of production team leaders and household heads made a significant difference under this system. While a household head would resist any resource transfer strongly, the resistance of a production team leader was much weaker. The marginal disutility to a team leader of a transfer of resources from the team was much smaller than in the case of a household head.

The three major components of the pre-reform agricultural institutions were closely related to each other and collectively implemented the heavy-industry oriented development strategy.

What institutional distortions have been corrected?

Pre-reform agricultural institutions helped the government to build a large-scale national industrial sector, but were unsuccessful in producing agricultural growth and economic efficiency. In the reform period, the government made efforts to change almost every aspect of the 'old' institutions in agriculture.

The most successful institutional change was the household responsibility system reform. While only 0.02 per cent of the production teams had adopted the household responsibility system in 1979, the proportion rose quickly to 97.8 per cent by the end of 1983. The rapid spread of the household responsibility system was a result of changes in government policy but, more importantly, a result also of its superiority as demonstrated by improved agricultural performance.

Though small in scale, the household responsibility system is an efficient institution when compared with the commune system. It reduces transaction costs and promotes productivity in at least three ways. First, it avoids the negative impact brought about by the egalitarian distribution system used in production teams which essentially reduces the marginal return to any given effort. Second, collectives are superior to household farming only if the production technology exhibits large economies of scale. A production team's total output would, in the presence of economies of scale, be higher than the sum of the output of individual farms. Agricultural collectives have their shortcomings – in particular the difficulties in monitoring efforts. Owing to the characteristics of agricultural production, it is extremely costly to monitor each part of the production process. Shirking is a common phenomenon in agricultural collectives. Moreover, there will be sufficient provision of monitoring only when the incentives to supply such monitoring are right. The distribution system established under production teams does not provide sufficient incentives for team leaders to monitor effort carefully.

Household farming under the household responsibility system avoids these problems and its implementation produced astonishing output and productivity growth. Output growth jumped from 2.4 per cent in 1952–78 to 5 per cent in 1978–84 for grain and from 1.9 to 7.4 per cent for agricultural production. A dominant proportion (78–96 per cent) of the productivity growth in 1978–84 can be attributed to improvements through the household responsibility system reform (see chapter 3).

Significant efforts were also made to reform the unified purchase and marketing system by first raising state purchase prices and then introducing free markets for agricultural products. This reform was largely successful for most agricultural products.

In the early stage of the reform, the government focused on narrowing the gap between state and market prices. In 1979, for instance, state purchase prices for agricultural products were raised on average by 20 per cent. The increases in state prices in those years were crucial for the growth of agricultural output. This was because free markets were largely not available and increased state prices directly raised farmers' marginal returns, resulting in higher levels of agricultural inputs. Even in cases where free markets existed at the margin, they were often too small in size to make an impact and non-state transactions were far from well developed. State prices still served as effective marginal prices.

Alongside increases in state prices, the government gradually opened rural and urban fairs as markets for agricultural products, on the condition that state procurement quotas would be fulfilled. Some less important agricultural products were slowly released from the influence of state plans. Market mechanisms played an increasing role in the determination of the structure of agricultural production. In 1985, the unified purchase and marketing system was abolished for all agricultural products except grain, cotton and edible oil. This was an important step in the establishment of the market in China's agricultural reform. Major structural changes in the following years were a result of farmers' responses to changes in agricultural institutions.

Reform of the unified purchase and marketing system for grain took a more difficult path. Mandatory procurement and low state prices were many times removed but then quickly resumed. The unified purchase and marketing system for grain and cotton changed to a contract system in 1985 but quickly changed back. Various national and regional efforts were made after 1985 to reform grain policies. In 1991 and 1992, a significant step was taken to unify purchase and marketing prices and to introduce market mechanisms – the 'third revolution'. This 'revolution', however, was not a clear-cut success. Some of the old administrative policy measures were adopted again in response to the grain market in 1993–95.

A big change in government policy in the post-reform period was the adoption of the open door policy, which resulted in extraordinary export growth – around 20 per cent per annum from 1978 to 1994. Steps toward reform were also taken in the agricultural sector, although to a much lesser extent. Restrictions on imports and exports of many agricultural products were gradually loosened. The proportion of agricultural products in total exports declined sharply during the reform period, as China's trade pattern moved closer to its resource endowments. Grain trade was also increasingly used by the government to balance domestic demand and supply.

Incomplete agricultural reform

Nineteen years of agricultural reform in China have achieved significant results. But, at the same time, it is incomplete in many aspects. This incompleteness is an important factor that hampers further growth of agricultural production and the whole economy.

The household responsibility system reform stimulated productivity growth in the agricultural sector and contributed significantly to rural economic development. While new production institutions were implemented, however, new mechanisms to encourage investment in agriculture were not established. Constrained by land tenure contracts, farmers did not have enough incentive to make long-term investments. This led to a widespread decay of agricultural infrastructure. Agricultural yields in the second half of the 1980s largely stagnated or decreased. Owing to equal division of the collectives' land in the household responsibility system reform, agricultural production could not achieve economy of scale. Because the land still belonged to the collectives and farmers only had the right to plant, land circulation among farmers was difficult. Even those farmers who obtained off-farm jobs did not want to return the contracted land to the collective. They would rather have kept the land for employment insurance and food security. It was almost impossible to concentrate land into the hands of a small number of skilled farmers. Given such a production institution, further increases in productivity seem difficult.

While removing the unified purchase and marketing system and introducing free markets, the government did not build effective measures to cushion the economy from the large fluctuations that occurred because reform was incomplete. Market reform does not necessarily mean that the government should never be involved in the operation of the market. The government had a role to play in the transition stage to prevent large fluctuations. As it happened, the Chinese government resumed its old administrative measures in the face of sharp changes that it could not otherwise control. This greatly increased uncertainties in markets and made difficulties for producers' and consumers' decision-making. Because of the incompleteness of the reform, state departments required to play policy roles did not perform their duties. Instead they speculated in markets for their own profit, utilising advantages gained as government bodies. Market fluctuations were thus magnified. The behaviour of many state grain stores over the years 1993–95 is a good illustration.

The government has not completely freed itself from grain market operations. Local governments are responsible for grain supply in their own regions and the link between government budgets and grain prices has not yet been cut. These strange policy-settings are largely responsible for the blockages in regional grain trade and the segmentation of regional markets, and further increase market instability.

There has been less progress in the reform of the inward-looking approach for agriculture. Although the open door policy was one of the major reforms contributing to rapid economic growth, there was little change in the agricultural sector. Grain imports and exports, although expanding, are still strictly controlled by state agencies. The government still focuses on basic self-sufficiency in grain as one of its major objectives for agricultural policy.

Reluctance to liberalise trade in agriculture is based on a number of considerations. China is worried that the internationalisation of its agricultural trade may increase the instability of the domestic market, threaten its food security, worsen income equity and create difficult adjustment problems for Chinese farmers. These considerations are groundless or could be solved if a cautious approach were taken. Internationalisation, appropriately introduced, will help to raise domestic productivity, increase food security and promote income growth.

Sequencing and reform

The Chinese government did not have a blueprint at the beginning of agricultural reform. Economic reform in China is now termed a 'gradual approach' – 'crossing the river by touching the stone' – in comparison with the 'shock therapy' adopted in Eastern Europe and the former Soviet Union. The evidence is still largely inconclusive as to which approach is superior although it seems that the gradual approach is working well in terms of output and productivity growth (Lin, Cai and Li 1994a). The gradual approach has the advantage that policy mistakes can be corrected at every step of the reform to avoid wide fluctuations. On the other hand, it is argued that the gradual approach jeopardises the building of significant support and allows enough time for opposition to reform to accumulate.

In retrospect, agricultural reform in China clearly exhibited the characteristics of a gradual approach, but at the same time had a strong logical base. It proceeded from easy to more difficult policy reforms. Policy changes introduced at earlier stages called for further reform policies at later stages.

From easy to difficult policy reforms

China's agricultural reform over the past nineteen years started with increases in state purchase prices and the household responsibility system reform. It then proceeded to the opening up of small rural and urban fairs for agricultural products. The introduction of free markets was the last step taken by the government and is still far from complete for grain products. In the later years of the reform, trade liberalisation for some agricultural products was attempted but the regime for the major ones remains largely the same.

The timing of policy change reflects a clear sequencing of China's agricultural reform. Given the overall economic environment in China at the end of the 1970s, it would have been difficult to introduce free markets or to switch to outward-looking policies for agriculture. With the commune system and central planning in place, a sudden change in the market environment would have caused dramatic adjustment. Whether or not producers could have responded sensitively to market changes under the special institutional arrangement remains in question.

Increases in state purchase prices and changes in production institutions from production teams to household farming, however, promoted agricultural production without affecting the rest of the economy significantly. Most of the effects resulting from these policy changes remained within the agricultural sector, although some spillover may have occurred even during this period. On account of increases in output prices and more direct linkages between effort and reward, farmers increased their inputs (both in quantity and quality) and raised agricultural output.

After the distortions to production institutions were corrected and the gaps between state and market prices narrowed, it was possible for the government to introduce free markets for agricultural products. This step was accompanied by the gradual reform of the whole economy. Market reforms engaged other parts of the economy in the process of adjustment and change. But the adjustment required was limited because the state and market prices were already close and farmers could make sensitive supply responses given that appropriate household farming institutions were in place.

From the product side, reforms started with relatively less important policies. Rural and urban fairs were first opened for products that were made in small quantities. Because these products were less critical to the basic standard of living for most of the population, the damage from any mismanagement of reforms was potentially less harmful. In 1985, free markets were introduced for these less important agricultural products. In May 1988, the Chinese government first reformed its marketing policies for non-staple food before it took action on staple food in 1991 and 1992.

Earlier policy changes called for later reforms

Earlier reform measures set the necessary conditions for later reforms so that the reform process proceeded logically. From 1978 to 1984, the most important reforms were the implementation of the household responsibility system and state price reform. Both promoted agricultural production because the energies released were directly channelled to agriculture as non-agricultural opportunities were largely unavailable.

Agricultural growth in the first half of the 1980s, however, presented new problems. Grain output experienced extraordinary growth, surpassing the growth in consumption by a large margin. The temporary grain surplus became a nationwide problem imposing burdens on both the government and farmers. A more important implication was that, given the institutional settings, farmers' income was not to be raised without further policy changes. An effective way to continue farmers' income growth, given the temporary supply surplus, was to diversify farmers' production activities. A rural market reform programme was introduced in 1985 to encourage non-grain and non-agricultural production.

Again, the story was similar in grain policy reform. Changes in price policy in the 1980s concentrated on the state purchase side. Grain output increased quickly partly because of increases in state purchase prices. Because urban marketing prices remained unchanged, however, the government faced a policy dilemma. On the one hand, it had to raise purchase prices to encourage grain production but, on the other hand, every price increase had to be financed by government subsidies because marketing prices were fixed. This called for further reforms in marketing policies for grain in urban areas. This was the main reason behind the policy changes at the beginning of the 1990s.

Current market reform in China presents an even clearer case. Domestic markets for agricultural products including grain have been opened. Consumers and producers are assumed to be subject to any changes in the market while prices are solely determined by demand and supply conditions. Because of the special characteristics of China's agricultural market and factor endowments, however, the government is anxious that opening markets could cause unexpected results – intermittent grain shortages and rapid price increases. This anxiety, to some extent, reflected the government's inexperience in indirectly managing markets. But, more importantly, it reflected a lack of freedom to trade both in domestic markets among different regions and in the international markets.

Further reforms to internationalise the agricultural sector are necessary, although not yet widely accepted among Chinese economists and policy analysts. The analysis in this study suggests that internationalisation may be unavoidable, given the worldwide trend of agricultural trade liberalisation, and the problems will become increasingly severe if this step is not taken quickly.

Institutional learning as a way of reform

One important characteristic of China's experience of agricultural reform has been that of institutional learning. Both official and unofficial policy experiments were undertaken before nationwide policy reforms were introduced. The learning process ensured that the disadvantages of any policy reform were kept to a minimum and the best policy choices were undertaken (although not necessarily in all cases).

The household responsibility system reform began with experiments in the 1950s and 1960s. Even within the severe political constraints of that time, farmers continued to experiment with different systems for appropriating responsibility for production decisions. The household responsibility system was widely accepted by farmers because of the clear relationship it established between effort and reward, given the condition of public ownership. The household responsibility system reform was also a learning process for the government. The government first permitted the adoption of various special management systems contracting agricultural work to groups, individuals and households. Then the contracting of output was allowed. When the government realised that the household responsibility system was the most effective and accepted production institution, it moved quickly to adopt it as a national policy. This occurred within a changed domestic political economy – the government had already switched its policy priority from class struggle to economic development.

Market reform was also a process of institutional learning. The two-tier price system was adopted as an intermediate stage between central planning and fully functioning free markets. Under the two-tier price system, the government was able to control certain agricultural products, ensuring stability of supply, while some products were allowed to enter the markets. This enabled the market mechanisms to develop, and consumers and producers to adapt gradually to a market environment.

The experiments with grain policy reform provide a good example. In the late 1980s, the government intended to reform its grain marketing policy but lacked knowledge as to how to proceed. In 1988, it carried out reform of non-staple foods to gain experience of how production and markets would be affected. At the same time, about a dozen experimental zones (including some administered by the central and some by local governments) were established to try out different approaches to reform in grain policy. These practices accumulated important knowledge for the 'third revolution' in 1992.

The gradual approach

China's agricultural reform so far has been largely successful. The gradual approach allowed it to continue to move forward while minimising any negative effects. Not only has agricultural productivity, and therefore output, grown quickly, but resources that moved out of the agricultural sector also contributed to rapid economic development. Although the process of agricultural reform after 1985 was problematic, disastrous changes did not occur. This was also largely attributable to the gradual approach – as soon as problems emerged, the government applied measures to eliminate potentially greater fluctuations.

The problem (rather than disadvantage) is that the gradual approach sometimes can delay reform policies. Moving forward then backward has been a common pattern during China's agricultural reform. Because policies are implemented step by step, problems arise because of the incompleteness of reform. The danger then is that these problems are attributed to the reform itself rather than to the incompleteness of reform. The direction of policy reforms can easily be turned back instead of being pushed forward. This may result in a slow and painful process of economic reform and stretch out the period of transition. The frequent removal and resumption of mandatory procurement of grain and state purchase prices is an example of this.

Agricultural reform: implications for China and the world

China's agricultural reform has come to a historical turning point – what direction China chooses to take, and when it implements this choice, is important not only for China but also the world. Since economic reform began, China has been increasingly integrated into the world economy. The Chinese economy grew at 9 per cent per annum in 1978–94, and its exports grew even faster. According to the income levels used in this analysis (Garnaut and Ma 1993; Garnaut, Ma and Huang, forthcoming), China is already the world's fourth largest economy, following the United States, Japan and Germany. In 1994, it was the world's eleventh largest trading nation. At the beginning of the 1990s, China also became the largest recipient of foreign direct investment among developing economies. It is likely that China will overtake Germany in size by the early twenty-first century. China's trade is expected to grow faster than its domestic output, although this growth may be less than in other East Asian economies. China will rise to become one of the world's top trading economies in a decade or two.

Despite the fact that China is already an important player in the world economy, it is still outside the international trading system. In December 1994, China's application to rejoin the General Agreement on Tariffs and Trade as a founding member was rejected by the major contracting parties. In 1995 and 1997, negotiations between China and other contracting parties of the World Trade Organisation continued. It is expected that this issue will be resolved in late 1997 or during 1998.

Against such a background, what are the implications of China's further agricultural reform for both China and the world trading system? The general direction of China's economic reform has been consistent and clear. China's rise in the international economy in the past decade has been largely facilitated by its rapid expansion of labour-intensive manufactured exports. Reform has increasingly brought China's trade pattern into conformity with its resource endowments and comparative advantages (Garnaut and Huang 1995; Song 1996). Shares of agriculture and resource-intensive exports have been declining, reflecting China's limited resource (agricultural and non-agricultural) endowments on a per capita basis, while the share of labour-intensive exports, especially textiles and clothing, has grown strongly.

The continued growth of China's exports requires a stable and expanding international market. This is where multilateral trade arrangements can play a role. Under the auspices of the World Trade Organisation and the Asia Pacific Economic Cooperation, an individual economy is disciplined by international rules and conventions. Such discipline can facilitate China's smooth integration into the world economy.

How does China's agricultural policy fit into this international play? China's current inward-looking agricultural policy not only contradicts its own overall reform objective, but also makes other economies reluctant to accommodate it within international institutions. The international community imposed some requirements that were beyond China's grasp – most importantly, the requirement that China join the World Trade Organisation as an industrial economy. Given China's current institutional settings and income levels, it is impractical to require China to meet all the industrial economy standards. A more realistic way to solve this problem is for China to join the World Trade Organisation as a developing economy, with a commitment to a reform agenda such that it will achieve industrial economy status within a finite period.

It is important, however, for China to understand the actual (both static and dynamic) gains from trade and the conventions of international trade practice. China must proceed with reforms in areas where it is both beneficial and feasible. Agricultural policy is one such area. Liberalisation of agricultural trade will bring welfare and income benefits to China, and will indicate China's belief in free trade to the international community. Such a signal is critical for winning the trust and co-operation of the international community and for making negotiations in other areas easier.

If China does not do so, it will gradually lose the co-operation it now receives from many economies, not only increasing China's difficulties in achieving further integration into the world economy but also reducing its probability of maintaining rapid growth. If China fails to join the international trading community soon, huge resources will be wasted on tough and time-consuming bilateral trade negotiations with individual trading partners. Uncertainty will greatly increase and resistance to China's labour-intensive exports will be stronger. Agriculture will certainly become a constant source of trade conflict. At the same time, China will not be able to share completely in the fruits of the Uruguay Round settlement, such as the removal of the Multifibre Arrangement.

It is not in the international community's interest to exclude China from international trade agreements such as the World Trade Organisation. The East Asian experience in the past decade has demonstrated that those who co-operate closely and trade intensively with China also benefit greatly from China's rapid growth. It is expected that agricultural trade liberalisation in China will result in huge agricultural imports from the rest of the world, while exports will grow more rapidly. To exclude China from the international trading system is to bring uncertainty to the international markets, especially for a number of commodities. China's is such a large economy that fluctuations in international markets can be created by China's residual behaviour in trade arising from temporary changes in domestic market conditions. Unstable cotton trade policies in China created related fluctuations in the world cotton market (figure 9.1). Grain policies are likely to have similar effects in the future if Chinese agriculture is not integrated into the world market.

The international community can only benefit from taking a more positive approach to accommodating China in both the international trading system and the world economy. International trade negotiations are an important factor influencing China's domestic political economy in agricultural trade liberalisation. The international community can also help China to build confidence in agricultural trade liberalisation. Some special agreements between China and the major agricultural exporting economies on issues related to the supply of grain in case of emergencies and political conflicts will be helpful in securing liberalisation of Chinese agriculture. Further removal of restrictions on China's labour-intensive exports, such as the Multifibre Arrangement, is another way to build China's confidence.

Toward a market economy

The Chinese government has as its goal of economic reform the establishment of a socialist market economy. The definition of a market economy may vary, especially in China where the 'Chinese characteristics' are often stressed in the process of reform. But an efficient agricultural market would at least contain sensitive price determination mechanisms, sufficient autonomy for consumers and producers in decisionmaking,

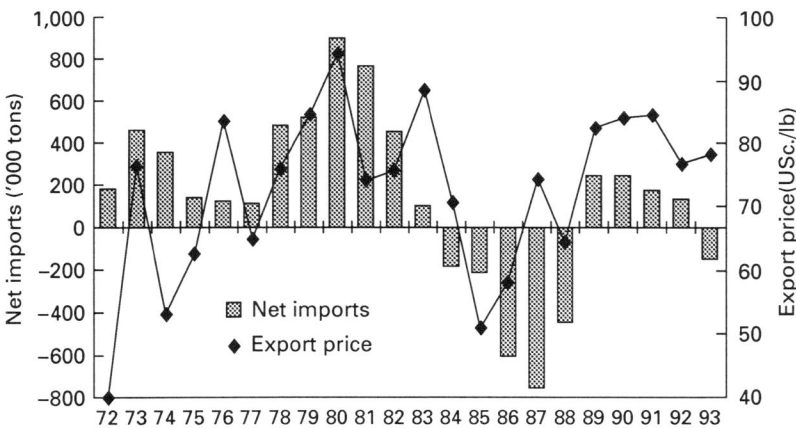

Fig. 9.1. China's net imports of cotton and world cotton prices, 1972 to 1993. (*Sources*: International Economic Databank, The Australian National University, Canberra; Australian Bureau of Agricultural Research Economics 1992.)

freedom to trade in both domestic and international markets and an effective market management scheme by the government.

There are a number of areas in the agricultural sector that require further reform. An effective and efficient land tenure system is necessary (whether or not the property rights issue is dealt with) to facilitate land concentration for skilled farmers and the realisation of scale economies. The government needs to build skills in the management of market fluctuations using more indirect measures such as grain stocks. The most important problem with the current agricultural institutions, however, is the lack of freedom to trade. Regional agricultural trade is blocked because of fiscal interests. Regional agricultural markets are segmented. The domestic market is strictly isolated from the international market, except for a small amount of agricultural trade monopolised by state agents. These were the dominant factors behind the agricultural crisis of the early 1990s. As Chinese agriculture is already at a turning point, it is necessary for the Chinese government to take action quickly before the adjustment process becomes too costly.

Agricultural problems in recent years have not been caused solely by agricultural institutions. The special mechanisms of the monetary and fiscal policies and the soft-budget problem of the state sector, for instance, magnified price fluctuations in grain markets, transforming some into more serious macroeconomic problems. Reforms in these areas are necessary for the establishment of both the efficient agricultural sector and the effective market economy that China needs.

Changes in agricultural policies at the end of the 1970s were the beginning of China's economic reform, and these have led to a long period of rapid economic growth. While most other parts of the economy, especially the manufacturing sector, are now widely open to the international market, the agricultural sector remains inward-looking. It is now time for Chinese policymakers to stimulate another round of rapid growth by creating a smooth passage for the Chinese economy into the international trading system.

Appendix: The China model

Sector details

One important decision in computable general equilibrium modelling is the degree to which production is disaggregated. This is a crucial determinant of a model's potential usefulness in policy analysis. Disaggregation and detailed sector structure are distinctive features of computable general equilibrium models, particularly when they are compared with macroeconomic models. This China model uses detailed agricultural sector data, since the primary interest lies in the impact of incentive distortions on the sector as a whole and on individual farm commodities. Grain (rice and wheat), cotton and wool are distinguished from other products. Disaggregation does not come without cost, however. A detailed model structure provides insights into structural change, but demands higher quality inputs. Computable general equilibrium models are built on parameters and coefficients characterising economic agents' behaviour. Data availability (for both input–output parameters and behavioural elasticities) is therefore important in determining the model's structure. In view of the limited resources available, non-agricultural sectors are treated at an aggregated level. In combining individual industrial sectors, attention is given to distinguishing export-oriented and import-competing industries (Clarete and Warr 1992) and to separating activities that use different production techniques (input combinations) (NCDS 1990).

The China model contains twenty-two sectors, of which four are agricultural and eighteen are non-agricultural (table A.1). Agriculture is of particular interest in this study. About two-thirds of the value of agricultural production comes from food and other crop production. Over half of this is in the production of food crops including rice, wheat and other grain crops. A further quarter of the value of agricultural output comes from livestock production which produces wool and non-wool animal commodities. Forestry and fishing each account for about 5 per cent of the value of agricultural production.

Agriculture is disaggregated into four sectors: farming, livestock, forestry and fishing. Farming and livestock sectors are multi-product industries, while forestry and fishing are single-product industries.

In the production process, each agricultural sector uses two categories of production input (intermediate inputs and primary factors) to produce either a single output (for a single-product industry) or a composite output (for a multi-

172 *Agricultural reform in China*

Table A.1. *Sector details of the China model*

Industry number	Industry description	Product number	Product description
1	Farming	1	Rice
		2	Wheat
		3	Other grains
		4	Cotton
		5	Other crops
2	Livestock	6	Wool
		7	Other livestock
3	Forestry	8	Forestry products
4	Fishing	9	Fish
5	Mineral (urban)	10	Minerals
6	Mineral (rural)	10	Minerals
7	Food processing (urban)	11	Processed food
8	Food processing (rural)	11	Processed food
9	Textile (urban)	12	Textile products
10	Textile (rural)	12	Textile products
11	Non-metal manufacture (urban)	13	Non-metal products
12	Non-metal manufacture (rural)	13	Non-metal products
13	Metal manufacture (urban)	14	Metal products
14	Metal manufacture (rural)	14	Metal products
15	Electricity (urban)	15	Water and electricity
16	Electricity (rural)	15	Water and electricity
17	Construction (urban)	16	Construction
18	Construction (rural)	16	Construction
19	Trade and transportation (urban)	17	Trade and transportation
20	Trade and transportation (rural)	17	Trade and transportation
21	Service (urban)	18	Service
22	Service (rural)	18	Service

product industry) (figure A.1). The composite output is then transformed into individual commodities through a specified mechanism. Intermediate input is distinguished as domestically produced or imported, while primary factors include labour, capital and land. The key characteristic of the China model is that the rural and urban sectors are separated because of differences in production technology, operating mechanisms and labour, and other factor sources.

China has relatively small mining sectors, particularly when compared to resource-rich economies like those of Australia and the Middle Eastern countries. Their output value corresponds to about a quarter of agriculture's. The mining sectors, however, distinguish themselves from other sectors in that they are both resource- and capital-intensive (compared to some other industrial sectors) and their outputs are relatively stable (compared to agriculture). In addition, because China is a very large economy the performance of its mining sectors is critical to overall growth.

Mining in the China model is aggregated at two sectors: mineral (urban) and mineral (rural). Both sectors include coal mining, oil and gas extraction, other

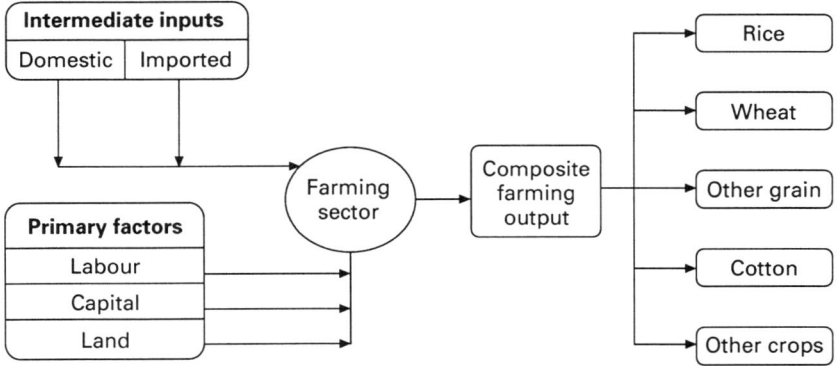

Fig. A.1. Agricultural production.

minerals and their products (thirteen sub-sectors). The so-called urban mining sector is not necessarily located in urban areas. The urban sector is distinguished from the rural sector in the sense that it is not managed by rural townships, villages or farm households.

Manufacturing has the largest number of sectors (eight) in the China model. The classification of manufacturing sectors reflects the focus of this study. A more detailed structure was specified for those manufacturing industries heavily dependent on agricultural outputs such as raw materials. The interactions between agriculture and these manufacturing industries are expected to be significant. The upstream or downstream effects of any exogenous changes and their feedback influences are of particular interest. On the other hand, textile industries – urban and rural – not only consume agricultural products, such as cotton and wool, directly but contribute significantly to export growth. Other manufacturing industries in the model are separated according to production process and exporting/importing behaviour. These include food processing, non-metal manufacture and metal manufacture (each of these sectors is further split into urban and rural sub-sectors).

Service industry is small in the Chinese economy. A policy was announced recently to encourage the development of the service sector, and non-state enterprises are becoming increasingly important to this sector. Six service sectors stand out as requiring particular emphasis in the China model: construction (urban), construction (rural), trade and transportation (urban), trade and transportation (rural), service (urban) and service (rural). Trade and transportation industry contains communications, domestic and foreign trade, marketing and storage, restaurants and transportation by railway, highway, water, air and pipeline. Other services include public utilities, health, education, scientific services, sports and financial institutions.

174 *Agricultural reform in China*

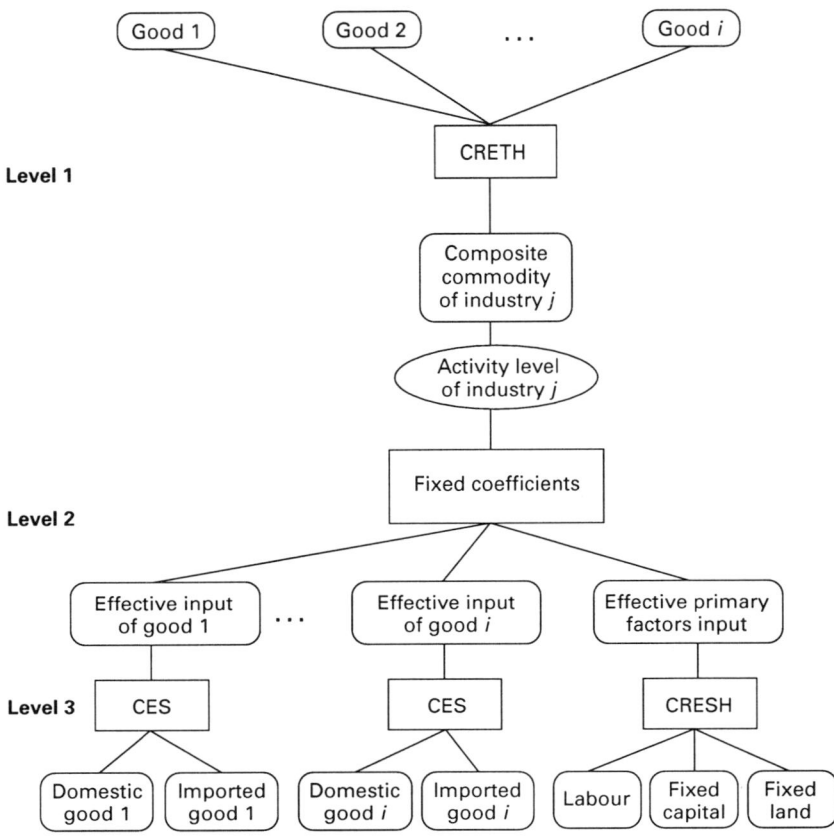

Fig. A.2. Technology of current production.

Theoretical structure

Production activities

Since producers are assumed to be price takers in both output and input markets, they choose input levels subject to production technologies to minimise production costs. The industrial technology of current production is illustrated in figure A.2. The production function is described in levels 2 and 3. At the third level, effective levels of inputs of commodity g ($g = 1, 2, \ldots, 18$) are defined as constant elasticity of substitution $(CES)^1$ combinations of domestic supplies and imports of the particular commodity classification; that is, the demand for intermediate input i ($i = 1, 2, \ldots, 18$) from source s ($s = 1$, domestically produced, $s = 2$, imported) by industry j ($j = 1, 2, \ldots, 22$), $x^{(1)}_{(is)j}$, can be expressed as

$$x^{(1)}_{(is)j} = z_j - \sigma^{(1)}_{ij}(p_{(is)j} - \sum_s S^{(1)}_{(is)j} p_{(is)j}) \tag{A.1}$$

by ignoring technological progress. Here, $\sigma^{(1)}_{ij}$ is the elasticity of substitution between two sources of intermediate inputs. The effective units of primary factors are defined as $CRESH^2$ combinations of fixed capital, labour and agricultural land. The demand for primary factor v by industry j, $x^{(1)}_{vj}$, in the simplest form, is

$$x^{(1)}_{vj} = z_j - \sigma^{(1)}_{vj}(p^{(1)}_{vj} - \sum_v S^{*(1)}_{vj} p^{(1)}_{vj}) \tag{A.2}$$

where $\sigma^{(1)}_{vj}$ is the CRESH parameter reflecting the degree of substitutability between primary factor v and other primary factors in the production process. Capital and agricultural land are treated as though they are non-shiftable between industries (fixed in modelling). In effect, it is assumed that there is a rental market for the capital and agricultural land of each industry and that each producer in industry j treats the rental prices of capital and agricultural land of type j as given. The rental rates adjust so that for each j, the sum of the demands from all producers in industry j equals the available supplies of capital and agricultural land of type j.

At level 2, effective inputs of each g of produced commodities and effective primary factor inputs are required for the production process in fixed proportion

$$z_j = \min\left\{\frac{X^{(1)}_{1j}}{A^{(1)}_{1j}}, \frac{X^{(1)}_{2j}}{A^{(1)}_{2j}}, \ldots, \frac{X^{(1)}_{gj}}{A^{(1)}_{gj}}, \frac{X^{(1)}_{vj}}{A^{(1)}_{vj}}\right\} \tag{A.3}$$

The industry is viewed as buying an activity level or general production capacity (z_j).

The supply decision (which bundle of commodities to produce) is based on producers' objective of maximising total revenue subject to the purchased activity level and given technology. The livestock industry in the China model produces two products: wool and non-wool livestock products (figure A.3). The livestock industry purchases the activity level or the production frontier AA. Area OAA represents the feasible production combinations of wool and non-wool products. It is not difficult to determine the output levels for two products (point X), given the price levels (p_w and p_n).

Assuming that the price of wool increases from p_w to p'_w (a rotation from the original iso-revenue line to the new iso-revenue line), a producer will make two adjustments. First, a higher activity level of wool production, z'_j, will result owing to the higher composite price of wool. The production frontier shifts outward to BB, which is a product-neutral (homothetic) expansion of the old transformation frontier. This is the expansion effect (from point X to Y). Second, the product mix will change in favour of wool. Since the relative price of wool to non-wool products increases, product mix will move along the new transformation frontier to Z. This is referred to as the 'transformation effect'.

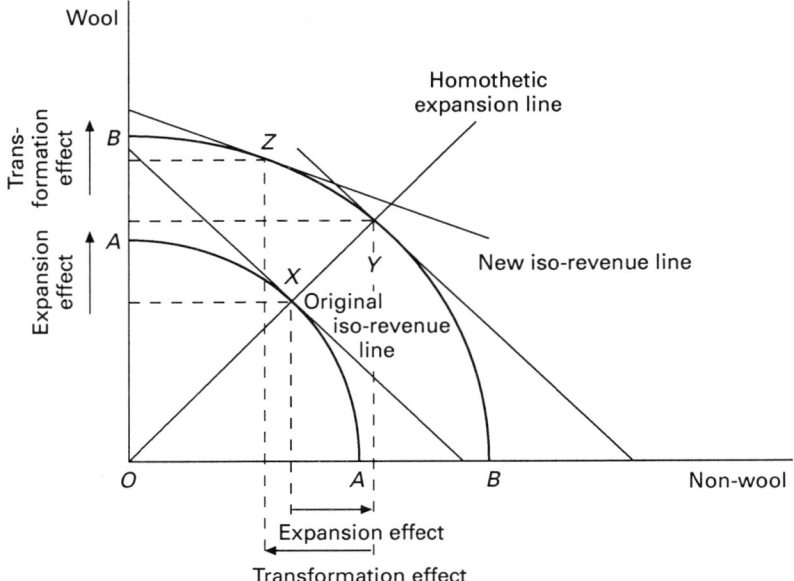

Fig. A.3. Industry output decisions: the case of the livestock industry.

In the model, the supply behaviour is specified as a CRETH[3] relation between products

$$x_{ij}^{(0)} = z_j + \sigma_{ij}^{(0)*}(p_i^{(0)} - \sum_i S_{ij}^{(0)*} p_i^{(0)}) \tag{A.4}$$

where $x_{ij}^{(0)}$ is the supply of commodity i by industry j, $p_i^{(0)}$ is the producer price of good i, $\sigma_{ij}^{(0)*}$ is the CRETH parameter reflecting the ease of transformation between commodity i and other commodities in the output bundle of industry j, and $S_{ij}^{(0)*}$ is the modified output share of good i in sector j.

Household and other final demands

There are two household groups in the present China model, one urban and one rural, reflecting model structures on the production side and labour market characteristics. Each group is assumed to be homogeneous and the behaviour of the households in each group can be characterised by a single representation.

Each household in the model derives its income from returns to factors: capital, labour and land. It is assumed that the household, as a price taker in the market, maximises a single utility function subject to an aggregate expenditure constraint. Substitutions are allowed between goods (by applying the linear expenditure system) and between domestically produced or imported sources

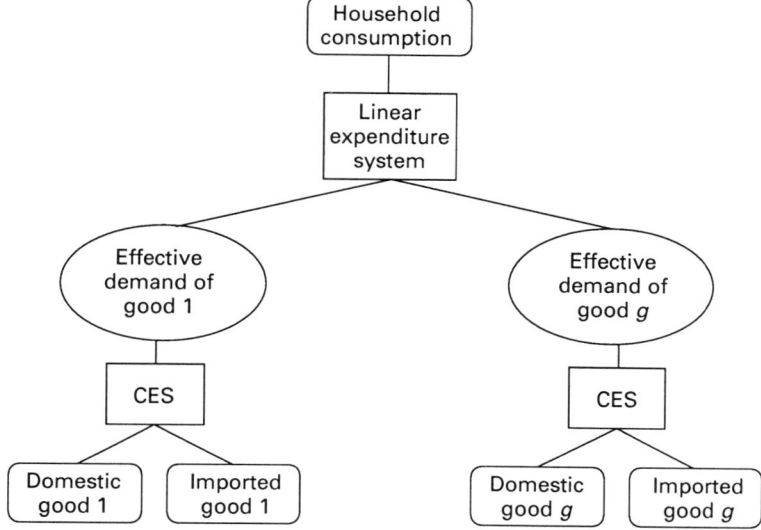

Fig. A.4. Household consumption

(through a CES mechanism) (figure A.4). The effects of changes in household preferences can be simulated via quantity-augmenting variables, $a_i^{(3)}$, with the demand specification

$$x_i^{(3)} = \varepsilon_i * c + \sum_l \eta_{(il)} p_l^{(3)} + a_i^{(3)} + \sum_l \eta_{(il)} (a_l^{(3)} + \sum_s S_{(ls)}^{(3)}) \qquad (A.5)$$

in which a positive value of the quantity-augmenting variable indicates a change in preference in favour of good i.

The other final demands include capital investment, stock and government consumption demands. As a short-run model, these demands are assumed to be changed proportionally to changes in absorption.

External sector

The external sector mainly involves two activities: exporting and importing. Import supply of each good to China from the world economy is specified as a function of the import price with an elasticity set empirically. The export market is separated into two parts: exports from China and exports from the rest of the world. The total world demand for exported goods from these two regions is elastic with respect to changes in composite export prices. Demand is substitutable between alternative sources and the substitution is modelled by a CES mechanism.

Equations of the model

Tables A.2, A.3 and A.4 present the equations, variables and parameters of the China model. All variables in the model are in the form of percentage change, unless otherwise indicated.

The equations of the model can be classified into nine groups (I–IX in table A.2). Group I defines the input demands (both intermediate inputs and primary factors) of the industry production. Equation (I.1) specifies the demand for intermediate inputs of commodities in the production process. This is derived from the producers' cost-minimisation problem according to the assumption, with possible technical changes incorporated (Dixon et al. 1982). It is first assumed that there is no change in relative prices, so a change in z_j will lead to a proportional change in demand for each intermediate input by sector j. This reflects the assumption of constant returns to scale. Suppose that the price of intermediate input m relative to that of n increases, then demand for m would increase less rapidly than n. Substitution will occur between the demands for m and n. The strength of this substitution will depend on the value of $S_{ji}^{(1)}$.

Equation (I.2) defines the demands for the primary factors – labour, capital and land – by each industry as a function of the output level in the industry and relative prices of each of the primary factor inputs.[4] The assumption is that factors can be aggregated into a composite primary factor bundle using a CES function. This demand equation form is obtained by imposing the first-order conditions for cost minimisation and is linearised in percentage changes. Similarly, substitutions between primary factors are assumed and the strength of the substitution depends on the value of $\sigma_{vj}^{(1)}$.

Equations (I.3)–(I.6) give the characteristics of the labour market segmentation between rural and urban areas. Equations (I.3) and (I.4) calculate the composite wage rates in the two broad sectors. Equations (I.5) and (I.6) show how the two labour markets are cleared. Within the rural labour market, labour supply is set equal to total demands by the agricultural and rural industrial sectors, while the supply of urban labour is set equal to total demands by urban sectors in the urban labour market.

Equation group II deals with the commodity supply in the economy. Supply of commodities is modelled at two levels. Total amounts of a commodity to be produced are determined and then a transformation mechanism is introduced to determine the proportion of output for domestic and export markets. The specification for non-agricultural sectors follows the usual ORANI format (equation II.1). The amount produced depends on activity levels, technical factors and output prices. It is assumed that only its own price and the general price of the group it produces affect the supply level of a particular commodity. For agricultural sectors, individual price elasticities are included in the equation determining output levels (equation II.2). Since urban and rural industries make the same products, however, total supply of one industrial product equals the sum of the outputs of both rural and urban industries (equation II.4). Equation (II.5) specifies the imperfect transformation between domestically produced goods supplied to domestic and export markets. This equation is a linearisation in percentage changes of the constant elasticity of transformation (CET) function. The interpretation of this equation is similar to that of previous ones. When there is no change in the relative prices of domestic and exported goods, the amount supplied to each destination will change proportionally to total output of the product. Whenever the price for one destination increases relatively, the amount supplied to this destination will rise more rapidly. Finally, equation (II.6) gives the composite commodity price for producers.

Household income and consumption are characterised in equation group III. As assumed, the households receive income from returns to factor (equation III.1). The functional forms for consumption demand – equations (III.2) and (III.3) – contain two levels. The total demand for one commodity is dependent on income and prices (represented by relevant elasticities) and changes in preference ($a_i^{(3)}$). The distribution of a commodity between domestic and imported sources is determined by the price difference and substitution elasticity ($\sigma_i^{(3)}$ for commodity i).

Other final demands are specified in equation group IV. Investment in fixed capital (equation IV.1), investment in stock (equation IV.2) and government consumption (equation IV.3), differentiated by sources of commodities, all keep step with the growth rate of real absorption. These functional forms are perhaps too simplified for any further analysis related to these areas. This study, however, does not investigate in detail the changes in capital stock or government consumption behaviour.

Foreign trade involves seven equations (equation group V). Demand for China's export of each commodity of equation (V.1) is represented by applying a CES function consistent with the Armington (1969) model. Whether China's exports could grow faster than the rest of the world depends crucially on the relative prices of its exports in the world market and the relevant substitution elasticities. Equation (V.2) specifies total world demand as a linear function of the weighted average price for the particular good where the weights are the shares of China and the rest of the world in total exports of this good. Following Martin (1990), supply of imports in equation (V.3) is specified as a function of the world price of imports, allowing for the possibility of China dominating particular markets. Equation (V.4) specifies the imports volume by summing all the imports components, and equations (V.5) and (V.6) calculate the foreign currency value of imports and exports. The balance of trade is reflected in equation (V.7).

Equation group VI is a set of zero profit conditions. Equation (VI.1) states that the total revenue from production is equal to the intermediate inputs plus the returns to primary factors. This condition implicitly involves the assumption of constant returns to scale of the technology and the assumption of sufficient competition to drive the pure profit at the margin to be zero. Although the zero profit in equations (VI.2) and (VI.3) for importing and exporting is easy to understand and interpret, there exists a gap between producer and user prices for the textile and commerce industries due to incentive distortion.

Equation group VII, specifying market-clearing conditions, contains seven equations. Equation (VII.1) shows that the domestic demand for good i from domestic sources must equal domestic production for the home market. Similarly in equation (VII.2), the export of good i from China must be equal to domestic

180 *Agricultural reform in China*

production for export. Equation (VII.3) implies that the demand for labour by the two broad sectors – agriculture and non-agriculture – is equated to the total supply of labour. Equations (VII.4) and (VII.5) specify the equilibrium between labour demand and supply within each of the two broad sectors. The stock of capital and that of land in each sector are specified exogenously (equations VII.6 and VII.7).

Equation group VIII comprises mostly identities or indices. Equations (VIII.1)–(VIII.3) compute domestic absorption, GDP and absorption. Equation (VIII.4) is an index of the GDP deflator.

Equation (IX.1) is the equilibrium condition for the money market, with money supply on the left and money demand on the right. Martin's (1990) model adopted a simpler equation for the purpose of price determination. Since Chow (1987) had found that a 1 per cent increase in the money supply would raise official prices by one-third of 1 per cent, and if the true inflation in China is 2.5 times the official rate as Chow estimated, Martin (1990) argued that using unit elasticity as in his model was reasonable. In equation (IX.1), a simple money market (money demand equals money supply) is incorporated explicitly to introduce some monetary effects in the Chinese economy.

Construction of a 22-sector input–output table for China, 1987

This table is constructed on the basis of the 117-sector input–output table constructed by the State Statistical Bureau and the Office of the National Input–Output Survey (1991). Building this 22-sector input–output table has three steps. The first is to derive new sectors by splitting some of the existing sectors in the larger table according to input–output information; the second is to aggregate the other sectors; and the third is to estimate the value-added shares for each primary factor.

Deriving the new sectors

Some of the sectors required in the 22-sector version do not appear individually in the 117-sector version. For instance, there is only one grain-cropping sector in the original table, so this grain sector has been split into rice, wheat and other grains. Likewise, cotton and other crops have to be separated from the existing 'other crop' classification. Wool has to be derived from the livestock sector.

Martin derived a new sector from an aggregate sector by estimating a gross output value for the new sector using the value of its imports and the ratio of gross output to imports (Martin 1990). In this work, the gross output value of paddy rice, wheat and other grain is obtained by multiplying the gross output and the average prices, both obtained from SSB (*China Statistical Yearbook 1988*). The values of imports and exports are also obtained from the *China Statistical Yearbook 1988*, and converted from US dollars to yuan, accounting for changes in the exchange rate. In forming the three grain sectors from an aggregate grain-cropping sector, assumptions were made that the shares for all intermediate inputs and value-adding factors were the same as those for the total grain-cropping sector, and that shares of intermediate and final use of each grain were the same. The net exports were directly derived from the *China Statistical Yearbook*, however, and adjustment was made to the grain's intermediate use as an input of the husbandry sector and final use for consumption. In China, very little rice and wheat is used as feed for livestock. Since there is no better information, it is assumed that of the total grain input to the husbandry sector, 85 per cent was grains other than wheat and rice, 10 per cent was wheat and 5 per cent was rice. The allocation of grain for consumption was also readjusted in the same way. This second adjustment is consistent with an increasingly high share of rice and wheat in direct consumption in China. Furthermore, this adjustment guarantees the sum of intermediate and final use of each grain to be consistent with that in the aggregate sector.

The wool sector was derived from the livestock sector in the same manner. More adjustments were made to the wool sector as it has some general differences from the aggregate husbandry sector, in the sense of both production inputs and the use of its output. Gross output value and net exports were obtained from the *China Statistical Yearbook*. Following Martin, wool input use was allocated to sectors which used animal husbandry inputs since in most cases these allocations involved very small amounts – the exception being the textile industry, which was assumed to use more than 90 per cent of the total value of wool. Wool investments into capital formation and stock change were set at zero. The input–output coefficients implied by the database of the Martin model were applied here to derive the input use in wool production.

Aggregating sectors

In the 117-sector version, 'other agricultural production' contains wild-plant collecting, wild-animal hunting and small-scale craftwork and industrial production. It is difficult to add it to any of the 22 newly created sectors. Since gross output value was not large (a little more than 6 per cent of total agricultural output value in 1987), it was added to the livestock and livestock products sector.

The other sectors are aggregated to accord with production technology. Care was also taken to distinguish the export-competing and import-substituting sectors, following Clarete and Warr (1992).

Estimating shares of primary factors

By deducting the value of intermediate inputs from gross output, the net revenue for each sector can be obtained. Following Martin (1990), the return to land was assumed to be zero for the non-agricultural sectors. The return to capital was derived by deducting the total wage bill (which was the return to labour) from the net revenue. For eight agricultural sectors, the situation is complicated, owing to self-employment, by the total wage bill containing certain parts of the return to labour, profit, and returns to capital and land. The results of McMillan, Whalley and Zhu (1989) are applied: that is, of the total net revenue, factor shares of 59 per cent for labour, 12 per cent for capital and 29 per cent for land are given.

Table A.2. *Equations of the China model* (a linear system in percentage changes)

I.	Demands for intermediate and primary inputs	
I.1	Demands for intermediate inputs, domestic and imported	2gh

$$x^{(1)}_{(is)j} = z_j - \sigma^{(1)}_{ij}\left(p^{(1)}_{(is)j} - \sum_s S^{(1)}_{(is)j} p^{(1)}_{(is)j}\right) + a^{(1)}_j + a^{(1)}_{ij} + a^{(1)}_{(is)j} - \sigma^{(1)}_{ij}\left(a^{(1)}_{(is)j} - \sum_s S^{(1)}_{(is)j} a^{(1)}_{(is)j}\right)$$

($s = 1$, domestic; 2, imported)

I.2	Industry demands for primary factors	3h

$$x^{(1)}_{vj} = z_j - \sigma^{(1)}_{vj}\left(p^{(1)}_{vj} - \sum_v S^{(1)*}_{vj} p^{(1)}_{vj}\right) + a^{(1)}_j + a^{(1)}_{vj} - \sigma^{(1)}_{vj}\left(a^{(1)}_{vj} - \sum_v S^{(1)*}_{vj} a^{(1)}_{vj}\right)$$

(v = labour, capital and agricultural land)

I.3	Composite rural wage	1

$$p^{(1)}_{1A} = \sum_j L^*_j p^{(1)}_{1j}$$

($j \in R$, rural sectors)

I.4	Composite urban wage	1

$$p^{(1)}_{1N} = \sum_j L^\#_j p^{(1)}_{1j}$$

($j \in U$, urban sectors)

I.5	Rural labour market equilibrium	1

$$l_R = \sum_j L^*_j x^{(1)}_{\text{labour}', j}$$

($j \in R$, rural sectors)

I.6	Urban labour market equilibrium	1

$$l_U = \sum_j L^\#_j x^{(1)}_{\text{labour}', j}$$

($j \in U$, urban sectors)

II.	Supply of commodities	
II.1	Supply of commodity by non-agriculture, undifferentiated by destinations	gN

$$x^{(0)}_{ij} = z_j - \sigma^{(0)*}_{ij}\left(p^{(0)}_i - \sum_l S^{(0)*}_{lj} p^{(0)}_l\right) - a^{(0)}_j - a^{(0)}_{ij} - \sigma^{(0)*}_{ij}\left(a^{(0)}_{ij} - \sum_l S^{(0)*}_{lj} a^{(0)}_{lj}\right)$$

($l \in n$, commodities supplied by sector j; $j \in N$, non-agricultural sectors)

II.2	Supply of commodity by agriculture, undifferentiated by destination	gA

$$x^{(0)}_{ij} = z_j + \sum_l \sigma^{(A)*}_{(il)j} p^{(0)}_i - a^{(0)}_j - a^{(0)}_{ij}$$

($l \in a$, commodities supplied by sector j; $j \in A$, agricultural sectors)

| II.3 | Total supply of agricultural commodities | g |

$$x_i^{(0)} = \sum_j S_{ij}^{(0)} x_{ij}^{(0)}$$

($j \in A$, agricultural sectors; $i \in a$ agricultural products)

| II.4 | Total supply of non-agricultural commodities | g |

$$x_i^{(0)} = \sum_j S_{ij}^{(0)} x_{ij}^{(0)}$$

($j \in N$, non-agricultural sectors; $i \in n$, non-agricultural products)

| II.5 | Transformation in production, domestic and export | $2gh$ |

$$x_{(id)j}^{(0)} = x_{ij}^{(0)} + \sigma_{ij}^{\tau}\left(p_{(id)j}^{(0)} - \sum_d S_{(id)j}^{(0)} p_{(id)j}^{(0)}\right) - a_{(id)j}^{(0)}$$

($d = 1$, domestic; 2, export)

| II.6 | Producers' commodity price | g |

$$p_i^{(0)} = \sum_d S_{(id)j}^{(0)} p_{(id)}^{(0)} + \sum_d S_{(id)j}^{(0)} a_{(id)j}^{(0)}$$

($d = 1$, domestic; 2, export)

III. Household income and consumption

| III.1 | Consumer nominal income | 2 |

$$c_T = \sum_j \sum_v S_{(vj)T}^{(c)} \left(p_{vj}^{(1)} + x_{vj}^{(1)}\right)$$

($T = r$, rural household for which $j \in R$; $T = u$, urban household for which $j \in U$; v = labour, capital and agricultural land)

| III.2 | Household demands for commodities classified by source | $4g$ |

$$x_{(is)T}^{(3)} = x_{iT}^{(3)} - \sigma_{iT}^{(3)}\left(p_{(is)}^{(3)} - \sum_s S_{(is)T}^{(3)} p_{(is)}^{(3)}\right) + a_{iT}^{(3)} + a_{(is)T}^{(3)} - \sigma_{iT}^{(3)}\left(a_{iT}^{(3)} - \sum_s S_{(is)T}^{(3)} a_{(is)T}^{(3)}\right)$$

($s = 1$, domestic; 2, imported; $T = r$, rural household; u, urban household)

| III.3 | Household demands for commodities, undifferentiated by source | $2g$ |

$$x_{iT}^{(3)} = \epsilon_{iT} * c_T + \sum_l \eta_{(il)T} p_l^{(3)} + a_{iT}^{(3)} + \sum_l \eta_{(il)T}\left(a_{iT}^{(3)} + \sum_s S_{(is)T}^{(3)} a_{(is)T}^{(3)}\right)$$

($s = 1$, domestic; 2, imported, $l \in g$)

| III.4 | Total household demand for commodities, differentiated by source | $2g$ |

$$s_{is}^{(3)} = \sum_T S_{iT}^{(3)} x_{(is)T}^{(3)}$$

($T = r$, rural household; u, urban household)

184 Agricultural reform in China

Table A.2. *(contd)*

III.5	General price of each commodity to households	g

$$p_i^{(3)} = \sum_s S_{(is)}^{(3)} p_{(is)}^{(3)} + \sum_s S_{(is)}^{(3)} a_{(is)}^{(3)}$$

($s = 1$, domestic; 2, imported)

IV.	Other final demands	
IV.1	Investment in fixed capital	$2g$

$$x_{(is)}^{(2)} = a_R$$

($s = 1$, domestically produced; 2, imported)

IV.2	Investment in stock	$2g$

$$x_{*(is)}^{(2)} = a_R$$

($s = 1$, domestically produced; 2, imported)

IV.3	Government consumption	$2g$

$$x_{(is)}^{(5)} = a_R$$

($s = 1$, domestically produced; 2, imported)

V.	Foreign trade	
V.1	Export demand from China	g

$$x_i^{(4)} = x_{wi}^{(4)} - \sigma_i^{(4)} \left(p_{(is)}^e - \sum_s S_{(is)}^{(4)} p_{(is)}^e \right)$$

($s = 1$, from China; 2, from the rest of the world)

V.2	World demand for export both from China and the rest of the world	g

$$x_{wi}^{(4)} = \beta_i \sum_s S_{(is)}^{(4)} p_{(is)}^e$$

($s = 1$, from China; 2, from the rest of the world)

V.3	Import supply to China by the rest of the world	g

$$x_i^8 = E_i p_i^m$$

V.4	Imports volume	g

$$x_{i2}^{(6)} = \sum_j C_{(i2)j}^{(1)} x_{(is)j}^{(1)} + C_{(i2)}^{(2)} x_{(is)}^{(2)} + C_{*(i2)}^{(2)} x_{*(is)}^{(2)} + C_{(i2)}^{(3)} x_{(is)}^{(3)} + C_{(i2)}^{(5)} x_{(is)}^{(5)}$$

($s = 2$, imported)

V.5	Foreign currency value of imports	1

$$m = \sum_i \left(p_i^m + x_{(i2)}^{(6)} + x_{(i2)}^{(6)} \right) * M_{(i2)}$$

| V.6 | Foreign currency value of exports | 1 |

$$e = \sum_i \left(p_i^e + x_i^{(4)}\right) * E_{i1}$$

| V.7 | The balance of trade | 1 |

$$100 * DB = E * e - M * m$$

| VI. | Zero pure profits in economic activities | |
| VI.1 | Zero pure profit in production | h |

$$\sum_i^{N(j)} \sum_d S_{(id)j}^{(0)} p_{(id)}^{(0)} = \sum_i \sum_s^g S_{(is)j}^{(1)} p_{(is)j}^{(1)} + \sum_v S_{vj}^{(1)} p_{vj}^{(1)}$$

($N(j)$ the number of goods produced by industry j)

| VI.2 | Zero pure profit for importing | g |

$$p_{(is)j}^{(1)} = p_i^m + t_i + \phi$$

($s = 2$, imported)

| VI.3 | Zero pure profit for exporting | g |

$$p_{(id)j}^{(0)} = p_i^e + v_i + \phi$$

($d = 2$, exported)

| VII. | Market-clearing conditions | |
| VII.1 | Market-clearing in the domestic market, domestically produced | g |

$$x_{(id)j}^{(0)} = \sum_j S_{(is)j}^{(1)\#} x_{(is)j}^{(1)} + S_{(is)}^{(2)\#} x_{(is)}^{(2)} + S_{*(is)}^{(2)\#} x_{*(is)}^{(2)} + S_{(is)}^{(3)\#} x_{(is)}^{(3)} + S_{(is)}^{(5)\#} x_{(is)}^{(5)}$$

($d = 1$, domestic destination; $s = 1$, domestic source)

| VII.2 | Market-clearing of exports | g |

$$x_{(id)j}^{(0)} = x_i^{(4)}$$

($d = 2$, for exporting)

| VII.3 | Supply of agricultural and non-agricultural labour | h |

$$x_{ih}^{(1)} = x_1^{(1)} + \sigma_l^{(1)} \left(p_{1h}^{(1)} - \sum_h S_{1h}^{(1)} p_{1h}^{(1)}\right)$$

($h = R$, agriculture; $h = U$, non-agriculture)

| VII.4 | Market-clearing for agricultural labour | h |

$$x_{ir} = \sum_j L_j^* x_{1j}^{(1)}$$

($j \in R$)

186 Agricultural reform in China

Table A.2. (contd)

VII.5 Market-clearing for non-agricultural labour   h

$$x_{iU}^{(1)} = \sum_j L_j^{\#} x_{1j}^{(1)}$$

$(j \in U)$

VII.6 Capital market-clearing   h

$$x_{2j}^{(1)} = k_j$$

VII.7 Agricultural land market-clearing   h

$$x_{3j}^{(1)} = l_j$$

VIII. GDP and real absorption

VIII.1 Domestic absorption of good i from all sources   g

$$x_i = \sum_i \sum_s \left(\sum_j B_{(is)j}^{(1)} x_{(is)j}^{(1)} + B_{(is)}^{(2)} x_{(is)}^{(2)} + B_{*(is)}^{(2)} x_{*(is)}^{(2)} + B_{(is)}^{(3)} x_{(is)}^{(3)} + B_{(is)}^{(5)} x_{(is)}^{(5)} \right)$$

$(i \in g, j \in h, \text{ and } s = 1, \text{ domestic}, s = 2, \text{ imported})$

VIII.2 Total output   1

$$x_R^{(0)} = \sum_i B_{(i1)j}^{(0)} x_{ij}^{(0)}$$

VIII.3 Real absorption   1

$$a_R = \sum_i A_i x_i$$

VIII.4 Price deflator for GDP   1

$$p^y = \sum_i S_i^{\#} p_i^{(0)}$$

IX. Money market

IX.1 Equilibrium in money market   1

$$m^s = \sigma_{mp} p^y + \sigma_{ma} a_R + \sigma_{mr} r$$

The China model 187

Table A.3. *Variables of the China model (all variables are percentage changes)*

Variable	Number	Description
z_j	h	Industry activity levels
$x^{(1)}_{(is)j}$	$2g$	Demand for inputs (domestic and imported) for current production
$x^{(1)}_{vj}$	$3h$	Demand for primary factors (labour, capital and agricultural land) for current production
$x^{(0)}_{(id)j}$	$2gh$	Supply of good i by industry j (domestic and exporting)
$x^{(0)}_{ij}$	gh	Supply of good i by industry j, undifferentiated by source
$x^{(2)}_{(is)}$	$2g$	Demand for investment in capital stock (domestic and imported)
$x^{(2)}_{*(is)}$	$2g$	Demand for investment in stock (domestic and imported)
$x^{(3)}_{(is)T}$	$4g$	Household demand for goods by type, source and household
$x^{(3)}_{iT}$	$2g$	Household demand for goods by type and household
$x^{(3)}_{is}$	$2g$	Household demand for goods by type and source
$x^{(3)}_i$	g	Household demands for goods, undifferentiated by source
$x^{(4)}_i$	g	Export demand from China by the rest of the world
$x^{(4)}_{wi}$	g	World demand for exports both from China and the rest of the world
x^*_i	g	Imports supply to China by the rest of the world
$x^{(5)}_{(is)}$	$2g$	Government demands for goods by type and source
$x^{(6)}_{i2}$	g	Imports volume
$x^{(1)}_{1h}$	2	Labour in agriculture and non-agriculture ($h = A, N$)
$x^{(1)}_1$	1	Total supply of labour
$x^{(0)}_{(r1)j}$	h	Total outputs by industry
$x^{(0)}_{(r1)}$	1	Total output
x_i	g	Domestic absorption of good i from all sources
$x^{(0)}_R$	1	Total output (GDP)
$p^{(1)}_{(is)j}$	$2g$	Purchasers' prices for produced inputs for current production
$p^{(1)}_{vj}$	$3h$	Purchasers' prices for primary factors for current production
$p^{(0)}_{(id)j}$	$2g$	Prices of outputs (domestic and export)
p^s_i	5	State prices for rice, wheat, other grain, cotton and wool
$p^{(3)}_{(is)}$	$2g$	Consumers' price of good i from source s
$p^{(3)}_i$	g	General price of commodity to household
$p^{(4)}_i$	g	Local currency price of export (including export tax)

188 *Agricultural reform in China*

Table A.3. *(contd)*

Variable	Number	Description
$p_{(i2)}^{(0)}$	g	Local currency prices of imports (including tariff)
$p_{(is)}^{e}$	$2g$	Foreign currency prices of exports from China and the rest of the world
p_i^m	g	Foreign currency prices of imports to China
$p_i^{(0)}$	gh	Prices of output
p^y	1	Price deflator for GDP
$p_{1h}^{(1)}$	2	Aggregate wage rates in agriculture and non-agriculture ($h = A, N$)
$a_j^{(1)}$	h	Neutral input-augmenting technical change
$a_{ij}^{(1)}$	gh	Input-i-augmenting technical change
$a_{(is)j}^{(1)}$	$2gh$	Input-(is)-augmenting technical change
$a_j^{(0)}$	h	Neutral output-augmenting technical change
$a_{ij}^{(0)}$	gh	Output-i-augmenting technical change
R	1	Growth rate of real absorption
$a_i^{(3)}$	g	Commodity-i-augmenting change in household preference
$a_{(is)}^{(3)}$	$2g$	Commodity-(is)-augmenting change in household preference
$a_{1h}^{(1)}$	2	Factor causing-h (A,N)-augmenting change in labour allocation
$a_{vj}^{(1)}$	$3h$	Factor-v-augmenting technical change
$a_{(id)j}^{(0)}$	$2gh$	Destination-d-augmenting technical change in transformation
DB	1	The balance of trade (this is the variable in *value* rather than in *percentage change*)
k_j	h	Fixed capital stock in industry j
l_j	h	Fixed land area in industry j
c	1	Disposable income of urban and rural consumers
m	1	Foreign currency value of imports
e	1	Foreign currency value of exports
t_i	g	Tariff on imports
ϕ	1	Exchange rate
v_i	g	Export tax
m^s	1	Money supply
r	1	Interest rate

Table A.4. *Coefficients and parameters of the China model*

Equation	Coefficients or parameters	Description
I.1	$\sigma_{ij}^{(1)}$	Elasticity of substitution between domestic and foreign sources of good i for use as a current input in the production of industry j.
	$S_{(is)j}^{(1)}$	Share of purchaser's price value of good i from source s ($s = 1$ for domestic, $s = 2$ for imports) in industry j's total purchases of good i for use as a current input to production.
I.2	$\sigma_{vj}^{(1)}$	CRESH parameter reflecting the degree of substitutability between primary factor v ($v = 1$, labour; $v = 2$, capital; $v = 3$, agricultural land) and other primary factors in the production process of industry j.
	$S_{vj}^{(1)*}$	Modified share of primary factor v in the total cost of primary factors used in industry j, defined as a function of the unmodified shares and the CRESH substitution parameters.
I.3, I.5	L_j^*	Share of labour in each rural industry ($j \in R$).
I.4, I.6	$L_j^\#$	Share of labour in each urban industry ($j \in U$).
II.1	$\sigma_{ij}^{(0)*}$	CRETH parameter reflecting the ease of transformability between commodity i and other commodities in the output bundle of industry j.
	$S_{ij}^{(0)*}$	Modified share of commodity i in total revenue of industry j defined as a function of unmodified share and the CRETH transformation parameter: $$S_{ij}^{(0)*} = \sigma_{ij}^{(0)*} S_{ij}^{(0)} \bigg/ \sum_{i}^{N(j)} \sigma_{ij}^{(0)*} S_{ij}^{(0)}$$
II.2	$\sigma_{(il)j}^{(A)*}$	Price elasticity of supply of agricultural product i by agricultural industry j with respect to price of agricultural product l.
II.3, II.4	$S_{ij}^{(0)}$	Share of industry j in total output of i.
II.5	σ_{ij}^T	Elasticity of substitution between domestic and export production of good i.
	$S_{(id)j}^{(0)}$	Revenue share of commodity i produced for destination d ($d = 1$ for domestic market, $d = 2$ for export) in total revenue derived from the production of commodity i.
III.1	$S_{vj}^{(c)}$	Household income share of return from factor v of industry j.
III.2	$\sigma_{iT}^{(3)}$	Elasticity of substitution between domestic and foreign sources of good i for use by household T.
	$S_{(is)T}^{(3)}$	Share of the purchaser's value of good i from source s in the total purchases of good i by household T.

Table A.4. (contd)

Equation	Coefficients or parameters	Description
III.3	ϵ_{iT}	Household expenditure elasticity of demand for good i from either source.
	$\eta_{(il)T}$	Household elasticity of demand for good i in general with respect to changes in the general household purchaser's price for good l.
III.4	$S^{(3)}_{iT}$	Household T's share in total household demand for i.
III.5	$S^{(3)}_{(is)}$	Share of good i from source s in total household demand for i.
V.1	$\sigma^{(4)}_i$	Elasticity of substitution between Chinese and rest of the world products in world market for commodity i.
	$S^{(4)}_{(is)}$	Share of China and the rest of the world in world export market for commodity i.
V.2	β_i	Global elasticity of excess demand for commodity i.
V.3	E_i	Elasticity of import supply for commodity i to China.
V.4	$C^{(1)}_{(i2)j}$	Share of imports of good i which is absorbed by industry j for purpose of intermediate input.
	$C^{(2)}_{(i2)}$	Share of imports of good i absorbed by fixed capital investment.
	$C^{*(2)}_{(i2)}$	Share of imports of good i absorbed by stock investment.
	$C^{(3)}_{(i2)c}$	Share of imports of good i for the use of households c.
	$C^{(5)}_{(i2)}$	Share of imports of good i for the use of government consumption.
V.5	M_{i2}	Share in foreign currency cost of total imports accounted for by imports of commodity i.
V.6	E_{i1}	Share in total export earnings accounted for by exports of commodity i.
V.7	M	Aggregate foreign currency value of imports.
	E	Aggregate foreign currency value of exports.
VI.1	$S^{(0)}_{(id)j}$	Revenue share of production of commodity i for destination d in total revenue of production of commodity i by industry j.
	$S^{(1)}_{(is)j}$	Cost share of intermediate input i from source s in total cost of production by industry j.
	$S^{(1)}_{vj}$	Cost share of primary factor v in total cost of production in industry j.
VII.1	$S^{(1)\#}_{(is)j}$	(For $s = 1$) Share of commodity i from domestic source used by industry j as intermediate input in total amount of domestic production for domestic market.

	$S^{(2)\#}_{(is)}$	(For $s = 1$) Share of commodity i from domestic source used for fixed capital investment in total amount of domestic production for domestic market.
	$S^{(2)\#}_{*(is)}$	(For $s = 1$) Share of commodity i from domestic source used for stock investment in total amount of domestic production for domestic market.
	$S^{(3)\#}_{(is)}$	(For $s = 1$) Share of commodity i from domestic source used for consumption by households c in total amount of domestic production for domestic market.
	$S^{(5)\#}_{(is)}$	(For $s = 1$) Share of commodity i from domestic source used for government consumption in total amount of domestic production for domestic market.
VIII.1	$B^{(1)}_{(is)j}$	Share of intermediate input i from source s used by industry j in total absorption of commodity i.
	$B^{(2)}_{(is)}$	Share of fixed capital investment i in total absorption of commodity i.
	$B^{(2)}_{*(is)}$	Share of stock investment i in total absorption of good i.
	$B^{(3)}_{(is)}$	Share of household consumption in total absorption of commodity i.
	$B^{(5)}_{(is)}$	Share of government consumption of good i in total absorption of this commodity.
VIII.2	$B^{(0)}_{(i1)}$	Share of output i in total output of the economy.
VIII.3	A_i	Share of good i in real absorption.
VIII.4	$S^{\#}_i$	Revenue share of good i in total GDP.
IX.1	σ_{mp}	Price elasticity of demand for money.
	σ_{ma}	Income elasticity of demand for money.
	σ_{mr}	Interest elasticity of demand for money.

Notes

1. The CES (constant elasticity of substitution) production function was developed by Arrow et al. (1961).
2. CRESH (constant ratio of elasticities of substitution, homothetic) is a generalisation of CES, which determines that the ratio of the elasticity between inputs h and j to the elasticity between h and k must be equal to the ratio of the elasticities between i and j, and i and k.
3. CRETH represents a transformation process with homothetic and constant ratios of elasticities of transformation.
4. Labour is assumed to be perfectly mobile within rural or urban areas.

References

Abbott, P. C., 1979, 'The Role of Government Interference in International Commodity Trade Models', *American Journal of Agricultural Economics*, 61: 22–31.

Abel, M. E., 1978, 'Hard Policy Choices in Improving Incentives for Farmers', in T. W. Schultz (ed.), *Distortions of Agricultural Incentives*, Bloomington: Indiana University Press.

Adulavidhaya, Kamphol, Yoshimi Kuroda, Lawrence Lau and Pan Yotopoulos, 1984, 'The Comparative Statics of Behaviour of Agricultural Households in Thailand', *Singapore Economic Review*, 29: 67–96.

Adulavidhaya, Kamphol, Yoshimi Kuroda, Lawrence Lau, Pichit Lerttamrab and Pan Yotopoulos, 1979, 'A Microeconomic Analysis of Agriculture in Thailand', *Food Research Institute Studies*, 17: 79–86.

Ahn, Choong Yong, Inderjit Singh and Lyn Squire, 1981, 'A Model of an Agricultural Household in a Multi-crop Economy: The Case of Korea', *Review of Economics and Statistics*, 63: 520–5.

Albacea, Zita V. and Peter Warr, 1991, 'Agricultural Parameter Estimates for the APEX CGE Model of the Philippines Economy', paper presented to the *Workshop on General Equilibrium Modelling for Agricultural Policy Analysis*, Pattaya, Thailand, 21–25 May 1991.

Alston, J. M., C. A. Carter, R. Green and D. Pick, 1990, 'Whither Armington Trade Models?', *American Journal of Agricultural Economics*, 72: 455–67.

Amsden, A. M., 1989, *Asia's Next Giant*, New York: Oxford University Press.

Anderson, K., 1989, 'Rent-Seeking and Price Distorting Policies in Rich and Poor Countries', Seminar Paper 428, Institute for International Economic Studies, University of Stockholm.

1990a, *Changing Comparative Advantage in China: Effects on Food, Feed and Fibre Markets*, Paris: OECD.

1990b, 'Urban Household Subsidies and Rural Out-migration: The Case of China', *Communist Economies*, 2: 525–31.

Anderson, K. and Y. Hayami, 1986, *The Political Economy of Agricultural Protection: East Asia in International Perspective*, Sydney: Allen & Unwin.

Anderson, K. and R. Tyers, 1987, 'Economic Growth and Market Liberalization in China: Implications for Agricultural Trade', *The Developing Economies*, 25: 124–51.

Anderson, K. and P. Warr, 1987, 'General Equilibrium Effects of Agricultural

Price Distortions: A Simple Model for Korea', *Food Research Institute Studies*, 20: 245–63.

Annual Analytical Group on Rural Economy, 1995, *The Annual Report on China's Rural Economic Development in 1994 and an Analysis of the Development Trend for 1995*, Beijing: China Social Sciences Press.

Armington, P., 1969, 'A Theory of Demand for Products Distinguished by Place of Production', *IMF Staff Papers*, 16: 179–201.

Arrow, K. J., H. B. Chenery, B. S. Minhas and R. M. Solow, 1961, 'Capital–Labour Substitution and Economic Efficiency', *Review of Economics and Statistics*, 63: 225–47.

Ash, R., 1988, 'The Evolution of Agricultural Policy', *China Quarterly*, 116: 529–55.

Ash, T. G., 1989, *The Uses of Adversity*, Cambridge: Granta Books.

Ashton, Basil, Kenneth Hill, Allen Piazza and Robin Zeitz, 1984, 'Famine in China, 1958–61', *Population and Development Review*, 10: 613–45.

Asia Pacific Economics Group, 1994, *Asia Pacific Profiles, 1994*, National Centre for Development Studies, The Australian National University, Canberra.

1996, *Asia Pacific Profiles, 1996*, National Centre for Development Studies, The Australian National University, Canberra.

Åslund, A., 1985, *Private Enterprise in Eastern Europe: The Non-agricultural Private Sector in Poland and the GDR, 1945–83*, London: Macmillan.

1991, 'Gorbachev, Perestroyka, and Economic Crisis', *Problems of Communism*, January-April: 77–89.

Australian Bureau of Agricultural Research Economics, 1992, *Commodity Statistical Bulletin*, Canberra: ABARE.

Ball, V. E., 1988, 'Modeling Supply Response in a Multiproduct Framework', *American Journal of Agricultural Economics*, 70: 813–25.

Banfield, E. C., 1958, *The Moral Basis of a Backward Society*, Glencoe: Free Press.

Barclay, G. et al., 1976, 'A Reassessment of the Demography of Traditional Rural China', *Population Index*, 42: 624–5.

Barnum, Howard, and Lyn Squire, 1978, 'Technology and Relative Economics Efficiency', *Oxford Economics Papers*, 30: 181–9.

1979a, 'An Econometric Application of the Theory of the Farm Household', *Journal of Development Economics*, 6: 79–102.

1979b, *A Model of an Agricultural Household*, Washington, D.C.: World Bank.

1980, 'Predicting Agricultural Output Response', *Oxford Economic Papers*, 32: 284–95.

Baruch, B., 1989. 'China's Environmental Prospects', *Asian Survey*, 29: 669–86.

Basu, K. et al., 1987, 'The Growth and Decay of Custom: The Role of the New Institutional Economics in Economic History', *Explorations in Economic History*, 24: 1–21.

Becker, G. S., 1983, 'A Theory of Competition Among Pressure Groups for Political Influence', *Quarterly Journal of Economics*, 98: 371–400.

Beghin, J. C., 1990, 'A Game-Theoretic Model of Endogenous Public Policies', *American Journal of Agricultural Economics*, 72: 559–73.

Beghin, J. C. and L. S. Karp, 1991, 'Estimation of Price Policies in Senegal: An

Empirical Test of Cooperative Game Theory', *Journal of Development Economics*, 35: 49–67.
Berliner, J. S., 1978, *The Innovation Decision in Soviet Industry*, Cambridge, Mass.: MIT Press.
Bhagwati, J. N. and T. N. Srinivasan, 1975, *Foreign Trade Regimes and Economic Development: India*, New York: Columbia University Press.
Bianco, L., 1971, *Origins of the Chinese Revolution, 1915–1949*, Stanford University Press.
Bird, I. L., 1983,*The Golden Bird*, London: Century Books.
Biswas, A. K. *et al.* (eds.), 1983, *Long-Distance Water Transfer: A Chinese Case Study and International Experience*, Dublin: Tycooly.
Blanchard, O. J., 1990, 'Why Does Money Affect Output? A Survey', in B. M. Freedman and F. H. Hahn (eds.), *Handbook of Monetary Economics*, vol. II, Amsterdam: Elsevier Science Publishers B.V.
Blanchard, O., R. Dornbusch, P. Krugman, R. Layard and L. Summers, 1991, *Reform in Eastern Europe*, Cambridge, Mass.: MIT Press.
Bland, J. O. P., 1912, *Recent Events and Present Policies*, Philadelphia: J. B. Lippincott Co.
Blejer, M. I. and G. Szapary, 1990, 'The Evolving Role of Tax Policy in China', *Journal of Comparative Economics*, 14: 452–72.
Blejer, M., D. Burton, S. Dunaway and G. Szapary, 1991, 'China: Economic Reform and Macroeconomic Management', *IMF Occasional Papers* 176.
Bordo, M. D., 1980, 'The Effects of Monetary Change on Relative Commodity Prices and the Role of Long-Term Contracts', *Journal of Political Economy*, 88: 1088–109.
Borrie, W. D., 1970, *The Growth and Control of World Population*, London: Weidenfeld and Nicolson.
Brandão, A. and W. Martin, 1993, 'Implications of Agricultural Trade Liberalisation for the Developing Countries', *Agricultural Economics*, 8: 313–43.
Brandt, L. and B. Sands, 1990, 'Beyond Malthus and Ricardo: Economic Growth, Land Concentration, and Income Distribution in Early Twentieth-Century Rural China', *Journal of Economic History*, 50: 807–27.
Brock, W. A. and S. P. Magee, 1978, 'The Economics of Pork-Barrel Politics', Working Paper 78–80, Bureau of Business Research, University of Texas at Austin.
1979, 'Tariff Formation in a Democracy', in J. Black and B. Hindley (eds.), *Current Issues in International Commercial Policy and Economic Diplomacy*, London: Macmillan.
Buchanan, J. M. and G. Tullock, 1962, *The Calculus of Consent*, Ann Arbor: University of Michigan Press.
Byrd, W. A., 1987a. 'The Impact of the Two-Tier Plan/Market System in Chinese Industry', *Journal of Comparative Economics*, 11: 295–308.
1987b, 'The Market Mechanism and Economic Reform in Chinese Industry', Ph.D. dissertation, Harvard University, Cambridge, Mass.
1989, 'Plan and Market in Chinese Economy: A Simple General Equilibrium Model', *Journal of Comparative Economics*, 13: 177–204.

Byrd, W. A. and Q. S. Lin, 1990, *China's Rural Industry*, Oxford University Press.
Cai, Fang, 1993, 'China's Agricultural Comparative Advantage and Internationalisation', paper presented to the international workshop *China's Rural Reform and Development in the 1990s*, Beijing.
Camm, F., 1976, 'The Political Economy of Agricultural Marketing Orders: Some Empirical Evidence', Department of Economics, University of Chicago, mimeo.
Carter, C. and F. Zhong, 1988, *China's Grain Production and Trade*, Boulder, Colo.: Westview Press.
Central Committee of the Communist Party of China, 1979a, 'Communiqué of the Fourth Plenary Session of the 11th Central Committee of the CPC', *Beijing Review*, no. 40 (5 October 1979).
—— 1979b, 'Decisions on Some Questions Concerning the Acceleration of Agricultural Development (Draft)', *Beijing Review*, no. 11 (16 March 1979).
—— 1983, 'Questions of the Current Policies of Rural Economy', Document no. 1, Research Centre for Rural Development, January 1983.
—— 1984a, 'A Circular on the Rural Work in 1984 . . .', Document no. 1, Research Centre for Rural Development, January 1984.
—— 1984b, 'Decision on Reform of the Economic Structure', *Xinhua*, 21 October.
—— 1985, 'On Ten Points of Policy Concerning Invigorating the Rural Economy . . .', Document no. 1, Research Centre for Rural Development, January 1985.
Chai, J. C. H., 1991, 'Agricultural Development in China, 1979–1989', Discussion Paper in Economics 70, Department of Economics, University of Queensland.
Chan, A. and J. Unger, 1990, 'Voices from the Protest Movement, Chongqing, Sichuan', *Australian Journal of Chinese Affairs*, 24 (July), 1–21.
Chan, T., 1989, 'China's Foreign Exchange and Trade Controls: What Next?', paper presented to Centre for Chinese Political Economy seminar, Macquarie University, Sydney, 3 August.
'Changjiang Sanxia Gongcheng Touzi Jisuan, Zonghe Jingji Pingjia Zhuanti Lunzheng Baogao', 1992. [Demonstration reports on the topics of estimated investments and comprehensive economic evaluation of the Yangtze Three Gorges project, synopses of 1988 reports], *Zhongguo Shuili* [*China's Water Conservancy*], (2): 22–9.
Chayanov, A. V., 1925, 'Peasants Farm Organization', Moscow: Cooperative Publishing House. Translated in A. V. Chayanov, *The Theory of Peasant Economy*, ed. D. Thorner, B. Kerblay and R. E. F. Smith. Homewood, Ill.: Richard Irwin (1966).
Chen, Deqiu, 1989, *New Stage of Export-oriented Economy in Xiamen SEZ*, Fujian: Committee of the Economic and Trade of the Xiamen Municipality.
Chen, Dong and Zhili Niu (eds.), 1990, *Zhongguo Jingji Tongji Shiyong Daquan* [*Practical Manual on Economic Statistics of China*], Beijing: China People's University Press.
Chen, J., 1992, 'Oil and gas prospecting and development in China', *Zhongguo Nengyuan* [*Energy in China*] (2): 6–8.
Chen, Jiyuan, and Yimin Deng, 1993, 'On Influences of Resumption of the GATT

Membership on Grain Production and Policy Response', *China's Rural Economy*, 9: 48–51.

Chen, K., H. Wang, Y. Zheng, G. Jefferson and T. Rawski, 1988a, 'Productivity Change in Chinese Industry: 1953–85', *Journal of Comparative Economics*, 12: 570–91.

1988b, 'New Estimates of Fixed Investment and Capital Stock for Chinese Industry', *China Quarterly*, no. 114 (June): 243–66.

Chen, M., 1990, 'Meet the Challenge, Protect the Environment', *Huanjing Baohu* [*Environmental Protection*], (1): 2–7.

Chen, N. and S. Lu, 1991. 'Dui 90-niandai Xiangzhen Qiye Fazhandi Chanwang' [Prospects of the Development of Rural and Township Enterprises into the Nineties], *Zhongguo Gongye Jingji Yanjiu* [*Research on China's Industrial Economy*],(6): 61–4.

Chen, Rengxing, 1983, 'Shilun Wo Guo Xian Jieduan De Geti Jingji' [A Tentative Discussion of the Individual Economy in China's Current Stage], *Xinhua Wenzhai* [*New China Digest*], 4: 60–1.

Chen, Xiangqing, Bojun Li and Huafei Xu, 1989, 'Siying Qiye Fazhan Xianzhuang Yu Mianlin De Wenti' [Current Conditions and Problems in the Development of Private Enterprises], *Zhongguo Nongcun Jingji* [*China's Rural Economy*], Chinese Township Enterprises Yearbook, 1989, no. 2: 24–31.

Chen, Yun, 1984, *Selected Works 1949–1956*, Beijing: The People's Press.

Cheng, E., 1991a, 'Power to the Centre', *Far Eastern Economic Review*, 24 January.

1991b, 'Credit Needs Fuel Inflation', *Far Eastern Economic Review*, 8 August.

Cheng, Guoqiang, 1993, 'Nonye Baofu Yu Jinji Fazhan' [Agricultural Protection and Economic Development], *Jingji Yanjiu* [Economic Research], 4: 27–34.

Cheng, X., 1991. 'Woguo Ziyuan Xiquexing yu Ziyuan Chanyedi Fazhan Xuanze (The Scarcity of Natural Resources of Our Country and the Selection of Productive Development of Resources), *Jingji Yanjiu* [*Economic Research*], 9: 67–71.

China Environment News. Monthly edited by the State Environmental Protection Agency, Beijing.

Chinn, D. L., 1980, 'Cooperative Farming in North China', *Quarterly Journal of Economics*. 94: 279–97.

Chow, G., 1987, 'Money and Price Level Determination in China', *Journal of Comparative Economics*, 11: 319–33.

Christensen, L. R., D. W. Jorgenson and L. J. Lau, 1971, 'Conjugate Duality and the Transcendental Logarithmic Production Function', *Econometrica*, 39: 255–6.

1973, 'Transcendental Logarithmic Production Frontiers', *Review of Economics and Statistics*, 55: 28–45.

Chu, Kim Yu, and Kwan Yiu Wong, 1985, 'Modernization and the Lessons of the Special Economic Zones', in Kim Yu Chu and Kwan Yiu Wong (eds.), *Modernization in China: The Case of the Shenzhen Special Economic Zone*, Hong Kong: Oxford University Press.

Chui, Xiaoli, 1988, 'China's State Procurement Policy and Industrial Accumulation', Development Research Report [*Fazhan Yanjiu Baogao*], no. 5, Beijing:

The Development Institute, Research Centre for Rural Development of the State Council, Beijing.
Clarete, R. I. and P. D. Warr, 1992, *The Theoretical Structure of the APEX Model of the Philippine Economy*, Canberra: Australian Centre for International Agricultural Research.
Coates, A., 1955, *Invitation to an Eastern Feast*, New York: Harper and Brothers.
1975, *Myself a Mandarin*, Hong Kong: Heinemann Educational Books.
Cohen, B., 1991, 'Freedom and the Chain Reaction', *The Weekend Australian*, 6 April.
Collins, R., 1986, *Weberian Sociological Theory*, Cambridge University Press.
Corden, W. M., 1974, 'The Theory of International Trade', in J. H. Dunning (ed.), *Economic Analysis and the Multinational Enterprise*, London: George Allen & Unwin.
1985, *Protection, Growth and Trade: Essays in International Economics*, Oxford: Basil Blackwell.
Cowitt, P. P. (ed.), 1986, *World Currency Yearbook 1985*, Brooklyn: International Currency Analysis Inc.
Cramer, G., E. Wailes and S. Shui, 1993, 'Impacts of Liberalizing Trade in the World Rice Market', *American Journal of Agricultural Economics*, 75: 219–26.
CRGRDI (Comprehensive Research Group, Rural Development Institute), 1987, 'Peasants, Market and Institutional Innovation', *Economic Research* [Beijing] (1): 1–32.
de Janvry, A. and K. Subbarao, 1984, 'Agricultural Price Policy and Income Distribution in India', Working Paper 274, Department of Agricultural and Resource Economics, University of California at Berkeley.
de Melo, J. and S. Robinson, 1981, 'Product Differentiation and the Treatment of Foreign Trade in Computable General Equilibrium Models of Small Economies', *Journal of International Economics*, 27: 47–67.
Decaluwe, B. and A. Martens, 1988, 'CGE Modelling and Developing Economies: A Concise Empirical Survey of 73 Applications to 26 Countries', *Journal of Policy Modelling*, 10: 529–68.
Delfs, R., 1991, 'Saying No to Peking', *Far Eastern Economic Review*, 4 April.
Dervis, K., J. de Melo and S. Robinson, 1981, 'A General Equilibrium Analysis of Foreign Exchange Shortages in a Developing Country', *Economic Journal*, 91: 891–906.
1982, *General Equilibrium Models for Development Policy*, Cambridge University Press.
Desai, P. and J. Bhagwati, 1981, 'Three Alternative Concepts of Foreign Exchange Difficulties in Centrally Planned Economies', in J. Bhagwati (ed.), *International Trade: Selected Readings*, Cambridge, Mass.: MIT Press.
Deyo, F. C. (ed.), 1987, *The Political Economy of the New Asian Industrialism*, Ithaca: Cornell University Press.
Diewert, W. and T. Wales, 1987, 'Flexible Functional Forms and Global Curvature Conditions', *Econometrica*, 55: 43–68.
Dixon, P. B., B. R. Parmenter, J. Sutton and D. P. Vincent, 1982, *ORANI: A Multisectoral Model of the Australian Economy*, Amsterdam: North-Holland.

Dong, Fureng, 1982, 'Chinese Economy in the Process of Great Transformation', in G. C. Wang (ed.) *Economic Reform in the PRC*, Boulder, Colo.: Westview Press.
Dornbusch, R., 1974, 'Tariffs and Nontraded Goods', *Journal of International Economics*, 4: 177–85.
—— 1980, *Open Economy Macroeconomics*, New York: Basic Books.
Dowrick, S., 1992, 'Technological Catch Up and Diverging Incomes: Patterns of Economic Growth 1960–88', *Economic Journal*, 102: 600–10.
Drysdale, P., 1988, *International Economic Pluralism: Economic Policy in East Asia and the Pacific*, Sydney: Allen & Unwin.
Drysdale, P. and A. Elek, 1992, 'China and the International Trading System', seminar paper presented at the Australia–Japan Research Centre, The Australian National University, 13 April.
Drysdale, P. and R. Garnaut, 1993, 'The Pacific: An Application of a General Theory of Economic Integration', in C. F. Bergsten and M. Norland, (eds.), *Pacific Dynamism and the International Economic System*, Washington, D.C.: Institute for International Economics.
Drysdale, P. and Y. Huang, 1996, 'Growth, Energy and the Environment: New Challenges for the Asia Pacific Economy', *Asian-Pacific Economic Literature*, 9(2): 1–12.
Drysdale, P. and L. Song, 1994, 'China's Trade Policy Agenda in the 90s', paper presented to workshop on *China and East Asian Trade Policy*, The Australian National University, Canberra, 1–2 September.
Du, Rensheng, 1992, 'The Rural Reform Objective: Establishing the Market Economy under the Socialism System', *Chinese Rural Economy*, 12: 3–8.
Du, Z., 1991, 'Qianyi Xiangzhen Meikuang Jinhou Shiniandi Fazhan Silu [On the Development of Rural and Township-owned Coal Mines in the Coming Decade]', *Zhongguo Nengyuan* [*Energy in China*], (12): 17–19.
Easterly, W. and S. Fischer, 1987, 'The Soviet Economic Decline: Historical and Republican Data', Policy Research Working Paper, World Bank, Washington D.C.
EBCCS (Editorial Board for Contemporary China Series), 1988, *Grain Work in Contemporary China*, Beijing: China Social Sciences Press.
Economics Research Institute, 1987, *Reports on the Organisation and Growth of China's Xiangzhen Enterprises*, Economic Research Materials, 7, Beijing: Chinese Academy of Social Sciences.
Eden, R. et al., 1981, *Energy Economics: Growth, Resources and Policies*, Cambridge University Press.
Ellis, Frank, 1988, *Peasant Economics: Farm Households and Agrarian Development*, Cambridge University Press.
—— 1992, *Agricultural Policies in Developing Countries*, Cambridge University Press.
Fan, Q. and P. Nolan (eds.), 1994, *China's Economic Reforms: Costs and Benefits of Incrementalism*, New York: St Martin's Press.
Fan, S., 1991, 'Effects of Technological Change and Institutional Reform on Production Growth in Chinese Agriculture', *American Journal of Agricultural Economics*, 73: 266–75.
Feltenstein, A. and Z. Farhadian, 1987, 'Fiscal Policy, Monetary Targets, and Price

Level in a Centrally Planned Economy: An Application to the Case of China', *Journal of Money, Credit, and Banking*, 19(2): 137–56.

Feltenstein, A., D. Lebow and S. Wijnbergen, 1990, 'Savings, Commodity Market Rationing, and the Real Rate of Interest in China', *Journal of Money, Credit, and Banking*, 22: 235–52.

Feng, L., 1992, 'Review of China's Steel Demand', in P. Drysdale (ed.), *The East Asia Steel Industry*, Economics Division Working Paper EA92/6, Research School of Pacific and Asian Studies, The Australian National University, Canberra.

——— 1993, 'Old and New Evidences of Steel and Economic Development: Implications for China', paper presented to the Annual Conference of the Chinese Economic Association, The Australian National University, Canberra, 30 November–1 December.

——— 1994, 'Changing Comparative Advantage and the Restructuring of the International Steel Industry', Ph.D. dissertation, The Australian National University, Canberra.

Feuerwerker, A., 1970, *China's Early Industrialization: Sheng Hsuan-Huai (1844–1916) and Mandarin Enterprise*, New York: Atheneum.

Field, R. M., 1988, 'Trends in the Value of Agricultural Output, 1978–86', *China Quarterly*, 116: 556–91.

Findlay, C., 1988, 'Developments in China's Open Door Policy and Integration with the World Economy: Implications for Further Reform', paper presented at Asian Studies Association of Australia (ASAA) Bicentennial Conference, Canberra, February.

——— (ed.), 1992, *Challenges of Economic Reform and Industrial Growth: China's Wool War*, Sydney: Allen & Unwin.

Findlay, C. and A. Watson, 1989, 'Risk and Efficiency: Contracting in the Chinese Countryside', Chinese Economy Research Unit, University of Adelaide.

——— 1990, 'China and Australian Wool', *Pacific Economic Papers* 180, Canberra: Australia–Japan Research Centre, The Australian National University.

——— 1992, 'The "Wool War" in China', in Findlay (ed.).

Findlay, C., A. Watson and W. Martin, 1992, 'Policy Reform, Chinese Agriculture and the Implications for China's Trade', University of Adelaide, mimeo.

Findlay, R., 1988, 'Trade Development and the State', in G. Ranis and T. P. Schultz (eds.), *The State of Development Economics*, Oxford: Basil Blackwell.

Fisk, E. K. and K. T. Shand, 1969, 'The Early Stage of Development in Primitive Economy: The Evolution from Subsistence to Trade and Specializations', in C. F. Wharton (ed.), *Subsistence Agriculture and Economic Development*, Chicago: Aldine.

Fitzgerald, C. P., 1985, *Why China? Recollections of China, 1923–1950*, Melbourne University Press.

Food and Agricultural Organization of the United Nations, *Production Yearbook*, Rome: FAO, various issues.

——— 1989, *Aspects of the World Feed-Livestock Economy*, Economic and Social Development Paper 80, Rome: FAO.

Foreign Broadcast Information Service, 1992, 'Regulations on Transforming the Management Mechanisms of State-Owned Industrial Enterprises', *Daily Report: China*, 28 July, pp. 27–37.
Forsyth, P., 1993, 'Trade Patterns and Labour Demand: International Influences on Wages and Unemployment in Australia', paper presented to conference on *Unemployment: Causes, Costs and Solutions*, The Australian National University and Department of Employment, Education and Training, Canberra, 16–17 February.
Frankel, J. A., 1986, 'Expectations and Commodity Price Dynamics: the Overshooting Model', *American Journal of Agricultural Economics*, 67: 344–8.
Fridley, D., 1991, 'China's Energy Outlook', in US Congress Joint Economic Committee, *China's Economic Dilemmas of the 1990s: The Problems of Reforms, Modernization, and Interdependence*, Armonk, N.Y.: M. E. Sharpe.
Friedman, J. W., 1986, *Game Theory with Application to Economics*, Oxford University Press.
Fry, M., 1988, *Money, Interest and Banking in Economic Development*, Baltimore: Johns Hopkins University Press.
Fuss, M., 1977, 'The Demand for Energy in Canadian Manufacturing: An Example of the Estimation of Production Structure with Many Inputs', *Journal of Econometrics*, 5: 89–116.
Gale, D., 1982, *Money in Equilibrium*, Welwyn: Nisbet.
1983, *Money in Disequilibrium*, Welwyn: Nisbet.
Gao, Xiaohang, 1993, 'China's Foreign Exchange Regime and Its Impact on Export and Growth', Ph.D. dissertation, National Centre for Development Studies, The Australian National University, Canberra.
Gao, Xiaomeng and Guoqing Song (eds.), 1987, *Research on China's Grain Issues*, Beijing: Economic Management Press.
Gao, Xiaomeng and Ning Xian, 1992, *China's Agricultural Price Policy Analysis* [*Zhongguo Nongye Jiange Zhence Fenxi*], Hangzhou: Zhejiang People's Press.
Garnaut, R., 1989, *Australia and the Northeast Asia Ascendancy*, Canberra: Australian Government Publishing Service.
1992, 'China's Reforms in International Context', in Garnaut and Liu (eds.).
Garnaut, R. and K. Anderson, 1980, 'ASEAN Export Specialisation and the Evolution of Comparative Advantage in the Western Pacific Region', in R. Garnaut (ed.), *ASEAN in a Changing Pacific and World Economy*, Canberra: The Australian National University Press.
Garnaut, R. and Yiping Huang, 1994, 'Grain in Developing Asia: A Comparative Review', paper presented to the workshop *Grain in Developing Asia*, The Australian National University, 28 February.
1995, *China's Trade Reform and Transition: Challenges and Opportunities for OECD Countries*, Paris: OECD.
Garnaut, R. and Guonan Ma, 1992a, *China's Grain Economy*, Canberra: Australian Government Publishing Service.
1992b, *Grain in China*, Canberra: Australian Government Publishing Service.
1993a, 'How Rich Is China: Evidence from the Food Economy', *Australian Journal of Chinese Affairs*, (30): 121–46.

1993b, 'Economic Growth and Stability in China', *Journal of Asian Economics*, 4: 5–24.
Garnaut, R., Fang Cai and Yiping Huang, 1996, 'A Turning Point in China's Agricultural Development', in Garnaut, Guo and Ma (eds.).
Garnaut, R. and Guoguang Liu (eds.), 1992, *Economic Reform and Internationalisation: China and the Pacific Region*, Sydney: Allen & Unwin.
Garnaut, R., S. Guo and G. Ma (eds.), 1996, *The Third Revolution in the Chinese Countryside*, Cambridge University Press.
Garnaut, R., Guonan Ma and Yiping Huang, forthcoming, 'How Rich Is China', in R. Garnaut (ed.), *Growth Without Miracles: The Chinese Economy in the Era of Reform*.
Garton-Ash, T., 1989, *The Uses of Adversity*, Cambridge: Granta Books.
Goldin, I. and E. Knudsen (eds.), 1990, *Agricultural Trade Liberalisation: Implications for the Developing Countries*, Paris/Washington, D.C.: OECD/World Bank.
Goulder, L. H. and B. Eichengreen, 1992, 'Trade Liberalization in General Equilibrium and Inter-Industry Effects', *Canadian Journal of Economics*, 25: 253–80.
Griliches, Z., 1963, 'The Source of Measured Productivity Growth: United States Agriculture, 1940–60', *Journal of Political Economy*, 71: 331–46.
Grossman, G., 1990, 'Sub-rosa Privatization and Marketization in the USSR', *Annals of the American Academy of Political and Social Science*, 507: 44–52.
Grow, R. F., 1991, 'In Search of Excellence in China's Industrial Sector: The Chinese Enterprise and Foreign Technology', in US Congress Joint Economic Committee, *China's Economic Dilemmas in the 1990s: The Problems of Reforms, Modernization, and Interdependence*, Armonk, N.Y.: M. E. Sharpe.
Guangdong Statistical Bureau, 1989, *Guangdong sheng tongji nianjian [Statistical Yearbook of Guangdong Province, 1989]*, Guangdong: Statistical Press.
Gunasekera, H. D. B. H., et al., 1991, 'Agricultural Policy Reform in China', *Discussion Paper 91.4*, Canberra: Australian Bureau of Agricultural and Resource Economics.
Guo, J. et al., 1989, 'Chengshi Daolu Jiaotong Raosheng Sunshi Fenxi [An Analysis of the Losses from Traffic Noise Along City Roads]', *Zhongguo Huanjing Kexue [Environmental Sciences in China]*, (6): 415–19.
Guo, Shutian, et al., 1989, *Forty Years of China's Countryside*, Beijing: Central China Farmers' Press.
Guo, Shutian, Xiaohe Ma, Fang Cai and Funing Zhong, 1993, 'An Analysis of the Current Situation of China's Agricultural Protection', *China's Rural Economy*, 3: 11–14.
Guo, Zhemin, 1991, 'Characteristics of Xiamen and its Development Tendency', paper prepared for Xiamen SEZ Conference, September.
Hamrin, C. L., 1990, *China and the Challenge of the Future: Changing Political Patterns*, Boulder, Colo.: Westview Press.
Han, G., 1989, *Jiujiu Zhongguo, Huanjing Fachudi Huangpai Jinggao [Save China, a Yellow Card Warning Given by the Environment]*, Beijing.
Han, J., 1992, 'Professor Gale Johnson on China's Grain Policy Issues', *Chinese Rural Economy* [in Chinese], 11: 58–60.

Han, Tong et al., 1992, 'Zengqiang Zonghe Kangzai Nengli, Wending Nongcun Jingji Fazhan [Strengthen the Capacity to Resist Disasters, Stabilize Rural Economic Development]', *Nongye Jingji Wenti [Agricultural Economic Problems]*, (2): 54–7.

Han, Zhirong, 1995, 'The Impact of Changes in Agricultural Prices on Overall Price Index', *Jingji Yangjiu [Economic Research]*, 3: 53–62.

Hanson, J. R., 1988, 'Third World Incomes before World War I: Some Comparisons', *Explorations in Economic History*, 25: 323–6.

Harding, H., 1987, *China's Second Revolution: Reform after Mao*, Washington, D.C.: Brookings Institute.

Harris, J. and M. Todaro, 1970, 'Migration, Unemployment and Development: A Two-Sector Analysis', *American Economic Review*, 60: 126–42.

Harsanyi, J. C., 1963, 'A Simplified Bargaining Model for the n-Person Cooperative Game', *International Economic Review*, 4: 194–220.

Haughton, J., 1986, 'Farm Price Responsiveness and the Choice of Functional Form: An Application to Rice Cultivation in West Malaysia', *Journal of Development Economics*, 24: 203–33.

Hayami, Yujiro, 1988, *Japanese Agriculture Under Siege*, London: Macmillan.

Hayami, Yujiro, and Yoshihisa Godo, 1995, 'Economics and Politics of Rice Policy in Japan: A Perspective on the Uruguay Round', paper presented to the *Sixth Annual East Asian Seminar on Economics: Regional and Multilateralism in International Economics*, Seoul, 15–17 June.

Hayami, Yujiro and V. Ruttan, 1985, *Agricultural Development: An International Perspective*, Baltimore: Johns Hopkins University Press.

He, Jianzhang, 1981, 'Jiji Fuchi, Shidang Fazhan Chengzhen Geti Jingji [Actively Support and Appropriately Develop the Urban Individual Economy]', *Hong qi [Red Flag]*, 24: 13–16.

Hegedüs, A. and M. Markus, 1979, 'The Small Entrepreneur and Socialism', *Acta Oeconomica*, 22: 267–89.

Hertel, T. W., R. L. Thompson and M. E. Tsigas, 1989, 'Economy-wide Effects of Unilateral Trade and Policy Liberalization in U.S. Agriculture', in A. Stoeckel, D. Vincent and S. Cuthbertson (eds.), *Macroeconomic Consequences of Farm Support Policies*, Durham N.C.: Duke University Press.

Higgs, P. J., 1986, *Adaptation and Survival in Australian Agriculture*, Oxford University Press.

Hochman, H. M. and J. D. Rodgers, 1969, 'Pareto Optimal Redistribution', *American Economic Review*, 59: 542–57.

Hoselitz, B., 1972, 'Agriculture in Industrial Development', in D. Wall (ed.), *Chicago Essays in Economic Development*, University of Chicago Press.

Houck, J. P. and M. E. Ryan, 1972, 'Supply Analysis for Corn in the United States: Impact of Changing Government Programs', *American Journal of Agricultural Economics*, 54: 184–91.

Howard, M., 1990, 'Industry, Energy and Transport: Problems and Policies', in T. Cannon and A. Jenkins, (eds.), *The Geography of Contemporary China*, London: Routledge.

Huang, W., 1989. 'Woguo Chuantong Jiuye Moshi De Chansheng, Yunxing He

Gaige [Emergence, Operation and Reform in China's Traditional Pattern of Employment]', *Jingji Yanjiu* [*Economic Research*], (7): 55–60.

Huang, Yiping, 1991, 'Price Policy of Grain in China', in *China: Trade and Reform*, Canberra: National Centre for Development Studies, The Australian National University.

― 1992, 'Farmers' Feasible Choice Set and Agricultural Performance in China: 1985–90', paper presented to the Australian Ph.D. Conference in Economics and Business, The Australian National University, Canberra 3–5 November.

― 1993a, 'Government Intervention and Agricultural Performance in China', Ph.D. dissertation, The Australian National University, Canberra.

― 1993b, 'Production Interactions in China's Semi-Marketized Farming Sector', *Economics Division Working Paper (East Asia)* 93/3, Canberra: Research School of Pacific Studies, The Australian National University, Canberra.

― 1994, 'The Uruguay Round and China's Agricultural Policy Choices', paper presented to an international workshop *China and East Asian Trade Policy*, The Australian National University, Canberra, 1–2 September.

― 1995, *China's Grains and Oilseeds Sectors: A Review of Major Changes Underway*, Paris: OECD.

Huang, Yiping, and Weiguo Lu, 1992, 'China's Import Demand for Wool by Source: Functional Forms and Elasticities', paper presented to the Annual Conference, Chinese Economic Association (Australia), Adelaide, 12–14 November.

Huanjing Baohu [*Environmental Protection*], monthly journal edited by NEPA, Beijing.

Hubeisheng Huanjing Baohu Zhi [*A Record of Environmental Protection in Hubei Province*], Beijing: CESP, 1989.

Hufschmidt, M. M. et al. (eds.), 1983, *Environment, Natural Systems, and Development: An Economic Evaluation Guide*, Baltimore: Johns Hopkins University Press.

― 1987, 'Water Management Policy Options for the Beijing-Tianjin Region of China', report by the Environment and Policy Institute North China Water Project Team, East-West Center, Honolulu.

Hughes, H., 1991, 'Constraints on Export Growth: Foreign or Domestic?', unpublished manuscript National Centre for Development Studies, The Australian National University.

― 1995, 'Why Have East Asian Countries Led Economic Development', *Economic Record*, 71: 88–104.

Hultman, Charles, 1990, 'China's Regional Foreign Exchange Transaction Centres: Market Orientation in a Modified Planned Economy', *Journal of Asian Economics*, 1: 309–17.

Industrial Development Problems Group, CASS Institute of Industrial Economics, 1991, 'Lun Jiushidai Woguo Gongyedi Fazhan yu Gaige [On the Industrial Development Problems of Our Country in the Nineties and Reforms]', *Zhongguo Gongye Jingji Yanjiu* [*Research on China's Industrial Economy*], (1).

International Energy Agency, 1993, *World Energy Outlook*, Paris: IEA.

International Monetary Fund, *International Financial Statistics*, Washington, D.C.: IMF, various issues.
International Monetary Fund, World Bank, Organisation for Economic Cooperation and Development, and European Bank for Reconstruction and Development, 1990, *The Economy of the USSR: Summary and Recommendations*, Washington, D.C.: World Bank.
Iqbal, F., 1981, 'The Demand and Supply of Funds among Agricultural Households', Ph.D. dissertation, Yale University, New Haven, Conn.
Jackson, S., 1991, 'The Market-Plan Controversy in China', *Discussion Paper in Economics* 63, Brisbane: Department of Economics, The University of Queensland.
Jao, Y. C., 1991, *The Financial System of China and Hong Kong*, Pacific Economic Papers, Australia–Japan Research Centre, The Australian National University, Canberra.
Jefferson, G. H., 1990, 'China's Iron and Steel Industry: Sources of Enterprise Efficiency and the Impact of Reform', *Journal of Development Economics*, 33: 329–55.
Jefferson, G. H. and T. G. Rawski, 1991, 'China: Urban Employment and Wage Study', report prepared for Asia Country III Department, World Bank, Washington, D.C.
Jefferson, G. H. and Wenyi Xu, 1991, 'The Impact of Reform on Socialist Enterprises in Transition: Structure, Conduct and Performance in Chinese Industry', *Journal of Comparative Economics* 1: 45–64.
Jefferson, G. H. and Yuxin Zheng, 1992, 'Growth, Efficiency and Convergence in China's State and Collective Industry', *Economic Development and Cultural Change*, 40: 239–65.
Jessop, B., 1977, 'Recent Theories of the Capital State', *Cambridge Journal of Economics*, 1: 353–73.
Ji, Jianlin, and Jun Zhu, 1989, 'Siying Qiye Lirun Liuxiang Fenxi [An Analysis of Profit Uses in Private Enterprises]', *Zhongguo Nongcun Jingji [China's Rural Economy]*, 9: 48–52.
Ji, Long and Nan Lu, 1980, 'A Discussion of the Scissors Differential between Industrial and Agricultural Product Prices', *Red Flag [Hong Qi]*, 6: 45–8.
Jiang, J., and X. Luo, 1988, 'Changes in Income of Chinese Peasants since 1978', in J. Longworth (ed.), *China's Rural Development Miracle: With International Comparisons*, Brisbane: University of Queensland Press.
Jiang, X. M., forthcoming, 'The Evolution of Property Rights in China: A Long-Run Analysis, with Special Reference to Hefeng Textile Mill', Ph.D. dissertation, Cambridge University.
Jiangsu Statistical Bureau, 1990, *Jiangsu Sheng Tongji Nianjian [Jiangsu Statistical Yearbook, 1990]*, Jiangsu: Statistical Press.
Johansen, L., 1960, *A Multi-Sectoral Study of Economic Growth*, Amsterdam: North-Holland.
Johnson, D. G., 1978, 'International Prices and Trade in Reducing the Distortions of Incentive', in T. W. Schultz (ed.), *Distortions of Agricultural Incentives*, Bloomington: Indiana University Press.

1988, 'Economic Reforms in the People's Republic of China', *Economic Development and Cultural Change*, 36: s225–45.
1991, *World Agriculture in Disarray*, 2nd edn, New York: St Martin's Press.
1995, 'Does China Have A Grain Problem?', *China Economic Review*, 1(5): 1–14.
Jones, E. L., 1987, *The European Miracle: Environments, Economies and Geopolitics in the History of Europe and Asia*, Cambridge University Press.
1988, *Growth Recurring: Economic Change in World History*, Oxford: Clarendon Press.
1990, 'The Real Question about China: Why Was the Song Economic Achievement Not Repeated?' *Australian Economic History Review*, 30: 5–22.
1991, 'The Ultimate Significance of East Asian Development', School of Economics and Commerce Discussion Paper 3/91, La Trobe University, Melbourne.
forthcoming, 'The European Background', in S. Engerman and R. Gallman (eds.), *The Cambridge Economic History of the United States*, vol. I, Cambridge University Press.
Jones, R. W., 1956, 'Factor Proportions and the Heckscher–Ohlin Theorem', *Review of Economic Studies*, 24: 1–10.
1971, 'A Three-Factor Model in Theory, Trade and History', in Jagdish Bhagwati et al. (eds.), *Trade, Balance of Payments and Growth*, Amsterdam: North-Holland.
1975, 'Income Distribution and Effective Protection in Multicommodity Trade Model', *Journal of Economic Theory*, 11: 1–15.
Jorgenson, Dale, and Lawrence Lau, 1969, 'An Economic Theory of Agricultural Household Behaviour', paper read at the Fourth Far Eastern Meeting of the Econometric Society, Tokyo, Japan.
Junankar, P. N., 1989, 'The Response of Peasant Farmers to Price Incentives: The Use and Misuse of Profit Functions', *Journal of Development Studies*, 25: 169–82.
Ke, Binsheng, 1993, 'China's Grain Trade Protection Coefficients and Policy Implications', *China's Rural Economy*, 3: 25–8.
Keeney, R. L. and H. Raiffa, 1976, *Decisions with Multiple Objectives: Preferences in Value Trade-Offs*, New York: Wiley.
Kehoe, T. J. and J. Serra-Puche, 1984, 'A General Equilibrium Analysis of Domestic Commerce in Mexico', *Journal of Policy Modeling*, 6: 1–28.
1986, 'A General Equilibrium Analysis of Price Controls and Subsidies on Food in Mexico', *Journal of Development Economics*, 21: 65–87.
Kessel, L., 1974, *Surgeon at Arms*, London: Futura.
Keynes, J. M., 1936, *The General Theory of Employment, Interest and Money*, London: Macmillan.
Khor, H., 1991, 'China: Macroeconomic Cycles in the 1980s', *IMF Working Papers*, WP/91/85, Washington, D.C.: IMF.
Kleinberg, R., 1990, *China's Opening to the Outside World: The Experiment with Foreign Capitalism*, Oxford: Westview Press.
Kohler, W., 1991, 'Multilateral Trade Liberalization: Some General Equilibrium Simulation Results for Austria', *Empirica*, 18: 167–99.

Kojima, R., 1989, 'Macroeconomic Development of China: "Overheating" in 1984–1987 and Problems of Reform', *Journal of Japanese and International Economics*, 3: 64–121.

   1990, 'Achievements and Contradictions in China's Economic Reform, 1979–88', *The Developing Economies*, 28: 265–389.

Kowalik, T. (ed.), 1994, *Economic Theory and Market Socialism: Selected Essays of Oskar Lange*, Aldershot: Elgar Press.

Krausse, A., 1900, *China in Decay*, London: George Bell and Son.

Krishna, Raj, 1964, 'Theory of the Firm: Rapporteur's Report', *Indian Economic Journal*, 11: 514–25.

Krissoff, B., J. Sullivan, J. Waino and B. Johnston, 1990, *Agricultural Trade Liberalisation and Developing Countries*, Washington, D.C.: United States Department of Agriculture.

Krueger, A., 1974, 'The Political Economy of the Rent-Seeking Society', *American Economic Review*, 64: 291–303.

Krueger, A., M. Schiff and A. Valdes, 1988, 'Agricultural Incentives in Developing Countries: Measuring Effect of Sectoral and Economywide Policies', *The World Bank Economic Review*, 2: 255–71.

Krugman, P. R. and R. Z. Lawrence, 1993, 'Trade, Jobs, and Wages', *NBER Working Papers* 4478, Boston: NBER.

Lardy, N., 1983, *Agriculture in China's Modern Economic Development*, Cambridge University Press.

   1986, 'Prospects and Some Policy Problems of Agricultural Development in China', *American Journal of Agricultural Economics*, 68: 451–7.

   1992, *Foreign Trade and Economic Reform in China, 1978–1990*, Cambridge University Press.

Lattimore, R. and G. E. Schuh, 1976, 'A Policy Model of the Brazilian Beef Cattle Economy', *Chilean Journal of Economics*, 39: 51–75.

Lau, Lawrence J., 1978, 'Testing and Imposing Monotonicity, Convexity and Quasiconvexity Constraints', in M. Fuss and D. McFadden (eds.), *Production Economics: A Dual Approach to Theory and Applications*, vol. I, Amsterdam: North-Holland.

Lau, Lawrence, Wuu-Long Lin and Pan Yotopoulos, 1978, 'The Linear Logarithmic Expenditure System: An Application to Consumption Leisure Choice', *Econometrica*, 46: 843–68.

Lawrence, D. and J. Zeitsch, 1989, 'Production Flexibility Revisited', contributed paper to the Thirty-third Conference of the Australian Agricultural Economics Society, Christchurch, New Zealand, 7–9 February.

Lee, K., 'The Chinese Model of the Socialist Enterprises: An Assessment of its Organisation and Performance', *Journal of Comparative Economics*, 87: 678–810.

Li, Maoshen, 1987, *Zhongguo Jinrong Jiegou Yanjiu* [Study on China's Financial Structure], Tayguan: Shanxi People's Press.

Li, P., 1991, 'Report on the Outline of the Ten-year Programme and of the Eighth Five-year Plan for National Economic and Social Development', *Fourth*

Session of the Seventh National People's Congress, 25 March. Rpt. *Xinhua*, 11 April 1991.

Li, Ying, Yiwei Jiang and Shulian Zhou (eds.), 1986, *Zhongguo Gongye Jingji Fazhan Zhanlüe Yanjiu* [Research into the Development Strategy for China's Industrial Economy]. Beijing: China Management Press.

Li, Yunhe, 1957, 'On The Farm Household Responsibility System' in O. C. Howe and K. Walker (eds.), *The Foundations of China's Planned Economy: A Documentary Survey 1953–5*, New York: St Martin's Press.

Lin, C. Z., 1988, 'China's Economic Reforms: Western Perspectives', *Asian-Pacific Economic Literature*, 2: 1–25.

Lin, Justin Yifu, 1987, 'The Household Responsibility System Reform in China: A Peasant's Institutional Choice', *American Journal of Agricultural Economics*, 69: 410–15.

1988, 'The Household Responsibility System in China's Agricultural Reform: A Theoretical and Empirical Study', *Economic Development and Cultural Change*, 36: s199–224.

1989, 'Farming Institution, Food Policy, and Agricultural Reforms in China', paper prepared for the World Food Colloquium on *Global Sharing of Food and Agricultural Innovation and Development*, Smithsonian Institution, Washington, D.C., 17–18 October.

1990, 'Collectivization and China's Agricultural Crisis in 1959–1961', *Journal of Political Economy*, 98: 1228–52.

1991a, 'Public Research Resource Allocation in Chinese Agriculture: A Test of Induced Technological Innovation Hypotheses', *Economic Development and Cultural Change*, 40: 55–73.

1991b, 'Technological Change and Agricultural Household Income Distribution: Evidence from Hybrid Rice Innovation in China', seminar paper presented at the Australia–Japan Research Centre, The Australian National University, 11 September.

1991c, 'Rural Reform and Development in China', *Pacific Economic Papers* 200, Australia–Japan Research Centre, The Australian National University, Canberra.

1992a, 'Rural Reforms and Agricultural Growth in China', *American Economic Review*, 82: 34–51.

1992b, 'Rural Reforms, Technological Innovation, and Nascent Factor Markets in China: An Empirical Study of Institutional Change', Seminar Paper, Department of Economics, Research School of Pacific Studies, The Australian National University.

1992c, 'Rural Reform and Development', in Garnaut and Liu (eds.).

1993, 'Government Procurement Price and Rice Supply Responses in China', seminar paper, Department of Economics, Research School of Pacific Studies, The Australian National University, 26 August 1993.

1994, *Institution, Technology and China's Agricultural Development*, Shanghai: Shanghai Sanlian Bookstore and Shanghai People's Press.

Lin, Justin Yifu, and J. B. Nugent, forthcoming, 'Institutions and Economic

Development', in T. N. Srinivasan (ed.), *Handbook of Development Economics*, Amsterdam: Elsevier Science Publisher B.V.

Lin, Justin Yifu, Fang Cai and Zhou Li, 1994a, 'China's Economic Reforms: Pointers for other Economies in Transition?' Policy Research Working Paper 1310, World Bank, Washington D.C.

1994b, *China's Miracle: Development Strategies and Economic Reform*, Shanghai: Shanghai Sanlian Bookstore and Shanghai People's Press.

Lin, Justin Yifu, Fang Cai and Minggao Shen, 1989, 'On Economic Reform and the Choice of Development Strategy', *Jingji Yanjiu* [*Economic Research*], 3: 1–5.

Lin, Shujuan, 1991a, *Application of Cost-Benefit Analysis in China: A Case Study of the Xiamen Special Economic Zone*, Ph.D. thesis, The Australian National University, Canberra.

1991b, *The Shadow Price of Capital*, China Paper 91/3, National Centre for Development Studies, The Australian National University, Canberra.

Little, I. M. D. and J. A. Mirrlees, 1969, *Manual of Industrial Project Analysis in Developing Countries: Social Cost Benefit Analysis*, Paris: OECD.

1974, *Project Appraisal and Planning for Developing Countries*, London: Educational Books Ltd.

Liu, A., 1991, 'Economic Reform, Mobility Strategies and National Integration in China', *Asian Survey*, 31: 396.

Liu, Long (ed.), 1986, *Zhongguo Xian Jieduan Geti Jingji Yanjiu* [*Studies on the Individual Economy in China's Current Stage*], Beijing: People's Press.

Liu, Sihua, 1990. 'Dui Xian Jieduan Shengtai Jingji Shengchanli Wentidi Tantao [Discussion of Problems of the Productive Capacity of an Ecological Economy at the Present Stage]', *Zhongguo Huanjing Nianjian* [*Chinese Environmental Yearbook*], 466–7.

Liu, S. and Wu Qungan (eds.), 1986, *China's Socialist Economy: An Outline History (1949–1984)*, Beijing: Beijing Review.

Liu, Wen and Yanyang Wang, 1989, *2000–nian Zhongguo Huanjing Jingji Yuce* [*A Prediction of China's Environment and Economy in the Year 2000*]. Beijing: CESP.

Liu, Z. et al., 1990, *Zhongguo Nongyezhi Yanjiu* [*Research into China's Agricultural System*], Beijing: Chinese Academy of Agricultural Sciences.

Longworth, J. W., 1989, *China's Rural Development Miracle: With International Comparisons*, Brisbane: University of Queensland Press.

1990, *The Wool Industry in China: Some Chinese Perspectives*, [Melbourne,] Victoria: Inkata Press.

Lu, Xianxi, 1989, 'Zaizhi Shiye Yu Tonghuo Pengzhang [On-the-Job Unemployment and Inflation]', *Jingji Guanli Yanjiu* [*Research on Economy and Management*], (4).

Luo, Xiaopeng, 1994, 'The Household Responsibility System and the Collective Land Ownership', in G. James Wen (ed.), *Mainland China's Contemporary Land System*, Changsha: Hunan Sciences and Technology Press.

Ma, Guonan, 1994, 'Budget Deficits and Fiscal Policy Targets in China', in Y. Wu and X. Zhang (eds.), *Chinese Economy in Transition*, National Centre for Development Studies, The Australian National University, Canberra.

Ma, Guonan, and R. Garnaut, 1992, 'Factor Accumulation, Market Expansion, and Structural Transformation: The Case of China's Agriculture', Department of Economics, Research School of Pacific Studies, The Australian National University, Canberra (mimeo).

Ma, Hong, 1991, 'Guanyu Gaohao Dazhongxing Qiye De Jige Wenti [Several Issues Concerning the Proper Operation of Large and Medium Enterprises]', *Jingji Yanjiu [Economic Research]*, (11): 3–8, 39.

Ma, H. and S. Shangqing, (eds.), 1990, *Economic Situation and Prospect of China 1989–1990* [in Chinese], Beijing: China Development Press.

—— 1991, *Economic Situation and Prospect of China 1990–1991* [in Chinese], Beijing: China Development Press.

Ma, Xiaohe, 1993, 'Analysing the Influences of the Resumption of the GATT Membership on China's Agricultural Production', *Agricultural Economic Issues*, 1: 27–30.

Malenbaum, W., 1990, 'A Gloomy Portrayal of Development Achievements and Prospects: China and India', *Economic Development and Cultural Change*, 38: 405.

Mäler, K., 1991, 'National Accounts and Environmental Resources', *Environmental and Resource Economics*, 1(1): 23–34.

Mann, S., 1987, *Local Merchants and the Chinese Bureaucracy, 1750–1950*, Stanford University Press.

Mao, Y. and P. Hare, 1989, 'Chinese Experience in the Introduction of a Market Mechanism into a Planned Economy: The Role of Pricing', *Journal of Economic Surveys*, 3: 137–58.

Mao Zedong, 1977, *Selected Works of Mao Zedong*, vol. V, Beijing: China People's Press.

Martin, W., 1990, *Modelling the Post-Reform Chinese Economy*, China Working Paper 90/1, Canberra: National Centre for Development Studies, The Australian National University.

—— 1992, 'Effects of Foreign Exchange Reform on Raw Wool Demand: A Quantitative Analysis', in C. Findlay (ed.), *Challenges of Economic Reform and Industrial Growth: China's Wool War*, Sydney: Allen & Unwin.

Marx, K., 1959, *Das Kapital*, Moscow: Foreign Language Publishing House.

McCloskey, D. H., 1983, 'The Rhetoric of Economics', *Journal of Economic Literature*, 21: 481–517.

McDougall, R. and R. Tyers, 1993, 'Developing Country Expansion and Factor Markets in Industrial Countries', paper presented at International Agricultural Trade Research Consortium Annual Meeting, San Diego, 12–14 December.

McFadden, D., 1975, 'The Revealed Preferences of a Government Bureaucracy: Theory', *Bell Journal of Economics*, 6: 401–16.

McKay, L., D. Lawrence and C. Valstuin, 1982, 'Production Flexibility and Technical Change in Australia's Wheat–Sheep Zone', *Review of Marketing and Agricultural Economics*, 50: 9–24.

McMillan, J. and B. Naughton, 1992, 'How to Reform a Planned Economy: Lessons from China', *Oxford Review of Economic Policy*, 8: 130–43.
McMillan, J., J. Whalley and L. Zhu, 1989, 'The Impact of China's Economic Reforms on Agricultural Productivity Growth', *Journal of Political Economy*, 97: 781–807.
McPhee, J. R., 1989, 'IWS Promotion Strategy: Selling Wool to the World', in R. J. Hart (ed.), *The Australian Bicentenary Wool Conference: Proceedings of an International Symposium*, Sydney: NSW Department of Agriculture and Fisheries.
Mellor, J., 1963, 'The Use and Productivity of Farm Labour in the Early Stage of Agricultural Development', *Journal of Farm Economics*, 45: 517–34.
Meng, S. and Z. Peng, 1989, *Zhongguo Zaihuang Shi (Xiandai Bufen)* [*A History of Calamities in China (Contemporary Part)*], Beijing: Water and Electricity Press.
Meng, Xin, 1993, 'Individual Wage Determination in Township, Village and Private Enterprises in China', Ph.D. dissertation, The Australian National University, Canberra.
Millar, J., 1970, 'A Reformulation of A. V. Chayanov's Theory of Peasant Economy', *Economic Development and Cultural Change*, 18: 219–29.
Ministry of Agriculture, 1982, *Zhong Guo Nongye Jingji Gaiyao* [*Outline of China's Agriculture*], Beijing: Agricultural Press.
  1988, *Statistical Abstract of China's Xiangzhen Enterprises* [*Quanguo Xiangzhen Qiye Tongji Zhaiyao*], Beijing: Department of Township and Village Enterprises.
Mitchell, D., M. Ingco and R. Duncan, 1997, *The World Food Outlook*, Cambridge University Press.
Montiel, Peter, and Ostry, Jonathan, 1993, 'Is Parallel Market Premium a Reliable Indicator of Real Exchange Misalignment in Developing Economies?', *IMF Working Papers*, WP/93/70, Washington, D.C.: IMF.
Morrison, G. E., 1985, *An Australian in China*, Oxford University Press.
Mundlak, Y., D. Cavallo and R. Domenech, 1989, *Agriculture and Economic Growth in Argentina, 1913–84*, Washington, D.C.: International Food Policy Research Institute.
Muth, S. L., 1987, 'Private Business under Socialism: An Examination of the Urban Individual Economic Sector in China', Ph.D. dissertation, George Washington University, Washington, D.C.
Nash, J., 1953, 'Two-Person Cooperative Games', *Econometrica*, 21: 128–40.
National Centre for Development Studies, 1990, *An Economy-wide Model of Papua New Guinea: Theory, Data and Implementation*, Canberra: The Australian National University.
National Research Council, 1992, *Grasslands and Grassland Sciences in Northern China*, a report of the Committee on Scholarly Communications with the PRC, Washington D.C.: National Academy Press.
Naughton, B., 1988, 'The Chinese Industrial Enterprise: Structure and Capabilities', World Bank Background Paper, World Bank, Washington, D.C.
  1990, 'Macroeconomic Obstacles to Reform in China', discussion paper, University of California, San Diego.

Nee, V., 1989, 'Peasant Entrepreneurship and the Politics of Regulation in China', in V. Nee and D. Stark (eds.), *Remaking the Economic Institutions of Socialism: China and Eastern Europe*, Stanford University Press.

Niu, R. 1988, 'China's Grain Production Toward 2000', in J. Longworth (ed.), *China's Rural Development Miracle: With International Comparisons*, Brisbane: University of Queensland Press.

Niu, R., and P. Calkins, 1986, 'Towards an Agricultural Economy for China in a New Age: Progress, Problems, Response, and Prospects', *American Journal of Agricultural Economics*, 68: 445–50.

Nolan, P., 1988, *The Political Economy of Collective Farms*, Cambridge: Polity Press.

—— 1994, 'Introduction: The Chinese Puzzle', in Qimiao Fan and P. Nolan (eds.), *China's Economic Reforms: The Costs and Benefits of Incrementalism*, New York: St Martin's Press.

North, D. C., 1990, *Institutions, Institutional Change and Economic Performance*, Cambridge University Press.

O'Connor, J., 1973, *The Fiscal Crisis of the State*, New York: St Martin's Press.

Odgaard, O., 1990a, 'Collective Control of Income Distribution: A Case Study of Private Enterprises in Sichuan Province', in J. Delman, S. Østergaard and F. Christiansen (eds.), *Remaking Peasant China*, Aarhus University Press.

—— 1990b, 'Inadequate and Inaccurate Chinese Statistics: The Case of Private Rural Enterprises', *China Information*, 5 (3): 29–38.

OECD, 1994, *Agricultural Policies, Markets and Trade: Monitoring and Outlook 1994*, Paris: Organisation for Economic Cooperation and Development.

Oehmke, J. F. and Xianbin Yao, 1990, 'A Policy Preference Function for Government Intervention in the U.S. Wheat Market', *American Journal of Agricultural Economics*, 72: 631–9.

Ofer, G., 1987, 'Soviet Economic Growth: 1928–85', *Journal of Economic Literature*, 4: 1767–833.

Outline, 1989, *Zhonghua renmin gongheguo 1985-nian gongye pucha ziliao – jianyaoben* [*Simplified Outline of People's Republic of China 1985 Industrial Census Materials*], Beijing: China Statistics Press.

Panagariya, A., 1990, 'The Parallel Market in Centrally Planned Economies: A Dynamic Analysis', *Journal of Comparative Economics*, 14: 353–71.

Parikh, K. S. and M. H. Suryanarayana, 1992, 'Food and Agricultural Subsidies: Incidence and Welfare under Alternative Schemes', *Journal of Quantitative Economics*, 8: 1–28.

Patinkin, D., 1965, *Money, Interest and Prices: An Integration of Monetary and Value Theory*, 2nd edn, New York: Harper & Row.

Pearce, D. W. and R. K. Turner, 1990, *Economics of Natural Resources and the Environment*, New York: Harvester Wheatsheaf.

Peebles, G., 1990, *China's Macroeconomy in the 1980s: The Impact of Reform on Structure and Performance*, China Working Paper 90/5, Canberra: National Centre for Development Studies, The Australian National University.

—— 1991, *Money in the People's Republic of China*, Sydney: Allen & Unwin.

Peltzman, S., 1976, 'Toward a More General Theory of Regulation', *Journal of Law and Economics*, 19: 211–40.

Peng, Z., 1992, 'Trade Reforms and Internationalizing Prices in the Chinese Economy', draft paper, Energy Economics Branch, Australian Bureau of Agricultural and Resource Economics, Canberra (mimeo).

Peng, Zhao-Yang, and W. Martin, 1991, 'Policy Responses to Terms of Trade Shocks in the Post-Reform Chinese Economy', Energy Economics Branch, Australian Bureau of Agricultural and Resource Economics, Canberra (mimeo).

Perkins, D. H., 1988, 'Reforming China's Economic System', *Journal of Economic Literature*, 26: 601–45.

1991, 'Markets vs. Plans: The Key Role of Enterprise Manager Behavior', in US Congress Joint Economic Committee (ed.), *China's Economic Dilemmas of the 1990s: Problems of Reforms, Modernization, and Interdependence*, Armonk, N.Y.: M. E. Sharpe.

1992, 'China's Economic Boom and the Integration of the Economies of East Asia', Korean Institute of Public Administration and the Economic Research Institute of the Daishin Group, Seoul.

Perkins, D. H. and Shahid Yusuf, 1984, *Rural Development in China*, Baltimore: Johns Hopkins University Press.

PLDRD (Policy and Law Department of the Ministry of Agriculture and Rural Department of the State Statistics Bureau, the People's Republic of China), 1989, *Forty Years of Rural China*, Henan: Zhong-Yuan Farmer Press.

Popper, K. R., 1960, *The Poverty of Historicism*, London: Routledge & Kegan Paul.

Portes, R. and A. Santorum, 1987, 'Money and the Consumption Goods Market in China', *Journal of Comparative Economics*, 11(3): 354–71.

Prybyla, J. S., 1986, 'Mainland China and Hungary: To Market, to Market', paper presented to the Fifteenth Sino-American Conference on Mainland China, Institute of International Relations, National Chengchi University, Taipei, 8–14 June.

1990, 'A Broken System', in G. Hicks (ed.), *The Broken Mirror: China after Tiananmen*, London: Longman.

Putterman, L., 1987, 'The Incentive Problem and the Demise of Team Farming in China', *Journal of Development Economics*, 26: 103–27.

1990, 'Efforts, Productivity, and Incentives in a 1970s Chinese People's Commune', *Journal of Comparative Economics*, 14: 88–104.

1992, 'Dualism and Reform in China', *Economic Development and Cultural Change*, 4: 467–93.

Qiang, Ru, 1992, 'Lun Woguo Caodi Ziyuandi Heli Kaifa Liyong [On the Rational Exploitation of our Country's Grassland Resources]', *Nongye Xiandaihua Yanjiu [Research on Agricultural Modernization]*, (1): 27–9.

Quanguo Gongye Wuranyuan Diaocha Pingjia yu Yanjiu (Zonglun) [Evaluation and Research of the National Survey of Industrial Sources of Pollution (General Discussion)], 1990, Beijing: CESP.

Raby, G., 1989, *Other Economic Systems*, Port Melbourne: Heinemann.
Ranis, G. and T. P. Schultz, 1988, *The State of Development Economics*, Oxford: Basil Blackwell.
Rausser, G. C. and J. W. Freebairn, 1974, 'Estimation of Policy Preference Functions: An Application to U.S. Beef Quotas', *Review of Economics and Statistics*, 56: 437–49.
Rausser, G. C. and D. P. Stonehouse, 1978, 'Public Intervention and Producer Supply Response', *American Journal of Agricultural Economics*, 60: 885–90.
Rausser, G. C., E. Lichtenberg and R. Lattimore, 1982, 'Developments in Theory and Empirical Applications of Endogenous Governmental Behavior', in G. C. Rausser (ed.), *New Directions in Econometric Modelling and Forecasting in U.S. Agriculture*, New York: North-Holland.
Rawski, T. G., 1982, 'The Simple Arithmetic of Income Distribution in China', *Keizai Kenkyû* [*Economic Research*], 33: 12–26.
  1989, *Economic Growth in Prewar China*, Berkeley: University of California Press.
  1992, 'Progress without Privatization: The Reform of China's State Industries', seminar paper presented at the Economics Department, Research School of Pacific Studies, The Australian National University, Canberra.
Rees, J., 1985, *Natural Resources: Allocation, Economics and Policy*, London: Methuen.
Reinhart, C. M. and V. R. Reinhart, 1991, 'Output Fluctuations and Monetary Shocks', *IMF Staff Papers*, 38(4), Washington, D.C.: IMF.
Ren, Jijun and Hung Yin, 1991, 'Senlin Gongye Chanye Zhengce Yanjiu [Research into the Production Policy of Forestry Industry]', *Zhongguo Gongye Jingji Yanjiu* [*Research on China's Industrial Economy*], (9): 30–5.
Reynolds, B. L. (ed.), 1987, *Reform in China: Challenges and Choices*, Armonk, N.Y.: M. E. Sharpe.
Reynolds, L. G., 1985, *Economic Growth in the Third World, 1850–1980*, New Haven: Yale University Press.
Riskin, Carl, 1987, *China's Political Economy – The Quest for Development Since 1949*, Oxford University Press.
Robinson, S., 1989, 'Multisectoral Models', in H. Chenery and T. N. Srinivasan, (eds)., *Handbook of Development Economics*, vol. II, Amsterdam: Elsevier Science Publishers B.V.
Rodzinski, W., 1984, *The Walled Kingdom: A History of China from 2000 BC to the Present*, London: Fontana.
Roemer, J. E., 1978, 'Neoclassicism, Marxism, and Collective Action', *Journal of Economic Issues*, 12: 147–61.
Roningen, V. O., 1986, 'A Static World Policy Simulation (SWOPSIM) Framework', *Economic Research Service Staff Report* AGES860625, Washington, D.C.: United States Department of Agriculture.
Roningen, V. O. and P. M. Dixit, 1989, 'How Level is the Playing Field? An Economic Analysis of Agricultural Policy Reforms in Industrial Market Economies', *Foreign Agricultural Economic Report* 239, Washington, D.C.: United States Department of Agriculture.

Rowe, W. T., 1984, *Hankow: Commerce and Society in a Chinese City, 1796–1889*, Stanford University Press.

Rybczynski, T. M., 1955, 'Factor Endowments and Relative Commodity Prices', *Economica*, 22: 366–41.

Sadoulet, Elisabeth and Alain de Janvry, 1992, 'Agricultural Trade Liberalisation and Low Income Countries: A General Equilibrium-Multimarket Approach', *American Journal of Agricultural Economics*, 74: 268–80.

Sarkar, H. and G. K. Kadekodi, 1988, *Energy Pricing in India: Perspective, Issues, and Options*, New Delhi: UNESCO.

Sarris, A. H. and J. Freebairn, 1982, 'Endogenous Price Policies and International Wheat Prices', *American Journal of Agricultural Economics*, 65: 214–24.

Schim van der Loeff, S. and R. Harkema, 1979, 'A Multiperiod Revealed Preference Approach to Estimating Preference Functions under Rational Random Behavior', Report 7925/E, Econometric Institute, Netherlands School of Economics, Rotterdam.

Schon, L., 1980, 'British Competition and Domestic Change inTextiles in Sweden, 1820–1870', *Economy and History*, 23: 61–76.

Schultz, T. W., 1964, *Transforming Traditional Agriculture*, New Haven: Yale University Press.

1978, *Distortions of Agricultural Incentives*, Bloomington: Indiana University Press.

Sen, Amartya K., 1966, 'Peasants and Dualism with and without Surplus Labour', *Journal of Political Economy*, 74: 425–50.

Serra-Puche, J., 1984, 'A General Equilibrium Model of the Mexican Economy', in H. E. Scarf and J. B. Shoven (eds.), *Applied General Equilibrium*, Cambridge University Press.

Service, 1988, *Disan Chanye* [*Tertiary Industry*], Zhongguo Tongji Chubanshe, Beijing.

Sevilla-Siero, 1991, 'On the Use and Misuse of Profit Functions for Measuring the Price Responsiveness of Peasant Farmers: A Comment', *The Journal of Development Studies*, 27: 123–36.

Shan, W., 1989, 'Reforms of China's Foreign Trade Systems: Experiences and Prospects', *China Economic Review*, 1: 33–55.

Shao, Ning and Wenxiu Han, 1991, 'Macroeconomic Analysis of Conditions Regarding the Economic Effectiveness of China's Industry', *Zhongguo Gongye Jingji Yanjiu* [*Studies in Chinese Industrial Economics*], (10): 18–24.

Shen, L. and Y. Dai, 1990, 'The Formation, Shortcomings and Origins of "the Economy Divided by Dukes and Princes under the Emperor" in China', *Jingji Yanjiu*) [*Economic Research*], 3: 14–19.

Shenzhen Investment Guide, 1991, Shenzhen Economic Development Bureau and Centre for Investment Promotion of the Shenzhen Municipality.

Shenzhen Special Economic Zone: 10 Years, 1990, Policy Research Office of the Shenzen Municipality.

Shenzhen Special Economic Zone Yearbook, various issues.

Shenzhen: Study on the New System, 1988, Policy Research Office of the Shenzhen Municipality

References 215

Shi, Shan, 1992, 'Shengtai Nongye Xian Jianshe yu Nongye Xiandaihua [The Construction of Counties with Ecological Agriculture and the Modernization of Agriculture]', *Nongye Xiandaihua Yanjiu* [*Research of Agricultural Modernization*], (1): 1–4.

Shoven, J. B. and J. Whalley, 1992, *Applying General Equilibrium*, Cambridge University Press.

Shu, H., 1991, 'Conscientiously Implement the State Council Decision of Further Strengthening Environmental Protection Efforts, Revamp Environmental Protection in the Electric Power Industry', *Dianli Jishu* (*Electric Power Techniques*), (11): 2–7, tr. in *JPRS Report, Science and Technology: China: Energy*, JPRS CEN-923-002: 3–9.

1992, 'Nengyuan he Huanjing Baohu Yao Tongbu Fazhan [Energy and Environmental Protection Must be Developed at the Same Pace]', *Zhongguo Nengyuan* [*Energy in China*], (1): 43–4.

Shue, V., 1988, *The Reach of the State: Sketches of the Chinese Body Politic*, Stanford University Press.

Sicular, T., 1986a, 'Prospects and Some Policy Problems of Agricultural Development in China: Discussion', *American Journal of Agricultural Economics*, 68: 458–60.

1986b, 'Using a Farm Household Model to Analyze Labor Allocation on a Chinese Collective Farm', in Inderjit Singh (ed.), *Agricultural Household Models*, Baltimore: Johns Hopkins University Press.

1988a, 'Plan and Market in China's Agricultural Commerce', *Journal of Political Economy*, 96: 283–307.

1988b, 'Agricultural Planning and Pricing in the Post-Mao Period', *China Quarterly*, 116: 671–705.

Sinha, S., 1988, 'Small Versus Large in the Indian Cement Industry – David and Goliath Hand-in-Hand', in M. Carr (ed.), *Sustainable Industrial Development: Seven Case Studies*, London: Intermediate Technology Publications.

SINOPEC Yearbook, 1991, *Zhongguo Shiyouhua Gongsi Nianjian 1991*, Beijing: China Petrochemical Press.

Smith, Victor E. and John Strauss, 1986, 'Simulating the Rural Economy in a Subsistence Environment: Sierra Leone', in Inderjit Singh (ed.), *Agricultural Household Models*, Baltimore: Johns Hopkins University Press.

Song, Guoqing, 1987, 'From the Unified Purchase and Marketing to Land Tax', in Gao and Song (eds.).

Song, L., 1996, *Changing Global Comparative Advantage: Evidence from Asia and the Pacific*, Sydney: Addison-Wesley Longman.

Squire, L. and H. van der Tak, 1975, *Economic Analysis of Projects*, Baltimore: Johns Hopkins University Press.

Srinivasan, T. N. (ed.), 1994, *Agriculture and Trade in China and India: Policies and Performance since 1950*, San Francisco: International Center for Economic Growth.

SSB (State Statistical Bureau), *China Agricultural Yearbook*, Beijing: China Statistics Press, annual.

China Price Statistical Yearbook, Beijing: China Statistics Press, annual.

China Statistical Yearbook, Beijing: China Statistics Press, annual.
Zhongguo Gongye Jingji Tongji Nianjian [*Economic Statistics on Chinese Industry*], Beijing: China Statistics Press, various issues.
Zhongguo Laodong Gongzi Tongji Ziliao [*Statistical Yearbook of Chinese Labour and Wages*], Beijing: China Statistics Press, various issues.
Zhongguo Nongcun Tongji Nianjian [*Chinese Rural Statistical Yearbook*], Beijing: China Statistics Press, various issues.
Zhongguo Jingji Nianjian [*Chinese Economic Yearbook*], Beijing: China Statistics Press, various issues.
Zhongguo Tongji Zhaiyao [*Statistical Survey of China*], Beijing: China Statistics Press, various issues.
1987, *Statistical Materials on Chinese Labour and Wages, 1949–85* [*Zhongguo Laodong Gongzi Tongjii Ziliao*], Beijing: China Statistics Press.
1989, *Zhongguo Renkou Tongji Nianjian* [*Statistical Yearbook of Chinese Population*], Beijing: Science and Technology Literature Press.
1990, *Lishi Tongji Ziliao Huibian* [*Compendium of Historical Statistical Materials, 1949–1990*], Beijing: China Statistics Press.
1991a, 'Statistical Communiqué of the State Statistical Bureau of the People's Republic of China on National Economic and Social Development in 1990', *Beijing Review*, 34, 22 February: 3–6.
1991b, *Zhongguo Shehui Tongji Ziliao 1990* [*Statistical Materials on China's Economy and Society, 1990*], Beijing: China Statistics Press.
SSTC and UNDP, 1991, 'Report of the International Workshop on the Control of Environmental Pollution in China', Beijing, mimeo.
State Science and Technology Commission Research Team, 1989, *Yanhai Kaifan Chenshi Waixianxing Jingji Faghan Ghanlue* [*Outward-Oriented Economic Development Strategy for Coastal Open Cities*], Beijing: Economic Management Press.
Stenvens, R. D. and C. L. Jabara, 1988, *Agricultural Development Principles: Economic Theory and Empirical Evidences*, Baltimore: Johns Hopkins University Press.
Stigler, G. J., 1970, 'Director's Law of Public Income Distribution', *Journal of Law and Economics*, 13: 1–10.
1971, 'The Theory of Economic Regulation', *Bell Journal of Economics*, 2: 3–21.
Strauss, John, 1982, 'Determinants of Food Consumption in Rural Sierra Leone: Application of the Quadratic Expenditure System to the Consumption-Leisure Component of a Household–Firm Model', *Journal of Development Economics*, 11: 327–53.
Su, Z. and J. Wang, 1992, 'Quanguo Bada Zhongdian Zhiliqu Shuitu Baochi Xiaoyi Fenxi [An Analysis of the Benefit of Water and Soil Conservation in Eight National Keypoint Treatment Areas]', *Zhongguo Shuitu Baochi* [*China's Water and Soil Conservation*], (3): 1–4.
Suanyu Wenji, 1989, [Collection of articles on acid rain], Beijing: CESP.
Summers, R. and A. Heston, 1991, 'The Penn World Table (Mark 5): An Expanded Set of International Comparisons, 1950–1988', *Quarterly Journal of Economics*, 106(2): 327–68.

Sung, Yun-Wing, 1991a, 'Hong Kong's Economic Value to China', in Yun-Wing Sung and Lee Ming-Kwan (eds.), *The Other Hong Kong Report 1991*, Hong Kong: Chinese University Press.
   1991b, 'Foreign Trade and Investment', in Kuan Hsin-chi and Maurice Brosseau (eds.), *China Review*, Hong Kong: Chinese University Press.
   1991c, *The China–Hong Kong Connection: The Key to China's Open Door Policy*, Cambridge University Press.
   1994, 'An Appraisal of China's Foreign Trade Policy, 1950–92', in T. N. Srinivasan (ed.), *Agriculture and Trade in China and India: Policies and Performance since 1950*, San Francisco: International Center for Economic Growth.
Sung, Yun-Wing, and T. M. H. Chan, 1987, 'China's Economic Reform I: The Debates in China', *Asian Pacific Economic Literature*, 2(1): 1–25.
Taylor, J. S. and J. Spriggs, 1989, 'Effects of the Monetary Macro-Economy on Canadian Agricultural Prices', *Canadian Journal of Economics*, 22: 278–89.
Taylor, L., 1988, *Varieties of Stabilisation Experience*, Oxford University Press.
Theil, H., 1971, 'An Economic Theory of the Second Moments of the Disturbances of Behavioral Equations', *American Economic Review*, 61: 190–4.
   1974, 'A Theory of Rational Random Behavior', *Journal of American Statistical Association*, 69: 310–14.
Thomson, W., 1981, 'A Class of Solutions to Bargaining Problems', *Journal of Economic Theory*, 25: 431–41.
Tidrick, H. G. and Chen Jiyuan, 1987, *China's Industrial Reform*, Oxford University Press.
Timmer, C. P., 1986, *Getting Prices Right: The Scope and Limits of Agricultural Price Policy*, Ithaca: Cornell University Press.
   1988, 'The Agricultural Transformation', in H. Chenery and T. N. Srinivasan (eds.), *Handbook of Development Economics*, vol. I, Amsterdam: Elsevier Science Publishers B.V.
Tisdell, C. A. and P. Maitra, 1988, *Technological Change, Development and the Environment: Socio-economic Perspectives*. London: Routledge.
Tom, C. F., 1957, *Entrepot Trade and the Monetary Standards of Hong Kong*, University of Chicago Press.
Tsui, K. Y., 1991, 'China's Regional Inequality, 1952–1985', *Journal of Comparative Economics*, 15: 1–15.
Tweeten, L., 1980, 'An Economic Investigation into Inflation Passthrough to the Farm Sector', *Western Journal of Agricultural Economics*, 5: 89–106.
Tyers, R. and K. Anderson, 1992, *Disarray in World Food Markets: A Quantitative Assessment*, Cambridge University Press.
Tzeng, Fuh-Wen, 1991, 'The Political Economy of China's Coastal Development Strategy: A Preliminary Analysis', *Asian Survey*, 31: 270–84.
United Nations, 1992, *Human Development Report*, New York: United Nations.
United Nations, Department of Economic and Social Development, *Energy Statistics Yearbook*, New York: United Nations, various issues.
United Nations Development Programme (UNDP), 1990, *Human Development Report*, Oxford University Press.

United States Department of Agriculture, 1993, *Large Grain Stocks Reported in China*, Washington, D.C.: USDA.

Usher, D., 1973, 'An Imputation to the Measure of Economic Growth for Changes in Life Expectancy', in M. Moss (ed.), *The Measurement of Economic and Social Performance, Conference Proceedings of Income and Wealth*, New York: National Bureau of Economic Research.

Vermeer, E. B., 1990, 'Management of Environmental Pollution in China: Problems and Abatement Policies', *China Information*, 5: 1–32.

—— 1991, 'Management of Pollution Abatement by Chinese Enterprises', *RVB Research Papers*, 1: 21–7.

—— (ed.), 1992, *From Peasant to Entrepreneur: Growth and Change in Rural China*, Wageningen, The Netherlands: Pudoc.

von Neumann, J., 1928, 'Zur Theorie der Gesellschaftespiele', *Mathematics Annual*, 100: 295–320.

von Neumann, J. and O. Morgenstern, 1944, *The Theory of Games and Economic Behavior*, Princeton University Press.

Vousden, N., 1990, *The Economics of Trade Protection*, Cambridge University Press.

Wade, R., 1990, *Governing the Market*, Princeton University Press.

Wakashiro, N., 1990, 'Rural Reform and Agricultural Production in China', *The Developing Economies*, 28: 382–502.

Walder, A. G., 1989. 'Factory and Manager in an Era of Reform', *China Quarterly* no. 118: 242–64.

Walker, K. R., 1988, 'Trends in Crop Production, 1978–86', *China Quarterly*, no. 116: 592–633.

Wall, D., 1976, 'Export Processing Zones', *Journal of World Trade Law*, 10: 478–89.

—— 1991, *Special Economic Zones in China: The Administrative and Regulatory Framework*, Canberra: National Centre for Development Studies, The Australian National University.

Walters, A., 1992., 'The Transition to a Market Economy', in C. Clague and G. C. Rausser (eds.) *The Emergence of Market Economies in Eastern Europe*, Oxford: Basil Blackwell.

Wang, F. (ed.), 1988, *Introduction to the Economics of Xiangzhen Qiye*, Beijing: New Age Press.

Wang, G., 1955, 'The Basic Tasks of China's First Five-Year Plan', *Jihua Jingji* [*Planned Economy*], no. 7, reprinted in C. Howe and K. R. Walker (eds.), 1989, *The Foundations of the Chinese Planned Economy*, Beijing: St Martin's Press.

Wang, H. (ed.), 1990, *Research into Economic Efficiency in Different Branches of the Chinese National Economy* [*Zhongguo Guomin Jingji Gebumen Jingji Xiaoyi Yanjiu*], Beijing: China Management Press.

Wang, R. and G. W. Hinman, 1992, 'Striving for Efficiency, Harmony and Vitality – A Human Ecological Approach to Urban Sustainable Development', paper presented at the conference on *China's Environment*, Portland.

Wang Z., 1991, 'Jieneng Duice Zhenyi' [Ideas on Energy Savings], *Zhongguo Nengyuan* [*Energy in China*], (9): 1–3.

Wang, Zhan'ao, 1988, 'Shi Lun Wo Guo Geti Jingji De Fazhan Yu Guanli [A

Tentative Discussion of the Development and Administration of China's Individual Economy]', *Caijing Yanjiu* [*Financial and Economic Research*], 7: 32.

Warr, P. G., 1983a, 'The Jakarta Export Processing Zone: Benefits and Costs', *Bulletin of Indonesian Economic Studies*, 19: 28–49.

—— 1983b, 'Korea's Masan Free Export Zone: Benefits and Costs', *The Developing Economies*, 12: 169–84.

—— 1987a, 'Export Processing Zones in China, East Asia and the Pacific', paper presented to *Foreign Investment in East Asia* conference, China State Planning Commission, Beijing.

—— 1987b, 'Export Promotion Via Industrial Enclaves: The Philippines' Bataan Export Processing Zone', *Journal of Development Studies*, 23: 220–41.

—— 1987c, 'Malaysia's Industrial Enclaves: Benefits and Costs', *The Developing Economies*, 25: 30–55.

—— 1990, 'Export Processing Zones', in C. Milner (ed.), *Export Promotion Strategies: Theory and evidence from Developing Countries*, New York: Harvester Wheatsheaf.

Watson, A., 1989, 'Investment issues in the Chinese countryside', *Australian Journal of Chinese Affairs*, 22: 85–126.

—— 1995, 'Conflict over Cabbages: The Reform of Wholesale Markets in China', in R. Garnaut, G. Ma and S. Shutian (eds.), *The Third Revolution in the Chinese Countryside*, Cambridge University Press.

Watson, A. and C. Findlay, 1992, 'The "Wool War" in China', in Findlay (ed.). *Challenges of Economic Reform and Industrial Growth: China's Wool War.*

Weaver, Robert D., 1983, 'Multiple Input, Multiple Output Production Choices and Technology in the U.S. Wheat Region', *American Journal of Agricultural Economics*, 65: 45–56.

Webb, S. H., 1989, 'Agricultural Commodity Prices in China: Estimates of PSEs and CSEs, 1982–87', China Agriculture and Trade Report, RS-89-5, Economic Research Service, US Department of Agriculture, Washington, D.C.

Wen, G. J., 1994, *Mainland China's Contemporary Land System*, Changsha: Hunan Sciences and Technology Press.

White, G., 1987, 'The Politics of Economic Reform in Chinese Industry: The Introduction of the Labour Contract System', *China Quarterly*, no. 111: 365–89.

White, K. J., 1993, *Shazam User's Reference Manual Version 7.0*, New York: McGraw-Hill.

Wiley, D., W. Schmidt and W. Bramble, 1973, 'Studies of a Class of Covariance Structure Models', *Journal of American Statistical Association*, 68: 317–23.

Wilhelm, R., 1982, *Chinese Economic Psychology*, New York: Garland.

Williamson, H. G., 1989, 'Potential Sources of Productivity Growth Within Chinese Industry', *World Development*, 17: 268–75.

Wong, C., 1990, 'Central–Local Relations in an Era of Fiscal Decline', discussion paper, University of California, Santa Cruz.

World Bank, *World Development Report*, Oxford University Press, various issues.

—— 1983, *China: Socialist Economic Development*, Washington, D.C.: World Bank.

1985, *China: Long-Term Development Issues and Options*, Baltimore: Johns Hopkins University Press.
1987a, *China: External Trade and Capital Reform Issues and Options*, Washington, D.C.: World Bank.
1987b, *China: Finance and Investment*, Washington, D.C.: World Bank.
1988a, *China: External Trade and Capital*, Washington, D.C.: World Bank.
1988b, *China: Finance and Investment*, Washington, D.C.: World Bank.
1989a, *India: Poverty, Employment, and Social Services*, Washington, D.C.: World Bank.
1989b, *India: Recent Developments and Medium-Term Issues*, Washington, D.C.: World Bank.
1989c, *World Development Report*, Oxford University Press.
1990a, *China between Plan and Market*, Washington, D.C.: World Bank.
1990b, *China: Macroeconomic Stability and Industrial Growth under Decentralised Socialism*, Washington, D.C.: World Bank.
1990c, *China: Reforming Social Security in a Socialist Economy*, Washington, D.C.: World Bank.
1990d, *World Development Report, 1990: Poverty*, Oxford University Press.
1990e, *World Population Projections, 1989–90*, Washington, D.C.: World Bank.
1991a, *World Development Report, 1991: The Challenge of Development*, Oxford University Press.
1991b, *World Tables 1991*, Baltimore: Johns Hopkins University Press.
1992, *World Development Report 1992: Development and the Environment*, Oxford University Press.
1993, *China Foreign Trade Reform: Meeting the Challenge of the 1990s*, Washington, D.C.: World Bank.
1994, *The East Asian Miracle*, Oxford University Press.
Wu, J. and R. Zhao, 1987, 'The Two-Pricing System in China's Industry', *Journal of Comparative Economics*, 11: 309–18.
Wulf, L. D. and D. Goldsbrough, 1986, 'The Evolving Role of Monetary Policy in China', *IMF Staff Papers*, 33(2): 38–49.
Xia, G. 1991, 'Zhongguo Dui Quanqiu Jihou Bianhuadi Lichang yu Duice [China's Position Towards Global Warming and Remedial Policies]', *Zhongguo Huanjing Kexue* [*Environmental Sciences in China*], (11): 457–9.
Xiamen Statistical Yearbook, Xiamen, China, annual.
Xiao, Geng, 1991a, 'The Impact of Property Rights on Productivity and Equity in Post-Mao Chinese Industrial Enterprises', Ph.D. dissertation, University of California, Los Angeles.
1991b, 'Managerial Autonomy, Fringe Benefits and Ownership Structure', *China Economic Review*, 2: 47–73.
Xu, K. and J. Hao, 1990, 'Woguo Suanyu Xianzhuang Tedian ji Duice Zouyi [Characteristics of the Present State of Acid Rain in Our Country and Proposals for Remedies]', *Zhongguo Huanjing Kexue* [*Environmental Sciences in China*], (11): 61–6.
Xue, Muqiao, 1981, *China's Socialist Economy*, Beijing: Foreign Languages Press.
Yang, J. and X. Jia, 1991, 'Woguodi Renkou Qianyi yu Huanjing Renkou

Rongliang' [Migration and Population Carrying Capacity of our Country], *Jingji Dili* [*Economic Geography*], (3): 39–41.

Yang, X., J. Wang and L. Wills, 1990, 'Economic Growth, Commercialisation, and Institutional Changes in Rural China, 1979–1987', seminar paper, Australia–Japan Research Centre, The Australian National University, Canberra.

Yang, Y., 1992, 'The Impact of the Multifibre Arrangement on World Clothing and Textile Markets with Special Reference to China', Ph.D. dissertation, The Australian National University, Canberra.

——1993, 'China, the New Giant: Is Its Trade Pattern Following?', paper presented at the conference on *Sustaining the Development Process*, National Centre for Development Studies, The Australian National University, Canberra.

——1994, 'Trade Liberalisation with Externalities: A General Equilibrium Assessment of the Uruguay Round', paper presented to the *Challenges and Opportunities for East Asian Trade* workshop, The Australian National University, Canberra, 13–14 July.

Yang, Y. Z. and Rodney Tyers, 1989, 'The Economic Costs of Food Self-Sufficiency in China', *World Development*, 17: 237–53.

Yao, C. and G. Ai, 1992, 'China's Natural Gas Industry Development Prospects in View of Natural Gas Exploration During the 8th 5-Year Plan', *Tianranqi Gongye* [*Natural Gas Industry*], (1): 10–15, trans. in *JPRS Report, Science and Technology, China: Energy* (JPRS CEN-92-003), pp. 17–24.

Yearbooks of China's Environment, 1990 and 1991 [*Zhongguo Huanjing Nianjian 1990, 1991*]. Beijing: CESP.

Yi, Gang, 1995, 'China's Demand and Supply of Money', *Economic Research*, 5(325): 51–8.

Yotopoulos, Pan, Lawrence Lau and Wuu-Long Lin, 1976, 'Microeconomic Output Supply and Factor Demand Functions in the Agriculture of Province of Taiwan', *American Journal of Agricultural Economics*, 58: 333–40.

Yu, T., 1987, 'Zhongguo Caidamu Bendi Lüzhou Nongye Shengtaidi Yanjiu [Research on the Agricultural Ecology of the Oases in the Tsaidam Basin in China]', in NEPA (ed.), *Nongcun Shengtai Xitong Yanjiu Guoji Xueshu Taolunhui Lunwenji* [*Collection of Papers on the International Conference on Rural Ecological System Research*], Beijing: CESP.

Yu, Zhida, 1990. 'Fazhan Waixiangxing Jingji yu Huanjing Baohu [The Development of an Outward-Oriented Economy and Environmental Protection]', *Chinese Environment Yearbook* [*Zhongguo Huanjing Nianjian*], pp. 456–7.

Zhang Houyi and Shaoxiang Qin, 1988, 'Siying Jingji Dangdai Zhongguo de Shijian [The Practice of the Private Economy in Contemporary China]', *Jingji Cankao* [*Economic Information*], 14 November: 4.

Zhang, J., 1987, 'Analysis of Ecological and Economical Results of Reclamation of Lakes and Marshes', *Shengtaixue Zazhi* [*Journal of Ecology*], 6: 19–24.

——1991, 'Woguo Nengyuan yu Guomin Jingji Fazhan Guanxidi Chubu Tantao [A Preliminary Investigation of the Relation Between our Country's Energy and national economic development]', *Zhongguo Gongye Jingji Yanjiu* [*Research on China's Industrial Economy*], (6): 57–60.

Zhang Q. et al. 1989, *Lun Huangtu Gaoyuan Nongye – Pinkun, Shengtai, Guotu*

Zhengzhidi Zhuti [On Agriculture on the Loess Plateau – Topics of Poverty, Ecology and Land Management], Beijing, China Statistical Press.

Zhang, S. and A. Zhang, 1987, 'The Present Management Environment in China's Industrial Management', in Chinese Economic System Reform Research Institute, *Reform in China*, Armonk, N.Y.: East Gate Press.

Zhang, X., W. Lu, K. Sun, C. Findlay and A. Watson, 1991, 'The "Cotton Chaos" and the "Wool War": Fibre Marketing in China', paper presented to the conference on *China's Reforms and Economic Growth*, The Australian National University, Canberra, 11–14 November.

Zhao, Y., 1989, *Huanjing Jiufen Anli* [Cases of Environmental Disputes], Beijing: CESP.

Zhao, Z., 1986, 'Report on the Seventh Five-year Plan', Fourth Session of the Sixth National People's Congress, 25 March. Rpt. *Xinhua*, 14 April.

——— 1987, 'Advance Along the Road of Socialism with Chinese Characteristics' *Thirteenth National Congress of CPC*, 25 October.

Zheng, X., 1991, 'Woguo Ziyuan Xiquexing yu Ziyuan Chanyedi Fazhan Xuanze [Resource Scarcity of Our Country and the Selection of Resource Development]', *Jingji Yanjiu* [Economic Research], (9): 67–71.

Zhong, Funing, 1994, 'China's Grain Trade After the Uruguay Round', *China's Rural Economy*, 3: 21–6.

Zhou, Zhangyue, 1992, 'Grain Producers' Responsiveness to Economic Incentives in China', paper presented at the Annual Conference of the Chinese Economic Association (Australia), Adelaide, 12–13 November.

Zhu, Z. and S. Liu, 1983, *Combating Desertification in Arid and Semi-arid Zones in China*, Lanzhou: CAS Institute of Desert Research.

Zhuang, C., 1990, *Zhongguo Xiangzhen Shengtai Jingjixue* [Ecological Economics of China's Villages and Townships], Beijing: CESP.

Zuo D., 1987, 'The Environmental Impacts of China's Water Transfer Project', in A. K. Biswas and Geping Qu (eds.), *Environmental Impact Assessment for Developing Countries*, Dublin: Tycooly.

Zusman, P., 1976, 'The Incorporation and Measurement of Social Power in Economic Models', *International Economic Review*, 17: 447–62.

Zusman, P. and A. Amiad, 1977, 'A Quantitative Investigation of Political Economy – The Israeli Dairy Program', *American Journal of Agricultural Economics*, 59: 88–98.

Index

Abel, M. E., 57
above-quota price, 119
administrative intervention, 33
agricultural institution, 10, 21
agricultural investment, 52
agricultural policy, 2, 6, 12, 16, 31, 60, 72–4, 77, 93, 118–19, 128, 129, 139–40, 146–8, 161, 167, 170
  agricultural trade policy, 129, 145–6
agricultural price, 1, 3, 6, 8, 12, 15, 20–1, 26, 33, 50, 54, 57, 61, 77, 124, 127, 147, 149–53
agricultural protection, 1, 15, 121, 123, 126–31, 133, 135–7, 145, 149, 154
agricultural reform, 1–3, 7, 9–12, 16, 54, 76–7, 103, 123, 145, 156, 159–66
Amiad, A., 60–1
Anderson, K., 59–60, 66, 75, 124, 129, 132, 145, 149
Annual Analytical Group on Rural Economy, 104–5
Armington, P., 143, 179
Ash, R., 16

Beghin, J. C., 60–1, 68–9, 75
Blejer, M. I., 91, 105
Brandão, A., 123–4, 147, 152
Brock, W. A., 60, 75
Buchanan, J. M., 58

Cai, F., 17, 36, 87, 119–20, 128, 162
Calkins, P., 2
central planning system, 4–6, 19–21, 77
  centrally planned economy, 6
  central planner(s), 5–6
Chai, J., 81, 84
Chen, J., 127
Chen, Yun, 27, 30
Cheng, G., 126
China model, 16, 139–44, 153
Chinn, D. L., 34, 42–3
Clarete, R. I., 177, 181

collective ownership, 51
collectivisation, 2, 11, 13, 22, 26–30, 34, 38–9, 44–5, 156–7
commune system, 6, 13, 22, 26, 30–1, 34, 42–4, 46–7, 51, 136, 157, 158, 162
comparative advantage, 22–3, 33, 47, 116, 124, 127, 130–1, 134, 154, 156, 167
Comprehensive Research Group, Development Institute (CRGDI), 37
computable general equilibrium (CGE), 13, 60, 139–47, 171
contracting everything to the household, 38

Deng, Y., 127
Development strategy, 5, 10, 13, 18–19, 22, 47, 86, 156–158
  heavy-industry oriented development strategy, 18, 22
distortion, 4–6, 58, 118, 121, 123, 133, 151, 155, 163, 171, 179
  price distortion, 6, 57, 60, 98
domestic consumption, 32, 128, 146
domestic production, 32
Dowrick, S., 135
Duncan, R., 131

Easterly, W., 35
economic growth, 13
economy-wide policy, 47
efficiency, 5–6, 23, 31–2, 35, 44, 47, 57, 59, 68, 111, 127, 135–6, 140, 158
endogenous government policy, 58
experiment, institutional, 38–9, 42

Fan, Q., 17
Fan, S., 50
First Five-Year Plan, 18–20
Fischer, S., 35
food security, 2, 9, 52, 102–3, 110, 114, 127, 130–2, 161
free trade, 15–16, 32, 119, 121, 123, 128, 132–3, 137, 146–7, 167

223

224 Index

Friedman, J. W., 68

Gao, X., 24, 35, 76, 79
Garnaut, R., 23, 81, 97, 100–1, 105, 119–20, 128, 138, 155, 166–7
Goldin, I., 123–4
Goldsbrough, D., 91
grain output, 1–2, 13–15, 17, 47, 76, 105, 113, 115–16, 130, 163–4
grain policy, 3, 8–9, 12, 14, 25, 62–3, 69, 71–4, 96–7, 102, 113, 165, 168
grain price, 2, 20, 54, 101–10, 116, 118, 123, 148, 161
grain support price, 101
growth accounting, 49
Gunasekera, H. D. B. H., 80–81, 83–84
Guo, S., 27–8, 34, 36, 41, 45, 97, 101

Hayami, Y., 129–30, 137
heavy industry, 19–20, 22
Hochman, H. M., 59
household farming, 51
household registration system, 30
household responsibility system (HRS), 7, 12, 38–52, 81, 83, 98, 115, 142, 158–9, 160, 162–5
Huang, Y., 1, 16, 23, 56, 110, 119–20, 123, 128, 138, 140, 144, 155, 166–7
Hughes, H., 32

import-substitution strategy, 32
industrialisation, 19–20, 26, 35
Ingco, M., 131
internationalisation, 1, 127, 134, 145, 153–4, 161, 164
Institutions, 4–7, 10–12, 17, 19–21, 30, 35, 42, 46–7, 52, 59, 98, 116, 118, 156–60, 162–3, 165, 167–9
   institutional change, 6–7, 11, 13, 42, 44, 96, 98, 158
   institutional distortion, 5–6, 10, 17, 158
   institutional innovation, 7, 12, 57, 96, 98
inward-looking approach, 22, 32–3

Jessop, B., 59
Johnson, G., 29, 104

Karp, L. S., 60–1, 68–9, 75
Knudsen, E., 123–4
Kojima, R., 91
Kowalik, T., 5
Krissoff, B., 152
Krueger, A., 60

Lardy, N., 22–3, 87
Lattimore, R., 57, 60

Li, Yunhe, 39, 52
Li, Z., 17, 36, 87, 162
Lichtenberg, E., 57, 60
Lin, J. Y., 14, 16, 27, 29, 34–7, 38, 42–4, 50, 56, 65, 78, 81, 83, 87, 94, 142, 162
Liu, A., 46
Longworth, J., 1
Luo, Y., 51, 53

Ma, G., 97, 100–1, 105, 166–7
Ma, X., 150
McMillan, J., 44, 49–50, 54, 83, 181
Magee, S. P., 60, 75
Mao, Zedong, 34–6
marginal return, 42–3
Martin, W., 123–4, 143, 147, 152, 180–1
Marx, K., 18
Mitchell, D., 131
mutual-aid team, 27–8

Nash, J., 68
Niu, R., 2, 78, 80–1
Nolan, P., 17
non-quota price, 54
North, D., 4
Nugent, J. B., 16

O'Connor, J., 59

Peltzman, S., 59, 75
Perkins, D., 16, 34, 42
policy decision, 14
private plot, 45–6
producer subsidy equivalent (PSE), 15
production team, 29, 40
productivity, 6, 13, 18, 22, 27, 33, 38–9, 42, 47, 50, 72, 77, 83, 85, 94, 128–36, 150, 157–61, 165
   agricultural, 54, 128, 131–2, 165
Putterman, L., 34, 42

quantitative assessment, 11, 50
quota price, 54

Rausser, G. C., 57, 60
Rodgers, J. D., 59
Roemer, J. E., 59
Rural Credit Co-operative (RCC), 28
rural market reform, 2
Rural Supply and Marketing Co-operative (RSMC), 28
rural–urban income gap, 48

Schultz, T. W., 57
self-sufficiency, 9, 16, 63, 66, 68, 102, 116, 128, 130–1, 136–7, 145, 147–9, 154, 161

Shoven, J. B., 140
Sicular, T., 56
Song, G., 36
Song, L., 167
Soviet Union, 17–20
specialisation, 31
special management system, 46
State Grain Department, 62, 65, 97–8, 102, 112–13
state intervention, 2, 6, 8–9, 24, 136
state plan, 4, 21, 62, 89, 159
state procurement, 54–7
state purchase, 7–8, 12, 24–6, 30, 35, 56, 66, 99, 101, 164
state purchase price, 1, 6–8, 14, 23, 26, 49–51, 54, 56–7, 66, 69, 97, 118, 159, 162, 164, 166
state purchase quota, 8, 25–6, 29, 64
State Statistical Bureau (SSB), 2, 18, 31, 48, 55, 79–80, 82–4, 89, 91–5, 102, 112, 125
Stigler, G. J., 58–9
Sung, Y., 24

Thomson, W., 68
Timmer, P., 6, 66, 126
township, village and private enterprises (TVPs), 12, 51, 91–2
trade liberalisation, 2, 9, 15–16, 118, 129, 131, 134–8, 139, 149, 152, 154–5, 162, 164, 168

transaction cost, 22
Tullock, G., 58
Tyers, R., 59–60, 66, 75, 124, 132, 149

unified purchase and marketing system (UPMS), 21–2, 25, 30, 101, 157–9
United States Department of Agriculture, 110–12

Vousden, N., 127

Wakashiro, N., 95
Wang, G., 19
Warr, P., 177, 181
Whalley, J., 44, 49–50, 54, 83, 140, 181
World Bank, 32, 91
Wulf, L. D., 91

Xiang, N., 24, 35, 76, 79
Xiaogang, 40–1
Xue, M., 17–18, 28, 35

Yang, X., 53
Ye, J., 22
Yi, G., 107
Yusuf, S., 34, 42

Zhang, H., 22
Zhu, L., 44, 49–50, 54, 83, 181
Zusman, P., 60–1, 75

HD 2098 .H82 1998
Huang, Yiping, 1964-
Agricultural reform in China